D1158321

PLATE I Don Quixote and Sancho in battle
(Brussels: Juan Mommarte, 1662)
      Courtesy of the British Library, 1074.i.5, vol. 1, facing p. 237

Juan de la Cuesta
Hispanic Monographs

Series: *Documentación cervantina* Nº 4

EDITOR

Thomas A. Lathrop
University of Delaware

EDITORIAL BOARD

Samuel G. Armistead
University of California, Davis

Alan Deyermond
Westfield College of the University of London

Manuel Durán
Yale University

Daniel Eisenberg
Florida State University

John E. Keller
University of Kentucky

Robert Lott
University of Illinois

José A. Madrigal
Auburn University

James A. Parr
University of Southern California

Julio Rodríguez-Puértolas
Universidad Autónoma de Madrid

Angel Valbuena Briones
University of Delaware

ASSOCIATE EDITOR

James K. Saddler

¿Sancho Panza Through Three Hundred Seventy-five Years of Continuations, Imitations, and Criticism, 1605-1980

by

R. M. ⌊Flores⌋

University of British Columbia

Newark, Delaware

WILLIAM MADISON RANDALL LIBRARY UNC AT WILMINGTON

The Trustees of the British Library have given
permission to reproduce the twelve plates
included in this volume.

Copyright © 1982 by Juan de la Cuesta—Hispanic Monographs
270 Indian Road
Newark, Delware 19711

MANUFACTURED IN THE UNITED STATES OF AMERICA

ISBN: 0-936388-06-4
Library of Congress Catalogue Card Number: 81-83663

PN57
·P27
·F4
1982

To W. F. Hunter

231687

PLATE 2 Sancho's blanketing
(Madrid: Andrés García de la Iglesia, 1674)
　　　　　　　Courtesy of the British Library, 1074.i.9, p. 92

TABLE OF CONTENTS

PLATES

PREFACE

HE FORTUNES OF *Don Quixote* in most Western countries and in Russia have already been recorded in detail in several treatises, where thousands of allusions and references to, and adaptations and imitations of Sancho are cited, but the emphasis has been placed, as is to be expected, on Cervantes, Don Quixote, and/or Cervantes's work as a whole. Sancho's overall character and his fortunes in Western literature have not been studied at any length. Having so many excellent sources of a general nature on which to draw, it would have been pointless to redo what had already been done, and given the awesome amount of Cervantine criticism, it would have been quixotic to attempt a detailed and all-encompassing survey of Sancho's fortunes through almost four centuries of criticism and imitations. There is always a chance that an exhaustive search might turn up the odd unrecorded reference to Sancho, or that under a close scrutiny a literary work might show some traces of Cervantine influence, but the findings would probably not justify the effort that such a project would require, because most of the allusions and references to Sancho show little or no critical insight, and most imitations and continuations only repeat commonplaces and one another.

This study does not purport to be comprehensive. Its purpose is merely to bring into focus the various, disparate, and frequently disparaging opinions that Sancho has elicited since his creation, and pinpoint their textual sources in *Don Quixote*. The following pages will present—through a sample of representative allusions, imitations, critical exegeses, and adaptations—a panoramic, impressionistic picture of how Sancho was treated across the centuries.

The University of British Columbia

November 15, 1981

ACKNOWLEDGEMENTS

AM GREATLY INDEBTED to Professor Keith Whinnom and Dr. William F. Hunter for their endless patience in reading several versions of this study, and for the invaluable help and advice they so generously gave me throughout this project. Their friendship, meticulousness, and scholarship have been a source of inspiration to me. Dr. Hunter will recognize his hand in more passages than I can count. I am proud to dedicate this book to him.

I also wish to thank The University of British Columbia for giving me a year's study-leave to pursue and complete this work, and the Trustees of the Izaac Walton Killam Memorial Fund for Advanced Studies, the Social Sciences and Humanities Research Councils of Canada, and The University of British Columbia Humanities and Social Science Grant Committee for their generous awards.

To Mary, Libby, Alex, Kenneth, and Tammy, my beloved wife and children, my love and devotion for their concern and constant support.

ON BIBLIOGRAPHICAL ENTRIES
AND QUOTATIONS

This study deals with works written in different centuries and countries; hence, no attempt has been made to correct or regularize the orthography or punctuation of quotations or titles of works.

References to works published in or after 1900 do not give the names of printers or publishers, except when the absence of these data could lead to confusion.

❦ 1 ❦

Sancho Panza in the Courts
and on the Stages
of Seventeenth-century Europe

Quem recitas meus est, o Fidentine, libellus:
Sed male cum recitas, incipit esse tuus.
MARTIAL, I, xxxviii

HE FIRST EDITION of *Don Quixote*, Part I, appeared in January 1605 (the date of the *tasa* is 20 December 1604), and Part II was published almost eleven years later in November 1615 (the date of the latest licence is 5 November 1615).[1] Eighteen editions were printed in Spain and Portugal during the seventeenth century, but this figure alone does not justly reflect the interest in Cervantes's work, especially when it is compared with the number of editions of other Spanish works printed during the same period.[2] It is necessary to take two other facts into account to appreciate the impact that *Don Quixote* had on seventeenth-century literature and the widespread popularity it enjoyed in those years,

---

[1] *El ingenioso hidalgo don Quixote de la Mancha. Con privilegio, en Madrid* (Madrid: Juan de la Cuesta, 1605), and *Segunda parte del ingenioso cavallero don Quixote de la Mancha* (Madrid: Juan de la Cuesta, 1615).

[2] See Daniel E. Quilter's "The Image of the *Quijote* in the Seventeenth Century" (unpublished dissertation, University of Illinois, 1962), Table 1, pp. 16-18 (there is an error in the column for 1615-1619: there should be four editions of *Don Quixote*, not three). *DQ*, Part I: Madrid, 1605 (2), 1608; Lisbon, 1605 (2); Valencia, 1605 (2). *DQ*, Part II: Madrid, 1615; Valencia, 1616; Lisbon, 1617. *DQ*, Parts I and II: Barcelona, 1617; Madrid, 1637, 1647, 1655, 1662, 1668 (2), 1674. For the number of editions of seventeenth-century translations of Spanish works printed in France and England see Quilter, Tables 2 and 3, pp. 226-27 and 246.

namely, the considerable number of adaptations, imitations, and translations, and the substantial number of editions printed abroad. Once these facts are taken into consideration, it becomes evident that, despite the relatively small number of seventeenth-century editions of *Don Quixote* published in the Peninsula, the novel had been instantly recognized as an exceptional work, and that its immediate success assured for its two principal characters lasting fame.

No sooner had the first edition of Part I appeared on the market than the popular imagination took Don Quixote and Sancho as an ideal source of entertainment and merrymaking. For instance, one day in Holy Week in 1605 two hundred persons gathered in a street in Valladolid to make fun of "un don Quijote,"[3] and in 1607 there was a parade in Pausa, Peru, with a Sancho "graciosamente vestido, caballero en su asno albardado y con sus alforjas bien proveídas, [el cual] 'echó unas coplas de primor, que por tocar en verdes no se refieren.'"[4] But the first fully-fledged apocryphal Sancho in literature was the Sancho of Alonso Fernández de Avellaneda, who made his ungracious entrance in 1614.

This spurious character is in most respects unlike the original Sancho. At times, like Cervantes's Sancho, he does show some affection for his master. For example, when the apocryphal Don Quixote tells his servant that, if he dies while fighting the *melonero* of Ateca, he wants to be buried at San Pedro de Cardeña, Sancho exclaims:

> —¡Oh señor!...por el arca de Noé le suplico que no me diga eso de morir; que me hace saltar de los ojos las lágrimas como el puño, y se me hace el corazón añicos de oírselo, de puro tierno que soy de mío. ¡Desdichada de la madre que me parió! ¿Qué haría después el triste Sancho Panza solo, en tierra ajena, cargado de dos bestias, si vuesa merced muriese en esta batalla?[5]

---

[3] José de Armas y Cárdenas, *El "Quijote" y su época* (Madrid, 1915), p. 76; reprinted in *Cervantes y el "Quijote"* (Havana, 1945), p. 95.

[4] Aurelio Miró Quesada S., *Cervantes, Tirso y el Perú* (Lima, 1947), p. 80. For the complete description of this celebration see the Appendix in Francisco Rodríguez Marín's *El "Quijote" y Don Quijote en América* (Madrid, 1911), pp. 97-118.

[5] Alonso Fernández de Avellaneda, *El Quijote: Segundo tomo del ingenioso hidalgo don Quijote de la Mancha, que contiene su tercera salida y es la quinta parte de sus aventuras*, second Aguilar edition (Madrid, 1947), Chapter 6, p. 102. All future references are to this edition by chapter and page.

Sancho worries once again when his master is about to be taken into the streets of Saragossa to be whipped publicly:

> Infinita fué la tristeza que en el corazón del pobre Sancho entró cuando oyó semejantes palabras al alguacil, y más cuando vió que todo se aparejaba para sacar a la vergüenza a su amo (8, 139).

But one cannot help questioning the sincerity of Sancho's feelings towards his master when, in Chapter 35, he abandons him to enter the service of the Archipámpano de Sevilla (the "Arcadepámpanos," according to the Sancho of Avellaneda) in the capacity of buffoon. In retrospect, it immediately becomes apparent that the spurious Sancho was worried not so much about the health and well-being of his old master as about himself being left alone without support. Hence, the only characteristics that the Sancho of Cervantes and the Sancho of Avellaneda have in common are their love for their asses, their comical use of malapropisms, and their outward appearance. In fact, the spurious Sancho is an uncouth glutton and a simpleminded, slanderous peasant, whose tiresome blabbing makes him unattractive to the reader. He lies continually for the sole sake of lying, and his lies are foolishly simple and inconsequential. In Chapter 2, for example, he says that he is the son of Pedro el Remendón (p. 52), but later on he contradicts himself by changing his father's trade for no reason whatsoever, making him a butcher (23, 370).

Cervantes was, of course, one of the first to notice the disparities between his Sancho and this unsavory imitation, and he defended his character in *Don Quixote*, Part II, through the mouth of Don Álvaro Tarfe, a character he cunningly borrowed from the apocryphal *Don Quixote* to discredit the work of Avellaneda. When, in Chapter 72 of Part II, Sancho says that "todo cualquier otro don Quijote y cualquier otro Sancho Panza es burlería y cosa de sueño," Don Álvaro replies:

> —¡Por Dios que lo creo... porque más gracias habéis dicho vos, amigo, en cuatro razones que habéis hablado que el otro Sancho Panza en cuantas yo le oí hablar, que fueron muchas! Más tenía de comilón que de bien hablado, y más de tonto que de gracioso.[6]

Avellaneda was the most audacious seventeenth-century imitator of Cervantes, but he was far from being the only Spanish writer of

---

[6] *Don Quijote de la Mancha*, edited by Luis Andrés Murillo, 3 vols. (Madrid: Clásicos Castalia, 1978), II, 577. For selected bibliographies on the various

the period who drew inspiration from Cervantes's novel, nor was he the most successful.[7] More fortunate than Avellaneda in passing off his version of Sancho as authentic was the anonymous writer of the passages describing the disappearance and reappearance of Sancho's ass, which were interpolated, unbeknown to Cervantes, in the second Madrid edition of *Don Quixote*, Part I (Cuesta, 1605).[8] The mourning of this spurious, though believable, Sancho when he discovers that his ass has been stolen was imitated by Lope de Vega in *El Antecristo, Barlán y Josafá, La mejor enamorada, la Magdalena*, and *Auto del Nacimiento de Nuestro Salvador*, by Tirso de Molina in *Antona García, El cobarde más valiente,El laberinto de Creta*, and *La mujer que manda en casa*, and by Pedro Calderón de la Barca in *La devoción de la cruz*.[9]

On the whole, however, Sancho's name was most often used to evoke separate vices or virtues. In 1617, scarcely two years after the publication of *Don Quixote*, Part II, Juan de Tarsis, Conde de Villamediana, referred to a known defaulter, the confessor of Philip III, as:

> Sancho Panza, el confesor
> Del ya difunto Monarca,
> Que de la vena del arca
> Fué de Osuna sangrador.
> (Herrero-García, p. 377)

---

topics discussed here see Volume III, *Bibliografía fundamental*. All future references are to this edition by volume/part, chapter, and page). For summaries of several monographs mentioned here see the very useful bibliographies compiled by Dana B. Drake, *"Don Quijote" (1894-1970): A Selective Annotated Bibliography* (Chapel Hill, North Carolina, 1974), and *"Don Quijote" (1894-1970): A Selective and Annotated Bibliography, Volume Two, with an Index to Volumes One and Two* (Miami, 1978).

[7] Quilter shows that at least thirty-two Spanish works written in that century used *Don Quixote* either directly or indirectly as a model, and he notes a further eighty-eight allusions to Cervantes's work; see pp. 23 and 43, and Appendix B. For plays dealing specifically with Sancho see pp. 160-03.

[8] For textual evidence supporting this assertion see my article "The Loss and Recovery of Sancho's Ass in *Don Quixote*, Part I," *Modern Language Review*, 75 (1980), 301-10.

[9] Miguel Herrero-García, *Estimaciones literarias del siglo XVII* (Madrid, 1930), pp. 413-20. For seventeenth-century imitations of *Don Quixote* for the stage see Gregory Gough LaGrone, *The imitations of "Don Quixote" in the Spanish Drama* (Philadelphia, 1937), especially pp. 8-12, and 25-32. Felipe Pérez Capo's *El "Quijote" en el teatro: Repertorio cronológico de 290 producciones escénicas relacionadas con la inmortal obra de Cervantes* (Barcelona, 1947) is a very unreliable and incomplete study which repeatedly fails to give credit to its sources and unashamedly passes off the work of Maurice Bardon and other scholars as original.

Sancho's loyalty to his master was referred to by Tirso in his play *No le arriendo la ganancia*: Recelo says to Honor, "Pues vas a la corte / Llévame contigo; / Y de un Don Quijote / Seré un Sancho Panza / Que andará a galope." His dreams and his faith in the prowess of his master are presented in Juan Vélez de Guevara's *Mancebón de los palacios*, and his complaints and demands in Lope's *Audiencias del rey don Pedro*. Sancho's simplicity is the characteristic used by the anonymous writer of the *Discursos de la viuda de veinte y cuatro maridos*, and his fondness for food is picked out by Josef de Valdivielso in his play *El hijo pródigo*: "Voy a hacer una mudanza / De la cena al mismo son, / Con el laúd de un jamón / Que tocará Sancho Panza." In *Testamento de don Quijote* Francisco de Quevedo used the disrespectful familiarity which at times Sancho shows towards his master, and his suffering when Don Quixote is about to die (Herrero-García, pp. 375-80). In two of his poems Juan de Salinas touched on a more delicate passage from *Don Quixote* (I, 20, 245-46)

> Sobre ciertas cosas de aire
> Tengo al Cabildo enojado
> Y no por ser Sancho Panza,
> Sí, por que la panza ensancho.

> En fin, hizo Sancho flux,
> Porque el miedo le envidaba
> Y el amo con el olfato
> Vió las cartas.
> Sancho Panza, tú lo has hecho
> Dijo con ira y con rabia;
> Y él replicó: Esto no es Sancho,
> Sino Panza.
> (Herrero-García, pp. 378 and 405-06)

Sancho's common sense did not pass unnoticed. In the anonymous "Fábula de Jesucristo y la Magdalena" a son reassures his father thus:

> ...No se alborote,
> Que no pretendo hacerme Don Quijote,
> Vengando ajenos duelos;
> ....
> Sea Usted don Quijote y Yo don Sancho.
> (Herrero-García, p. 365)

One of the episodes from *Don Quixote* which attracted the attention of a considerable number of seventeenth-century writers is that which shows Sancho as a frustrated and hungry governor on the *ínsula* Barataria (II, 47, 386-89). This passage was exploited at length by the anonymous writers of the farces *El visir de la Perdularia* and *El rey de los tiburones*. Neither of these farces mentions Sancho directly, but the similarities between the plots leave no doubt that they must have been inspired by Cervantes's episode. In *El visir de la Perdularia* the Sancho-like character is Lorenzo, and the dishes are taken away from him not by a doctor, as in *Don Quixote*, but by a Turk, a giant, and a Frenchman successively. In the second farce, it is four doctors who prevent the *rey de los tiburones* from eating. The stage direction states: "Sacarán una mesa acompañada de cuatro doctores, sirviéndole la vianda, sin dejar que coma de ningún plato." The doctors enter commenting on the unhealthy qualities of some fruits:

DOCTOR 1	La lima es húmeda y seca;
DOCTOR 2	Los orejones pesados;
DOCTOR 3	Las [fresas] son muy adustas;
DOCTOR 4	Basta un bizcocho mojado.
DOCTOR 1	Muy verdes están las guindas.
VALLEJO	Darélas su Santiago.
MÚSICOS	De que el rey coma poco
	Cuidad, doctores;
	Que pues tiene corona,
	Viva con orden.
VALLEJO	¡Qué aviso tan lastimoso!
	El corazón me ha quebrado.
DOCTOR 2	Del lechoncillo, un poquito
	Del cuero, muy bien tostado
	Podéis comer y no más
	. . . .
VALLEJO	Decidme, nobles vasallos,
	¿Los monarcas se sustentan
	Con platos imaginarios?
	(Herrero-García, pp. 402-04)

In *Olla podrida a la española* (Antwerp, 1655) Marcos Fernández introduces a grandson of Sancho, Toncho Panza, who tells his new master that when he was going to be baptized the sexton said to his mother: "lo más que yo he visto, señora Panza, es que el señor Gobernador de la Isla [Barataria] vive, digo el señor Sancho Panza, el cual gobierno los señores Duques le han dado hereditario para todos sus herederos; bebe y come a dos carrillos, porque el Doctor Recio murió; *ergo, ergo,* no es muerto; porque si lo fuera, se hubiera comido (por lo menos) tres cabrillas, y yo hallo todas siete en el cielo, *ergo, ergo*" Herrero-García, p. 382). Fernández also alludes to Sancho's common sense when describing the surroundings of the city of Munich with their windmills: Don Quixote attacked the windmills "haciéndose sordo a los gritos de Sancho Panza, su escudero. Hartos Don Quijotes había aquí, que aunque ven menear los brazos de los gigantes, ellos oyen los ecos de la voz de Sancho" (Herrero García, p. 409)

To conclude this brief survey of how seventeenth-century Spanish writers used Sancho in their works, a comment on his physical appearance: Sancho "tuvo por mejor partido caminar en una burra poco menos redonda con su preñado que él que iba en ella, con serlo tanto como una bola," says Páez de Valenzuela in his description of a masquerade presented in 1615 at Cordova (Quilter, p. 69).

It did not take long for *Don Quixote* to cross the English Channel and settle comfortably in the literary circles of post-Elizabethan England. The first edition in any foreign language of *Don Quixote*, Part I, was Thomas Shelton's English translation (1612), and his translation of the complete work was published only five years after the first edition of Cervantes's sequel.[10] The earliest known direct reference to Sancho by an English writer appeared in print in 1627:

> Men talke of the Adventures strange,
> Of Don Quishott, and of their change
> Through which he Armed oft did range,
> Of Sancha Panchas travell.[11]

Despite the lack of other references to Sancho, however, there can be no doubt that a scene in John Fletcher's tragedy *The Double Marriage* (London, c. 1620) was inspired by *Don Quixote*. The play is not as a whole indebted to Cervantes's novel, but there is one scene which is clearly a reminiscence of Sancho's troubles with the Baratarian doctor. In Act 1, Scene 1, the courtier Castruccio finds that the banquet he was hoping to enjoy is ruined by the officiousness of his doctor:

---

[10] *The History of the Valorous and Wittie Knight-Errant, Don-Quixote of the Mancha* (London: E. Blount, 1612), and *The History of Don-Quichote. The First Parte. (The Second Part of the History of the Valorous and Witty Knight-Errant, Don Quixote of the Mancha)*, 2 vols. (London: E. Blount, 1620).

[11] Michael Drayton's poem *Nimphidia, The Court of Fayrie*, edited by Herbert Francis Brett Brett-Smith (Oxford, 1921), p. 12, stanza 35. There is a mention of Sancho in Samuel Butler's "Wit and Folly,".(n. d.), MSS in the British Library, Addit. 32625-6. Butler writes: "the Author of Don Quixot, makes Sancho (though a Natural Fool) much more wise and Politique [than] his Master with all his Study'd, and acquir'd Abilities," see *Samuel Butler: Characters and Passages from Note-Books*, edited by Alfred Rayney Waller (Cambridge, 1908), p. 328.

Castruccio.	Where's this wine?
	Why, shall I choke? do ye long all to be tortur'd?
Doctor.	Here, sir.
Castruccio.	[tastes] Why, what is this? why, doctor!
Doctor.	Wine and water, sir:
	'Tis sovereign for your heat; you must endure it.
	. . . .
Castruccio.	Come, taste this dish, and cut me liberally;
	I like sauce well.
Doctor.	Fie, 'tis too hot, sir,
	Too deeply season'd with the spice. —Away with't!—
	. . . . [Servants take away the dish.
Castruccio.	But pray, stay, doctor,
	And let me have my meat again.
Doctor.	By no means:
	I have a charge concerns my life.
Castruccio.	No meat neither!
	Do kings never eat, doctor?
Doctor.	Very little, sir,
	And that too very choice.[12]

But the first Sancho-like character to appear on the English stage was
Borachio, a *"Rustick, Tennant, and Servant to* Lothario" in William D'Avenant's tragedy *The Cruel Brother* (1630).[13] The borrowing is unquestionable from the rising of the curtain. Borachio not only resembles
Sancho physically, but he also strings together proverb after proverb
at the beginning of the play, and complains that certain promises
made by his master have not as yet been fulfilled:

Lothario.	*Borachio.*
Borachio.	My Lord?
Lothario.	Survay my garments round, and then declare
	If I have hit it?
Borachio.	You have, sir: but not the marke.
Lothario.	What marke? thou bold Parishioner of Hell.

---

12 *The Works of Beaumont and Fletcher,* edited by Alexander Dyce, 11 vols.
(London: Edward Moxon, 1843-1846), VI (1844), 395-96. In his article "The
Relationship between Beaumont's *The Knight of the Burning Pestle* and Cervantes'
Don Quixote," Anales Cervantinos, 11 (1972), 87-96, Steven H. Gale compares
these two works and finds several similarities between them, but concludes
that "the difference between [Sancho and Ralph's squires George and Tim] is
enormous" (p. 95).

13 *The Cruell Brother* (London: A. Mathews, 1630), "The Persons of this
Tragedy," folio A4v.

BORACHIO. Why Sir, the marke I aime at: Preferment.
After a storme, comes a calme: the harder
You blow, the sooner your Cheekes will ake: and he
That cares for your anger, may have more of't
When he list, for my part, I know my Mother.

LOTHARIO. The froward Sisters have conspir'd. Slave! Dog!
Wilt thou never leave this immense folly?
Can nothing serve those dull Lippes but Proverbs?

BORACHIO. Sir, I know none of your Proverbs. First come,
First serv'd. Those words that are neerest the tongue,
Have opportunitie soonest to leave
The mouth.

LOTHARIO. Is it then decreed, I must grow mad?

BORACHIO. I'le be no more flowted, nor brus'd, not I.
What need my Lord, be beholding to me
For's mirth; when he may laugh at's owne folly?
Besides though motion and exercise
Be good for grosse bodies; therefore, must they
Of the Guard, pitch me up and downe like a barre?

LOTHARIO. Sa, sa, sa, A mutinie in Heaven!

BORACHIO. If there be; You are not likely to come
Thither to appease it, first end this quarrel
Upon earth, I have serv'd you this sixe Moneths,
In hope of an Office; and am no more
An Officer than she that bore me.

(Act 1, Scene 1, folios C3-C3v)

Borachio's complaint about being buffeted and bruised, and his asking Lothario, "must they Of the Guard, pitch me up and downe like a barre?" immediately bring to one's mind the tossing that Sancho suffered at the hands of the "alegre, bien intencionada, maleante y juguetona" company who were staying at the inn the morning Don Quixote refused to pay their board and lodging (I, 17, 213). This complaint of Borachio, his fondness for proverbs, his hopes to hold an "office," his gross constitution, and the familiarity and impoliteness with which he dares to address his master are an excellent sketch of Sancho; but the likeness between the two characters fades as the play unfolds and it is difficult to find any similarity between them at the end.

Sancho re-entered the world of English farce in James Shirley's *The Triumph of Peace*, performed by the four Inns of Court before Charles I at Whitehall on 3 February 1633. The masque includes a whimsical knight and his squire, who appear after the dotterels and immediately before the bowlers:

After the *Dotterels* are caught by
severall imitations, enters

A Windmill.	The phantastique Adventur-
A *phantastique Knight.*	er, with his lance makes
and	attempts upon the Windmill,
His Squire armed.	his Squire imitates: to them
	Enter
A Country Gentleman,	These are assaulted by the
and	Knight and his Squire, but
his servant.	are sent off lame for their
	folly.[14]

With two strokes of the pen Shirley has taken away from Sancho the
one quality which apparently no one had denied him before. Unlike
Sancho in the episode of the windmills in *Don Quixote* (I, 8, 128-30),
where he is the epitome of common sense, Shirley's squire is a
mindless character who simply apes his master's follies.

A potboiler that would have much to do with the distorted image
that Sancho would project on English literature was Edmund Gayton's *Pleasant Notes upon Don Quixot.* This work, published in 1654,
perpetuated the idea that Cervantes's characters were nothing but a
couple of unscrupulous rogues. Edward M. Wilson has accurately
summarized Gayton's style and his attitude towards the characters of
his text by pointing out that he "is diffuse, obscure, insensitive,
pornographic [and] sadistic.... He was incapable of perceiving any
admirable features in either Quixote of Sancho, and other characters
in the novel are crudely caricatured without necessity or without
excuse."[15] The following passages chosen at random attest the validity of Wilson's strictures:

> On Sancho's entering the service of Don Quixote: "*Sancho* hath
> bit at the ambitious baite, and is caught poor fellow, he knew
> not what a dance the *Don* would lead him, before he return'd to
> the shaking of the sheets, with his *Joan Gutierez*" (folio E1).

> On Sancho's statement that Teresa may become queen: "For a
> man of [Sancho's] expectations to be depressed with a slut, a
> whore, or a fool (or it may be all at once in one) was an
> intollerable weight" (folio E1v).

---

[14] *The Triumph of Peace* (London: John Norton, 1633), folio C2.

[15] "Edmund Gayton on Don Quixote, Andrés, and Juan Haldudo," *Comparative Literature,* 2 (1950), 65. See also Quilter, pp. 258-60.

After the defeat of the Vizcayan: "and now you see the chiefe of *Sancho's* service, he was for the plunder, the Squire for the bag, the Knight for the baggage, for he is with the *Biscaine* Lady, while his Squire made an adventure indeed, of robbery" (folio E4).

On Sancho's preparing to follow his master: "*Knight-Errants* and their Squires, like Ships, must be victuall'd, and *Sancho* was providing for a long voyage. The Cloak-bag in his belly, was of more capacity than that of his Ass; a corner of which, the whole Pye would not well fill" (folio Nn2v).

It is obvious that this extensive, unflattering treatment could not in the least improve matters for Sancho. Fortunately, Gayton only defiled Part I of *Don Quixote*.

A play which would have served ideally to test the theory that Gayton's pamphlet exerted a strong influence on the opinion that English playwrights would hold of Don Quixote and Sancho is *The History of Don Quixote*. This play seems to have been presented in London in 1658, but unfortunately there are no copies extant. "All we know of it consists of such advertisements as those by the printer Nathaniel Brook, who lists it as 'in presse' in the back of *The New World of English Words* and again in *Wit and Drollery*."[16]

Despite the scarcity of printed evidence, however, it is certain that seventeenth-century English writers were aware of the possibilities for farce offered by Sancho and the slapstick essence of many episodes in *Don Quixote*; but not until the end of the century were these elements exploited in full on the English stage.

Thomas D'Urfey's play *The Comical History of Don Quixote* was presented at the Queen's Theatre in May 1694. The comedy was received enthusiastically, and D'Urfey followed in the wake of its success with a second part in June of the same year and a third part in November 1695.[17] The first and second parts stage the principal adventures of Don Quixote with many personal touches and addi-

---

[16] Edwin B. Knowles, Jr., "*Don Quixote* in England before 1660," p. 7. This article is the first of four on *Don Quixote* in England in a collection entitled "Dissertations: Literature and Art," University of Oregon Library, 800/D632/v. 1.

[17] "Certain of the songs in the first and second parts of D'Urfey's 'Don Quixote' (1694) were by Purcell, the most famous of them being 'Let the dreadful engines;"...and the third part of 'Don Quixote,'...though it failed on the stage, became famous from its containing the song 'From rosy bowers.' This is said to be 'the last song the author sett, it being in his sickness,'" *Dictionary of National Biography*, VXI, 484-85.

tions of D'Urfey's own invention, but they follow Cervantes's plot closely and show thematic continuity. The third part, on the other hand, is largely the creation of D'Urfey himself and has little to do with the other two parts.

In the preface to the second part D'Urfey says: "*I have had the honour to have it judg'd that I have done both Don* Quixote *and Sancho Justice, making as good a Copy of the first as possible, and furnishing the last with newer and better Prove[r]bs of my own than he before diverted ye with;*" but whether or not critics agreed with this statement, they certainly did not think highly of the work as a whole. The first and second parts achieved great success amongst the nobility and the general public, but the third part was a failure, artistically as well as economically.

Sancho is described in the "Dramatis Personae" as a "dry shrewd Country Fellow, Squire to Don Quixote, a great speaker of Proverbs, which he blunders out upon all occasions, tho' never so far from the purpose." The play opens with Don Quixote and Sancho riding in the fields of Montiel. Sancho is hungry from the very first lines of the dialogue:

> SANCHO. . . . [aside. Now am I to be fed with a tedious Tale of Knight-Errantry, when my Guts are all in uproar within me for want of better provision.
> [*Exit with* Rosin, *and* Dapple.
>
> QUIXOTE. The gross and sordid quality of this Fellow, gives me the better reflection upon my self, for as his thoughts are grovelling like his Nature, so mine are elevate like my Profession . . .
> *Re-enter* Sancho.
> So, thanks be to *Lady Flora*, the Beasts are well provided for, *Dapple* is happy, he is exercising his Grinders yonder, whilst I carry mine here only for shew; for the Devil of any other use will my Master let me have for 'em; See—now is he making his Dinner upon Cogitations, and I am to have the Scraps of 'em for mine; Honour and Air is always our fare. Oh *Sancho, Sancho!* What hast thou brought thy self to?[18]
> (Part I, Act I, Scene I)

[18] *The Comical History of Don Quixote* (London: Samuel Briscoe, 1694); *The Comical History of Don Quixote. Part the Second* (London: Samuel Briscoe, 1694); *The Comical History of Don Quixote. The Third Part. With the Marriage of Mary the Buxome* (London: Samuel Briscoe, 1696).

Sancho seems to be paraphrasing here in a meditative mood Gayton's statement that when Sancho joined his master he was "caught poor fellow, he knew not what a dance the *Don* would lead him;" but the key sentence in this scene is when Don Quixote snobbishly places himself several pegs above Sancho, showing that D'Urfey had perceived not only a difference of outlook, but a clear-cut contrast between the personalities of Don Quixote and Sancho, a fact that escaped most of his contemporaries. It is also worth noting that the description of Sancho, although not flattering, shows some understanding of Cervantes's character: "he blunders out [proverbs] upon all occasions, tho' never so far from the purpose." These insights set D'Urfey apart, at least temporarily, from the insensitive and crude glossing of Gayton. D'Urfey's simplistic, though initially sober, overall view of Cervantes's novel led him, however, to overemphasize the differences between master and squire and to rely too heavily on Sancho for comedy. The Sancho of D'Urfey does not respect, far less admire, his master, an attitude that culminates with Sancho's getting drunk and beating Don Quixote. In *Don Quixote* Sancho does indeed overpower his master on one occasion and throw him flat on his back (II, 60, 492), but he does it in self-defense and not under the effects of alcohol. Moreover, *The Comical History of Don Quixote* has its own massive share of vulgarities and farcical excesses.

The third part bears the subtitle *With the Marriage of Mary the Buxome*, and in it D'Urfey marries off Sancho's daughter. Here D'Urfey almost abandons Don Quixote, and much of the play is taken up by sexual innuendo, with Sancho and Teresa Panza advising their daughter and their future son-in-law on what to expect on their wedding night. Sancho spends most of his time drunk and babbling nonsense, but his personality changes drastically from scene to scene and it is impossible to predict his moods. At times he is very learned (he speaks in Latin to the citizens of the Island of Barataria), but at other times he is an ignoramus; he is a religious man and a blasphemer at the turn of a page; he is a loving father in one scene and has no paternal affection in the next. Of the three parts, the second presents perhaps the least imperfect Sancho, although here too there are innumerable inconsistencies in his character.

The one characteristic of this unlovable Sancho that remains constant throughout the triad is his shocking irreverence towards sacred things, an attitude unthinkable in the Sancho of Cervantes. In Part I, Act 4, Scene 1, Sancho complains about his wife and about married life. The priest Perez tries to console him:

PEREZ.   In troth, my good Friend and Neighbour, honest
           Sancho, I am Sorry to hear this, for as I remember,
           'twas my luck to give *Teresa* and you the Blessing.

SANCHO.   A Plague on your Blessing; I perceive I shall have
           occasion to wish you hang'd for your Blessing—
           Good finisher of Fornication, good Conjunction
           Copulative.

NICHO.   The profane Wretch defame's the Holy Ordi-
           nance of Marriage, and ought to be presented to the
           Inquisition.

PEREZ.   Speak reverently of our Function, *Sancho*, or I'll
           Excommunicate you the Church.

SANCHO.   I care not; I should lose nothing by it if you
           should, but my Nap in an Afternoon.

It was mainly because of this blatant profanity that Jeremy Collier
was moved to attack D'Urfey's plays in his *Short View of the Immorality,
and Profaneness of the English Stage*.[19] D'Urfey, says Collier, "writes from
the *Romance* of an ingenious Author: By this means his Sense, and
Characters are cut out to his Hand. He has wisely planted himself
upon the shoulders of a *Giant*; but whether his Discoveries answer
the advantage of his standing, the Reader must judge" (p. 196).
Collier bitterly criticized *The Comical History* on three counts: D'Urfey's lack of concern for the moral and religious convictions of his
audience, his profanity towards religion and the Holy Scriptures, and
his abuse of the clergy. Although Collier's interest is focused principally on the religious and moral aspects of the comedy, his accusations are fully justified by the play itself. Collier remarks that "Smut
Sancho and *Teresa* talk it broad, and single sens'd, for almost a page
together. *Mary the Buxome* has likewise her share of this Accomplish-
ment" (pp. 202-03). "Collier's diatribe had at least one concrete result
as far as D'Urfey was concerned, for the justices of Middlesex
brought an indictment against him on May 12, 1698, for having
written [these plays]."[20] It is a bitter irony, as James Fitzmaurice-
Kelly has noted, that Collier's "fulminating protest should have been
called forth by a work professedly derived from Cervantes who justly
prided himself on the morality of his writings."[21]

[19] Second edition (London: S. Keble, 1698).

[20] *The Songs of Thomas D'Urfey*, edited by Cyrus Lawrence Day (Cambridge,
Massachusetts, 1933), p. 22.

[21] "Cervantes in England," *Proceedings of the British Academy 1905-1906*, 2
(1906), 11-29, at p. 25.

There are some short passages in *The Comical History* that can be described as amusing, such as the episode of the Dueña Dolorida:

MATRONA. ...I must desire to know whether the most puri-fiediferous Don *Quixote* of the *Manchissima* and and [sic] his Squireiferous *Panca* be in this Company or no.

SANCHO. Why look ye forsooth without any more flourishes, the Governour *Panca* is here, and Don *Quixotissimo* too, therefore most afflictedissimous Matronissima speak what you willissimus, for we are all ready to be your Servitorissimus.

(Part II, Act 3, Scene 2)

D'Urfey has, for once, retained the clean-natured humor of Cervantes's novel (II, 38, 330), but on the whole one can say without hesitation that the Sancho of D'Urfey is an unfortunate imitation of the original character. The coarse caricature that D'Urfey drew for the English public is neither accurate nor in the least sympathetic. D'Urfey's own words in the preface to the third part of *The Comical History* show how little he thought of Sancho when he finished this part. *"I know no other way in Nature to do the Characters right, but to make a Romp* [Mary the Buxome] *speak like a Romp, and a Clownish Boor* [Sancho] *blunder."* D'Urfey's initial insight in perceiving the contrast between the personalities of Don Quixote and Sancho and the difference in their outlooks became blurred as the action progressed, and his final opinion of Sancho is indicative of the concept in which Sancho was held by seventeenth-century English writers. Sancho was a "clown-ish Boor" who could only "blunder."

If, as Sancho states in *Don Quixote*, it is better to be ill-spoken of than not to be mentioned in books at all—"por verme puesto en libros y andar por este mundo de mano en mano, no se me da un higo que digan de mí todo lo que quisieren" (II, 8, 95)—his fortune in seven-teenth-century Germany was even more dismal than in England.

Don Quixote, Part I, as a whole was not the first work of Cervantes to attract the interest of German translators.[22] In fact, the first

---

[22] *Unzeitiger Fürwitz*, an anonymous German translation of the French version by Nicolas Baudouin of *El curioso impertinente*, one of the short stories interpolated in *Don Quixote*, Part I, appeared in 1617. In the same year an anonymous Germanized version of Cervantes's *Rinconete y Cortadillo* was pub-lished under the title *Isaac Winkelfelder und Jobst von der Schneid*. *Unzeitiger Fürwitz* was later adapted for the stage; see Christian Fritz Melz's excellent mono-graph "An Evaluation of the Earliest German Translation of *Don Quixote: Juncker Harnisch aus Fleckenland*," *University of California Publications in Modern Philology*, 27, N° 5 (1945), 302.

edition of Pahsch Bastel von der Sohle's incomplete German translation of *Don Quixote*, Part I, was not published until 1648 (second
edition 1669),[23] and the only two complete German translations
printed in the seventeenth century (1683 and 1696) were not rendered from the original Spanish but from the French version of
Filleau de Saint-Martin (1678). Despite, or perhaps because of, these
translations, neither Cervantes nor his characters seem to have been
household names in seventeehth-century Germany.

The only recorded mention of Sancho in Gemany in that century
occurred in 1613 at Heidelberg in a masquerade given to celebrate the
wedding of the Elector Frederick V of the Palatinate and Elizabeth
Stuart, eldest daughter of James I. "As part of the entertainment,
Don Quixote and Sancho Panza, in archaic German, challenge the
assembled guests to admit that Dulcinea is the most beautiful woman
in the world."[24] The early date on which the masquerade took place
and the fact that this is the only known occasion on which Sancho
was mentioned in seventeenth-century Germany seem to contradict
each other. *Don Quixote* was already known in Germany in 1613, and,
one may add, relatively well-known, or the name of Dulcinea and the
antics of Don Quixote and Sancho would not have produced the
desired comical effect on the audience; and yet, Sancho went practically unnoticed throughout the remaining eighty-seven years of
that century. It is also evident that the first German Sancho must
have been concocted following either the original Spanish text or,
more likely, Shelton's translation (1612).

The roles of Don Quixote and Sancho in the German masquerade
are in keeping with the roles they would play in the Duke's court in
Part II of *Don Quixote*, and with the pleasures and sense of humor of
the courtiers Cervantes would portray so vividly. The masquerade
shows that the sense of humor of the Duke, the Duchess, and their
court was common in the European courts of this period, where
refinement, elegance, beauty, luxury, and artistic genius were frequently interwoven with unpleasant and cruel mockeries. And, as
will be seen, the courts of Louis XIII and Louis XIV in France were no
exception to the general rule.

[23] The first edition has two title-pages: *Don Kichote ae la Mantzscha, Das ist:
Juncker Harnisch auss Fleckenland* (Frankfurt: Thomas Matthias Götz, 1648), and *Erster Theil der abenthewerlichen Geschichte des scharpffsinnigen Lehns- und Ritter-sassen Juncker
Harnisches auss Fleckenland* (Hofgeismar: Salomon Schadewitz, 1648). Pahsch Bastel was a pseudonym of Joaquim Caesar from Halle (Melz, pp. 302 ff.)

[24] Lienhard Bergel, "Cervantes in Germany," in *Cervantes Across the Centuries*, edited by Ángel Flores and Maír José Benardete (New York, 1947), p.
307.

As in Germany, Cervantes first found his way into the French literary milieu through Baudouin's translation of *El curioso impertinente* (*Le Curieux impertinent*; Paris: Jean Richer, 1608). The first complete French translation of *Don Quixote*, Part I, appeared six years later in 1614.[25] Apparently, however, the first artists to take advantage of Sancho's farcical possibilities were not playwrights, as in England, but a painter of religious themes, and an engraver.[26]

Sancho was painted by Jean Mosnier c. 1625, "avec ses jambes trop allongées pour son buste," and engraved by Jacques Lagniet as a short, fat, and bearded peasant wearing a ridiculous hat garnished with ribbons (Bardon, p. 59 and Appendix A; and p. 87 and Appendix B). Lagniet, a *marchant d'estampes*, etched thrity-eight plates for his series of engravings entitled *Les Advantures du fameux Chevalier Dom Quixot de la Manche et de Sancho Pansa, son escuyer*. The engravings depict episodes from both Parts. In one of these plates Lagniet "reproduit l'aventure des 'malliets de foulons'. ne peut aujourd'hui, par certain détail scatologique, que nous écœurer et révolter. Mais Lagniet n'avait cure du bon goût, ni des convenances" (Bardon, p. 87).

After Mosnier and Lagniet it was the writers' turn to abuse Sancho. In "La Chambre du débauché" Marc-Antoine Saint-Amant says that Sancho:

> Baigne ses yeux dans la clarté
> Des cent ducats qu'il accumule,
> Et, riant comme un farfadet,
> Se console auprès d'une mule
> De la perte de son baudet.
>   (Bardon, p. 89)

---

[25] *L'Ingénieux Don Quixote de la Manche. Traduit Fidellement d'Espagnol en François par Caesar Oudin* (Paris: J. Foüet, 1614). François de Rosset translated Part II under the title: *Seconde Partie de l'Histoire de l'Ingénieux, et Redoutable Chevalier Dom-Quichot de la Manche* (Paris: V. J. du Clou and D. Moreau, 1618).

[26] *Le Ballet de Don Quichot dansé par Mrs Santenir* was recorded as having been performed on 3 Februrary 1614, but there is some question as to the accuracy of the date given. The manuscript has an obvious error in the date 1600 it gives for the compilation of the separate ballets; hence, it is possible that the date given for *Le Ballet de Don Quichot* may be another mistake. See Maurice Bardon's Bibliography B in his definitive study *"Don Quichotte" en France au XVIIe et au XVIIIe siècle 1605-1815* (Paris, 1931), p. 854. *L'Entrée en France de Don Quichot de la Manche*, a masquerade, is believed to have been written between 1616 and 1625, but there is no evidence to establish the exact year when it was presented.

But the first full-fledged Sancho-like character to appear in a French literary work was the valet Carmelin in Charles Sorel's novel *Le Berger extravagant* (1627). Carmelin expresses himself in proverbs, like Sancho, but:

> Non seulement par son langage, mais, en certaines occasions, par ses attitudes ou ses grimaces, Carmelin rappelle Sancho. Et de même qu'on berne l'un, on frappe l'autre. Toutefois, ce qui n'était que plaisant dans l'original espagnol devient vite , ici, odieux: il n'y a pas de comique dans la souffrance, et rien ne porte moins à rire que les contorsions d'une bouche qui hurle.
> (Bardon, p. 128)

Carmelin's complaints when he loses his hat remind one of Sancho's mourning on the loss of his ass, but whereas the grief of Sancho both amuses and touches the reader, the exaggerated and misplaced sorrow of the valet only awakens his laughter. Like D'Avenant's Borachio, Carmelin is a crude caricature of Sancho. He is slovenly, with greasy hair, an unkempt and bushy beard, and dirty hands with black nails. He speaks like a parrot, incorrectly, without punctuation or pauses, and in a monotonous fashion. "Il reste, dans l'ensemble, grossier et vulgaire. En lui, la 'bête' domine: n'y voyons, en définitive, qu'une contrefaçon de Sancho" (Bardon, p. 130).

Adrien de Montluc, Count of Cramail, exploited *ad nauseam* one of Sancho's most endearing traits in *La Comédie de proverbes*, presented in Paris in 1633. All the characters of this comedy speak in proverbs. "Chacun, dans cette pièce, s'exprime en émule, mais en émule lourdaud, du plaisant écuyer" (Bardon, p. 153). Paul Scarron created another Sancho-like character for his *Jodelet ou le Maître valet* (1645) and *Les Trois Dorotées ou le Jodelet souffleté* (1646). "Qu'est-ce donc que Jodelet? C'est le *gracioso* espagnol, et c'est aussi Sancho Pança.... Ce caractère, d'une bassesse déjà marquée chez les dramaturges castillans, et même dans Cervantes, Scarron en a encore outré les défauts. Gourmand, lubrique, hâbleur, poltron, son Jodelet fait honte à Sancho Pança. C'est le type, poussé à l'extrême, de l'égoïsme et de la couardise" (Bardon, p. 100). Cervantes's episodes of the *ínsula* Barataria and Sancho's troubles with Pedro Recio de Agüero, *Medicinae Doctor*, were borrowed by Guyon Guérin de Bouscal for his comedy *Le Gouvernement de Sancho Pansa* (1641). The Advocate Fourcroy wrote a comedy entitled *Sancho Pança* (1659), but unfortunately no copy of this play has survived (Bardon, p. 231). One can be sure, however, that Sancho would not have received any better treatment from Fourcroy than he had received from other playwrights.

It can be seen that only the farcical side of Sancho's character fired the imagination of French writers. Throughout the first half of the seventeenth century Sancho and Don Quixote were a constant source of merriment at the courts of Louis XIII and Louis XIV, where they were repeatedly used, misused, and abused in numerous masquerades, ballets, burlettas, plays, and pageants (see Bardon, pp. 170-95). Writers, unable to understand and reproduce in their own works the complicated personalities of Cervantes's heroes, confined themselves to underlining the inelegant figure of Don Quixote and the graceless shape of Sancho. They reduced knight and squire to the same grotesque level by using in their works only the earthy attachments of Sancho and the comical antics of Don Quixote.

With the flourishing of *les grands classiques* (1660-1700) a new interpretation of *Don Quixote* began to emerge. Molière, Jean de La Fontaine, Madame de Sévigné, Nicolas Boileau, and Jean Baptiste Racine approached Cervantes's novel with more serious minds. Until then, Don Quixote and Sancho had been kept together, a laughable duet, a madman and a vulgar and greedy peasant. The Classics separated Don Quixote and Sancho and treated each character in a totally different fashion. The heavy burden of the ridiculous fell solely on the squire's shoulders. But of these writers only Molière needs to be mentioned here because of his Sancho-like characters.

Molière drew inspiration from Sancho for four of his characters. One of these French Sanchos, Monsieur Jourdain in *Le Bourgeois gentilhomme*, has resolved to marry his daughter to a son of the "Grand Turk," in spite of the many sensible reasons adduced by Madame Jourdain to dissuade him from his purpose (Bardon, pp. 233-34). Madame Jourdain's objections are faintly reminiscent of those advanced by Teresa when Sancho tells her that he is going to marry Sanchica to a Spanish nobleman and make her a countess (II, 5, 74-79). One is also reminded of Sancho when Monsieur Jourdain boasts of his friendly relationship with a count (Act 3, Scene 3):

MDM. JOURDAIN. Vous êtes fou, mon mari, avec toutes vos fantaisies, et cela vous est venu depuis que vous mêlez de hanter la noblesse.

M. JOURDAIN. Lorsque je hante la noblesse, je fais paroître mon jugement, et cela est plus beau que de hanter votre bourgeoisie.

MDM. JOURDAIN. Çamon vraiment! il y a fort à gagner à fréquenter vos nobles, et vous avez bien opéré avec ce beau Monsieur le comte dont vous êtes embéguiné.

M. JOURDAIN. Paix! Songez à ce que vous dites. Savez-vous
bien, ma femme, que vous ne savez pas de qui
vous parlez, quand vous parlez de lui? C'est une
personne d'importance plus que vous ne pensez,
un seigneur que l'on considère à la cour, et qui
parle au Roi tout comme je vous parle. N'est-ce
pas une chose qui m'est tout à fait honorable,
que l'on voye venir chez moi souvent une personne de cette qualité, qui m'appelle son cher
ami, et me traite comme si j'étois son égal? Il a
pour moi des bontés qu'on ne devineroit jamais;
et, devant tout le monde, il me fait des caresses
dont je suis moi-même confus.[27]

Monsieur Jourdain sounds very much like Sancho bragging about his
friendship with the Duke and Duchess.

The three other characters of Molière that remind one of Sancho
are Gros-René (*Sganarelle*), La Montagne (*Les Fâcheux*), and Du Bois (*Le
Misanthrope*), who, according to Bardon, resemble Sancho in their
gluttony, intemperate complaints against their masters, inopportun-
ity, and cowardice (pp. 236-37).

Little has been written about the fortunes of *Don Quixote* in Italy
or Cervantes's overall influence on Italian writers. The only two
seventeenth-century *drammi per musica* inspired largely by *Don Quixote*
which have received some attention are Marco Morosini's *Don Chisciotte della Mancia*, presented at Venice in 1680, and Girolamo Gigli's *Il
"Don Chisciotte," ovvero Un pazzo guarisce l'altro* (Siena, 1698).

Antonio Belloni notes in his *Il Seicento* that the melodrama *Don
Chisciotte della Mancia* is "una cosa puerile che non ha alcun rapporto col
capolavoro del Cervantes."[28] Nor is the Sancho in Gigli's *Un pazzo
guarisce l'altro* a faithful copy of Cervantes's squire, "ma conserva la
maliziosa arguzia che ha nel romanzo spagnuolo."[29] He is never
caught in the dream world of his master, but he resembles his

---

[27] *Le Bourgeois gentilhomme* in *OEuvres de Molière*, edited by Eugène André
Despois and Paul Mesnard, 13 vols. (Paris: Librairie Hachette, 1873-1900),
VIII (1883), 108-09. The first public performance took place at the Théâtre
du Palais-Royal in Paris in 1670, but the play had been previously staged at
the court of Louis XIV in October 1670.

[28] Paraphrased by Eugenio Mele in "Per la fortuna del Cervantes in Italia
nel Seicento," *Studi di Filologia Moderna*, 2 (1909), 234; see also footnote 30.

[29] Rosaria Flaccomio, *La fortuna del "Don Quijote" in Italia nei secoli XVII e XVIII
e il "Don Chisciotti" di G. Meli* (Palermo, 1928), p. 45.

Spanish model in some other aspects of his personality, as, for example, when he refers to a bunch of bananas as "bellissimi, vezzosissimi, platanissimi" (Flaccomio, p. 43). He too misuses words (*decapitare* in lieu of *recapitare*), but he is more learned than Cervantes's Sancho: "disserta sul conte Orlando, col quale mette a confronto il proprio padrone; cita 'il Signor Splandiano' (sic); definisce 'platonico' l'amore del suo padrone per la Sibilla; gli scrive lui le sue lettere perchè i cavalieri possono scrivere alle proprie dame solo col sangue; paragona il proprio stomaco alla luna che 'appena si empie una volta al mese'; dichiara di 'favorire le lettere'; si fa premura di precisare che la parola latina *Ius*, che vuol dire legge, significa ancora il brodo delle minestre (a. II, sc. 17); declina il latino: 'Sancius Sancij come Dominus Dei, Panza Panze, como Musa Musae' (a. II, sc. 7)."[30] But this benign treatment that Sancho received in *Un pazzo guarisce l'altro* is the exception that proves the rule, because the previous quotations and examples furnish sufficient reference points to show that Sancho had to travel an uphill path in seventeenth-century Europe.

From the very beginning of the century Sancho was tacitly accepted and used as a tool or vehicle to provoke laughter, to represent isolated human weaknesses, and/or to remind the public of passages or whole episodes from *Don Quixote* with a few strokes of the pen. But whether Sancho was being used as a simple mnemonic device or as a symbol of a human flaw, the final effect was always comical and, not infrequently, gross and derogatory.

Sancho fared worse abroad, needless to say, than in his native land, where some of his good qualities (humor, loyalty towards Don Quixote) were duly noted and praised. In Germany he was practically unknown, and his popularity in England, France, and Italy was also more limited than in Spain. Knowles has stated that "for some reason the English were even slower to appreciate Sancho than they were Don Quixote or Rocinante. Only eight of the eighty allusions to Cervantes' novel [made between 1605 and 1660] make mention of the squire."[31] This fact is, however, not surprising. In those years the English stage had an abundance of its own native stock of fools, jesters, unfaithful servants, and drunkards, whereas it was short of windmill-fighters and hacks. The same could be said of Germany,

---

[30] Giuseppe Carlo Rossi, "Una 'fantasia' italiana su *Don Chisciotte*," *Hispano-Italic Studies*, 2 (1979), 92.

[31] "The Vogue of *Don Quixote* in England from 1605 to 1660" (unpublished dissertation, New York University, 1938), p. 187.

France, and Italy. The French Classics recognized the spirited deed of
Don Quixote, but for them Sancho remained a court jester, as Molière's Monsieur Jourdain, Gros-René, La Montagne, and Du Bois
clearly attest.

In the seventeenth century Sancho conveyed very much the same
image throughout Europe. The great majority of writers who dealt
with him were satisfied with endowing their Sanchos or their Sancho-like characters with only the most earthy and comical traits of
the original Sancho, always exaggerating them until every bond
broke and pulled apart. The characteristics most commonly associated with Sancho were an immoderate fondness for proverbs, a
blatant disrespect towards his master, talking, eating, and, especially
in England, drinking. The very name of the Sancho-like character in
D'Avenant's tragedy *The Cruel Brother*, Borachio, gives a very precise
idea of the overall concept of Sancho held by English writers. In fact,
one wonders whether Gayton's grotesque and ludicrous gloss of *Don
Quixote* did indeed begin the harmful trend of misinterpretations and
abuse that both Sancho and Don Quixote suffered in England during
the seventeenth century, or merely reflected the low opinion in
which master and squire were held all along by English writers.

It is curious to note that, in contrast to England, where Sancho is
always a sot, a wineskin ready to burst, wine-producing Spain, Italy,
and France seldom exploited Sancho's soft spot for wine. It is interesting also to detect the class-consciousness of seventeenth-century
writers, who treated Sancho benignly only when they referred to, or
duplicated, his Solomonic judgments on the *ínsula*. Two distinct Sanchos, as it were, appear: one, Don Quixote's squire, is a crass,
deformed, pigheaded, and avaricious peasant; the other, the Governor of Barataria, is dignified and full of wisdom in his role of
magistrate, as though the status associated with the office and the
imposing aspect of a robe would have dazzled the reader, who would
no longer notice Sancho's paunchy shape or his rustic speech. The
works in which the episodes of the *ínsula* are treated in full deal with
Sancho's judgments and his frustrated banquet as if they were two
totally unrelated occurrences. On the one hand, writers admire and
present as exemplary the common-sense verdicts of the magistrate,
on the other, they laugh at, and make sport of, the helpless marion-
ette of the Duke, who must starve because he is only a puppet
playing Governor.

As in the Duke's court, Sancho was a puppet also in the hands of
seventeenth-century writers, who, perhaps with the only exception
of Gigli, misjudged and mistreated him remorselessly throughout the

century. A fitting finale for Sancho's unenviable seventeenth-century European tour is an anecdote recounted by Bardon (p. 509).

On 27 January 1694, so it goes, Charles Dufresny's comedy in three acts entitled *Sancho Pança* was presented by the Comédiens-François. At the opening of the third act the Duke exclaims: "I begin to grow tired of this Sancho!" "And I too!" yelled a groundling from the pit. The public approved this retort enthusiastically, and the comedy ended then and there.

PLATE 3 Sancho's departure for the island of Barataria
by Charles-Antoine Coypel (London: n.p., 1725).
Courtesy of the British Library, 12490.aaaa.20, vol. 4, after title page

✣ 2 ✣
Sancho in the Age
of Enlightenment

> Suffer [your wife] not to look into *Rabelais*, or
> *Scarron*, or *Don Quixote*—they are all books which
> excite laughter.
> LAURENCE STERNE, *Tristram Shandy*
> Book 8, Chapter 34

 HE NUMBER OF ALLUSIONS TO Cervantes by English writers, and of English continuations of, and works inspired by, *Don Quixote* increased substantially in the eighteenth century. Knowles has noted that "Sir William Temple, Addison, Steele, Swift, Arbuthnot, Pope, Fielding, Sterne, Smollett, Joseph [Warton], Dr. Johnson, and others in this satire-loving age considered Cervantes' book a classic,"[32] but it is well to point out that it was only after the publication of Henry Fielding's *Joseph Andrews* (1742) that the most important works directly or indirectly inspired by *Don Quixote* began to appear, and not until the publication of *Tom Jones* (1749) did Sancho become adapted to his new environment. Alexander Pope, for instance, alludes only once to Cervantes ("Whether thou choose Cervantes' serious air," *Dunciad*, Book 1, line 21; first published in 1728), and once to Sancho:

> A solemn Sacrifice, perform'd in state,
> You drink by measure, and to minutes eat.
> So quick retires each flying course, you'd swear
> Sancho's dread Doctor and his Wand were there.[33]

By now, it comes as no surprise to find that Pope's only allusion to

[32] "*Don Quixote* through English Eyes," *Hispania*, 23 (1940), 109-10.

[33] "Moral Essays, Epistle IV [to John Boyle]" (1731), in *The Works of Alexander Pope Esq.*, edited by William Warburton, 9 vols. (London: Printed for

25

Sancho links the squire with his frustrated meal at Barataria, and, in fact, is not even strictly a reference to Sancho but to the Baratarian doctor. While Pope's interest in Cervantes and *Don Quixote* was minimal, Fielding's was, on the other hand, lifelong and shows throughout his work.

Fielding was fascinated by *Don Quixote* from his youth. He began writing his short comedy *Don Quixote in England* in Leyden in 1728. The managers of Drury Lane rejected the play the following year, considering it unsuitable for the stage,[34] but the New Theatre in the Haymarket presented it with some success in 1734.[35]

Fielding expresses his admiration for Cervantes in his Preface to the play:

> This Comedy ... was originally writ for my private Amusement; as it would indeed have been little less than Quixotism itself to hope any other Fruits from attempting Characters wherein the inimitable Cervantes so far excelled. The Impossibility of going beyond, and the extreme Difficulty of keeping pace with him, were sufficient to infuse Despair into a very adventurous Author.

One need only compare these words with D'Urfey's boast only thirty-four years earlier in his Preface to the second part of *The Comical History of Don Quixote*, "*I have done both Don Quixote and Sancho Justice, ... furnishing the last with newer and better Prove[r]bs of my own than he before diverted ye with,*" to comprehend the radical turn that the appreciation of *Don Quixote* by English writers took in the eighteenth century.

The Sancho of Fielding is a brave and faithful squire. He loves his food, makes great use of proverbs throughout the play, and , more important, he now finds himself at home in England. He sings English folk-songs, drinks ale, and pines after English roast beef:

> SANCHO.   ...Ah, Madam, might I hope your Ladyship would speak a good Word for me?

J. and P. Knapton, 1751), III, p. 313. This epistle is known as the fourth Moral Essay, "Of the use of Riches." Pope also mentions "La Mancha's Knight" in *An Essay on Criticism* (lines 267-84), but he is referring there to a passage from Lesage's French rendition of the spurious *Don Quixote* of Avellaneda, not to Cervantes's character.

[34] Frederick Homes Dudden, *Henry Fielding: His Life, Works, and Times*, 2 vols. (Oxford, 1952), I, p. 126.

[35] *Don Quixote in England. A Comedy. As it is Acted at the New Theatre in the Hay-Market* (London: Printing-Office in Wild-Court, 1734).

DOROTHEA.   Name it, and be assur'd of any thing in my Power, honest *Sancho.*

SANCHO.   If your Princess-ship could but prevail on my Master, that I might not be sent home after my Lady *Dulcinea*; for, to tell you the Truth, Madam, I am so fond of the *English* rost Beef and strong Beer, that I don't intend ever to set my Foot in *Spain* again, if I can help it: Give me a Slice of roast Beef before all the Rarities of *Camacho's* Wedding.

DOROTHEA.   Bravely said, noble Squire.

(Act 1, Scene 6)

In Act 3, Scene 16, Sancho is caught by the cook eating every-thing he can in the kitchen and packing his wallet full for later consumption. When Don Quixote reprimands him, Sir Thomas Love-land pleads for the squire, and Sancho then jokingly states that he would change masters if in the exchange his stomach would be better provided for:

SIR THOMAS.   Dear Knight, be not angry with the trusty *Sancho*, you know by the Laws of Knight-Erran-try, stuffing the Wallet has still been the Privi-lege of the Squire.

SANCHO.   If this Gentleman be a Knight-Errant, I wish he wou'd make me his squire.

Fielding's character does not like to quarrel without a good reason, but when necessary he is as ready to fight as anyone else:

BADGE.   Stand away, Landlord, stand away. —If I don't lick him!

SANCHO.   Come along, out into the Yard, and let me have fair Play, and I don't fear you—I don't fear you.

(Act 2, Scene 7)

Unlike the Sancho of Avellaneda and the other seventeenth-century imitations, Fielding's Sancho would not consider serving another master unless he was a knight, and then only in the capacity of squire; nor does he hide leftover food *en el seno* (Avellaneda 12, 186); nor is he a coward. It is evident that Fielding regarded Sancho with sympathy, and that the adjectives "honest," "noble," and "trusty" with which Dorothea and Loveland preface Sancho's name are not meant ironically, but as compliments to the faithful companion of Don Quixote. Sancho's only condemnable weakness is his gluttony.

Taken as a whole, however, *Don Quixote in England* is not an accomplished comedy. It is too short for Fielding to present the personalities of his characters in full. But Fielding was only twenty-one years old when he wrote this play, and even though he departed from the original plot of Cervantes he was capable with so few strokes of conveying the general light tone of the original and sketching Sancho's complex personality. With this in mind, Fielding's achievement seems praiseworthy. Sancho's Cockneyfication had begun, but it would take him a hundred years to complete his adaptation to his new environment.

Fielding's interest in Cervantes's novel is also evident in *Joseph Andrews* (1742) and in *Tom Jones* (1749). Abraham Adams, from *Joseph Andrews*, reminds one of Don Quixote, but nowhere in this novel is there a Sancho-like character. in *Tom Jones*, on the other hand, Tom's companion, Benjamin Partridge, is a "thoroughly anglicized Sancho Panza" (Dudden, pp. 651-52).

Partridge is like Sancho in many ways: his sense of humor, which shows no respect of persons, time, or place; his inquisitiveness; his insatiable babbling; his inability to keep secrets; his variable definitions of "honesty," depending on whether it is his own or someone else's property which is in question; his love of comfort, food, drink, and a warm seat by the kitchen fire; his desire to advance himself in life; his willingness to do battle, despite earlier signs of cowardice. when fighting cannot be avoided; his good-natured personality; his loyalty to his master. Unlike Sancho, Partridge is a Jack-of-all-trades (schoolmaster, clerk, barber, surgeon, tailor, manservant), moderately literate, and chronically superstitious.[36] Physically, Sancho and Partridge could not be less alike; Partridge is "near six feet high" (*Tom Jones*, Book 8, Chapter 8) and slim; Sancho is fat and short.

From the character of the squire in *Don Quixote in England* and the general personality of Partridge one can see that Fielding sympathized with Sancho, who was for him "a Masterpiece in Humour, of which we never have, nor ever shall see the like."[37]

Amongst the several other English writers who exploited the vogue and acceptance that *Don Quixote* was enjoying in those years, Tobias Smollett and Richard Graves are especially worth noting here for the charaters they modeled after Sancho.[38]

[36] All these characteristics of Partridge are listed by Dudden (pp. 652-53), who refers his readers to the appropriate passages in the novel.

[37] "Proceedings at the Court of Censorial Enquiry," in *The Covent-Garden Journal*, edited by Gerard Edward Jensen, 2 vols. (Oxford, 1915), I, p. 280. This article, a review of Charlotte Lennox's *The Female Quixote*, appeared on 24 March 1752.

[38] There is a manservant in Laurence Sterne's *Tristram Shandy*, Corporal

Smollett began serializing his novel *The Adventures of Sir Launcelot Greaves* in the *British Magazine* in early 1760, the last chapters appearing in 1762.[39] Smollett's hero is a nobleman in his early thirties, who, upon a disappointment in love, takes to the road armed at all points. The ostensible purpose of Sir Launcelot's adventures is, like Don Quixote's, to protect the poor, weak, and oppressed, but his high-handed meddling is not always opportune or welcome. Unlike Don Quixote, however, Sir Launcelot has a patronizing and disdainful attitude towards the lowborn, and he always solves his and other people's problems by brandishing his name and titles, and resorting to his well-heeled purse. Smollett makes constant allusions to Sir Launcelot's madness (which in truth is only a self-assumed eccentricity), but he always describes and treats his knight as a paragon of virtue, prowess, and physical beauty.

Timothy Crabshaw, Sir Launcelot's squire, receives a completely different treatment. He is a "ploughman and carter" on the Greaves's estate,[40] married to a very practical woman, and father of several children.

> [Timothy] seemed in age to be turned of fifty. His stature was below the middle size; he was thick, squat, and brawny, with a small protuberance on one shoulder, and a prominent belly.... His forehead was remarkably convex, and so very low, that his black bushy hair descended within an inch of his nose [2, 11-12].... The fellow was a composition, in which [one] did not know whether knave or fool most predominated [2, 14].... [He had] a dry sort of humour about him; but he was universally hated among the servants for his abusive tongue and perverse disposition,... [and although he was] as strong as an elephant, he [had] no more courage naturally than a chicken—I say naturally, because, since his being a member of knight-errantry, he [had] done some things that [appeared] altogether incredible and preternatural [5, 61].

In actual fact, Timothy never does anything at all incredible or

---

Trim, and the novel is peppered with references to Cervantes and to *Don Quixote*, but Sterne did not create any of his human characters after those of Cervantes (the parson's horse "was full brother to Rosinante...for he answered his description to a hairbreath in every thing," Book 1, Chapter 10).

[39] Smollett's *réchauffé* of Charles Jervas's translation of *Don Quixote* was published in 1755.

[40] *The Adventures of Sir Launcelot Greaves*, Chapter 5, in *The Works of Tobias Smollett*, edited by William Ernest Henley, 12 vols. (Westminster, 1899-1901), X (1900), p. 61.

preternatural. True, he always joins, and at times even precedes, his master in the numerous fracas and skirmishes in which they get involved, but usually he finds himself accidentally in the midst of the melee, or starts abusing people out of sheer malice. He is also in it for the spoils. For instance, when, in Chapter 19, Sir Launcelot unhorses Esquire Sycamore, Timothy attacks a servant of the Esquire, pulls him off his horse, and, "alighting with great agility [tells him],... 'I think as haw yawrs bean't a butcher's horse, a don't carry calves well...now, you shall pay the score you have been running on my pate'.... So saying, he rifled his pockets, stripped him of his hat and coat, and took possession of his master's portmanteau. But he did not long enjoy his plunder," because Sir Launcelot forced him to return everything to its rightful owner (pp. 219-20).

Timothy also strings proverbs together (see Chapter 10, 116-17), is always hungry, constantly complains about everything, and has no trouble falling asleep even in the most adverse circumstances. Like Sancho, he too has a four-legged companion for the road, Gilbert, but the strange partnership between Timothy and his horse has masochistic overtones:

> Gilbert was the most stubborn and vicious [horse that could be found in Sir Launcelot's stable], and had often like to have done mischief to Timothy while he drove the cart and plough. When he was out of humour, he would kick and plunge as if the devil was in him. He once thrust Crabshaw into the middle of a quickset hedge, where he was terribly torn; another time he canted him over his head into a quagmire, where he stuck with his heels up, and must have perished, if people had not been passing that way; a third time he seized him in the stable with his teeth by the rim of the belly, and swung him off the ground to the great danger of his life; and I'll be hanged if it was not owing to Gilbert that Crabshaw was now thrown into the river (5, 63).

It is clear throughout the novel that Gilbert hates Timothy and loses no opportunity to show his dislike and contempt for the squire. And yet, when, in Chapter 8, Timothy loses his horse, he worries about it, and upon recovering the animal, "he imprinted a kiss on his forehead; and, hanging about his neck, with the tears in his eyes, hailed his return with the following [half-page long] salutation: 'Art thou come back, my darling?... What canst thou say for thyself, thou cruel, hard-hearted, unchristian tuoad?' To this tender expostulation...Gilbert answered not one word; but seemed altogether insensible to the caresses of Timothy" (p. 94). On another occasion, when the squire is told by a false conjurer that "Gilbert would die of the staggers, and his carcass be given to the hounds, ... [Timothy] shed a plenteous shower of tears, and his grief broke forth in some passionate expressions of tenderness" (22, 256). The following morning Timothy "visited [Gilbert] in the stable, and saluted [him] with the kiss of peace. Then he bemoaned his fortune with tears, and by the sound of his own lamentation was lulled asleep among the litter" (22, 259). Seeing the payment that Timothy receives in return for his caresses, it is no wonder that everyone thinks Timothy crazy when he chooses Gilbert for his companion rather than any of the other horses.

A similar reaction had followed Sir Launcelot's picking Timothy for his squire, and the text fully justifies this general surprise because the relationship between master and servant is no less strange than that between Timothy and his horse. "What should have induced our knight to choose this here man for his [squire] is not easy to determine," says another character, "for, of all the servants about the house, he was the least likely either to please his master, or engage in such an undertaking" (5, 60). Although Timothy makes his entrance on the shoulder of Sir Launcelot as "a bundle dropping with water" (2, 10), his master having fished him out of the river where he would almost certainly have drowned without his help, neither of them really likes or cares for the other. When the doctor tells Timothy: "You ought to thank God and your master ... for the providential escape you have had," the squire cries: "Thank my master! ... thank the devil! Go and teach your grannum to crack filberds. I know who I'm bound to pray for, and who I ought to curse the longest day I have to live" (2, 13). Timothy's unkind sentiments are heartily reciprocated by Sir Launcelot, who spends half his time beating, yelling at, insulting, or threatening to horse-whip the squire. What is worse, when Sir Launcelot sheds his armor he forgets about Timothy, and the squire all but disappears from the book. At the end of the novel one does not know what has happened to Timothy, because he is not mentioned at all in either the denouement or the last chapter of the story. Smollett forces Timothy to partake of all the misadventures that befall Sir Launcelot, and makes him pay dearly for them, but he does not allow him to be part of the general merriment and happy ending of the novel.

There is not the slightest doubt that Smollett drew heavily on *Don Quixote* for his novel, but, unfortunately, he neither kept sufficiently close to it to profit from Cervantes's already well delineated characters, nor did he distance himself enough from it to produce a consistent and independent narrative. The *Adventures* of Sir Launcelot *Greaves* is an entertaining novel, especially if one has read *Don Quixote* and notices the numerous similarities of detail between the two works, but it is marred by countless contradictions of both plot and characterization. Timothy was clearly modeled after Sancho, but it is difficult to ascertain exactly what Smollet thought of the original character. Timothy is not in the least a likeable character, and the only direct reference to Sancho that appears in the novel is derogatory: in Chapter 13 Timothy tells his master that the reason he has a bleeding nose is that he entered into an argument with two army officers (haberdasher's apprentices impersonating army officers), who had "basted" him in the kitchen with a poker and then "cursed and abused him, calling him Sancho Panza, and such dogs' names" (pp. 149-50). But whether or not Timothy's personality and the unkind words of the apprentices (or of Timothy) reflect Smollett's view of Sancho, one cannot say with certainty.[41]

A more skilfully drawn and more engaging character than Timothy Crabshaw is Richard Graves's Jeremiah Tugwell, who is introduced to the reader in the following fashion:

> Come! then, thou goddess Fame.... I do not blasphemously invoke thy power to record the humbler virtues of a rural craftsman; come to my aid! and bestow one blast in honour of the fidelity, courage, wit, and humour of the renowned Jeremiah Tugwell,...or Tagwell, or Tackwell.[42]

Jerry is "a thickset little fellow, near fifty; but of a strong constitution and hale complexion" (1, 7, 21), who has only one tooth left and is almost bald. He is fond of books, "chiefly those of the fabulous kind" (1, 7, 22), his language is "frequently interlarded with hard words, not always applied or pronounced with the utmost propriety"

---

[41] Edward L. Niehus, "Quixote Figures in the Novels of Smollett," *Durham University Journal*, 40 (1979), 233-43, considers that Smollett "fully realized that Don Quixote and Sancho were not meant to be contemptible and repulsive, but were, in fact, charming and appealing" (p. 237). If true, however, this appreciation is not at all reflected in Smollet's depiction of Timothy. Niehus thinks also that Sir Launcelot's servant "is more closely modelled on Sancho than his master is modelled on Don Quixote. Crabshaw is the target for much of the laughter and punishment which would ordinarily have been directed at the Quixotic hero" (p. 240).

[42] Book 1, Chapter 7 of *The Spiritual Quixote: or, The Summer's Ramble of Mr. Geoffry Wildgoose*, 3 vols. (London: Printed for J. Dodsley, 1773), I, 20-21. Future references are to Book (not volume), chapter and page.

(1, 8, 25-26), and he passes "amongst his more [provident], though really less sagacious, neighbours, for an half-witted fellow"(1, 7, 22). Jerry is "naturally tame and moderate, [and he is] not often guilty either of swearing or drinking" (2, 2, 42). He is married and in the past had had a son, a soldier, who is now supposed to have died in America.

Jerry's master and teacher is Mr. Geoffry Wildgoose, who, like Don Quixote, loses his mind reading books—religious treatises in this case—and goes tramping the roads trying to convert souls to a religion of his own. "Mr. Wildgoose, having determined to go on a pilgrimage to Bristol, after some deliberation, communicated his intention to his `...honest neighbour, Jeremiah Tugwell, but under a strict injunction of the greatest secrecy" (2, 2, 41), and invited him to become his assistant in his crusade. Mr. Wildgoose's only concern is to convert souls, and all earthly needs must be taken care of by Jerry. Jerry advises and warns his master about the convenience of taking some "money to pay for [their] lodgings, and to provide necessaries upon the road" (2, 3, 48), though Mr. Wildgoose questions "whether it be lawful, for a preacher of the Gospel to take any thought for the things of this life" (2, 3, 50). On Mr. Wildgoose's stating that there were no inns in the wilderness where Elijah traveled, Jerry remarks:

> "However, folks were not so hard-hearted in those days; but were more given to *hostility*, than they are now."
> "Hospitality, I suppose you mean," says Wildgoose.
> "Well, well, that is all one, replies Tugwell; but I am no Oxford scholar, that's *sartain*" (2, 3, 49)

Jerry's concern for their everyday needs and his down-to-earth prudence come to his aid many a time, and he loses no occasion to remind his master whose providence it is that saves them from going hungry.

> [Upon arriving at a] plain called Dover's-hill, . . . Jerry proposed resting under an oak, that cast an inviting shade near the side of a wall; and opening his wallet, he produced a large fragment of a brown loaf, and cheese in proportion, the reviving odour of which put Wildgoose in mind of his breakfast: for hitherto he had not bestowed a thought upon that article, nor on the means of procuring it.
> "Now, Master," (quoth Tugwell) "If we had trusted to Providence, and I had not brought some bread and cheese in my wallet, what would your Worship have done for a breakfast?"
> "Hold thy prophane tongue!" replies Wildgoose: "this is not a difficulty which requires the interposition of Providence" (2, 7, 70).

Jerry's weaknesses are his pipe, good liquor, and abundant food, and whenever he lies down to rest he right away goes "into a world of his own, snoring most profoundly" (2, 7, 71). On one occasion, Jerry abandons his master in the middle of a town battle, but when Mr. Wildgoose reprimands him and tells him that he would pursue his crusade with or without a servant, Jerry instantly repents and follows his master. Throughout the novel he contradicts, cajoles, talks back to, defends, makes fun of, helps, and misleads his master with his unceasing chatter.

Mr. Wildgoose's travelling lasts almost two months, at the end of which (Mr. Wildgoose having meanwhile recovered his senses), master and squire return to their sequestered village. Mr. Wildgoose returns to a loving mother and an advantageous marriage, which has been waiting for him. Poor Jerry, however, is being awaited by an "infinitely exasperated [wife] ... for presuming to elope from home, in downright defiance of her sovereign authority" (12, 15, 306); but when Jerry greets her with aplomb and a right hand "filled with silver, two or three half-guineas being [interspersed] amongst it" (12, 15, 307) she immediately unwrinkles her brow, smiles, and welcomes her husband with open arms, just as Teresa receives Sancho after he has told her that he is bringing "otras cosas de más momento y consideración" (I, 52, 602), mainly the hundred gold crowns he had found in his first sally with Don Quixote.

The textual parallels between *Don Quixote* and *The Spiritual Quixote* are countless. One can quote reminiscences of *Don Quixote* from practically every page of Graves's work. Even the purely religious disquisitions that take place between Mr. Wildgoose and his servant, friends, neighbors, and possible proselytes could be seen in the light of Don Quixote's arguments in defense of his statement that "religión es la caballería" (II, 8, 98-99).[43] The similarities between Sancho and Jerry could not be clearer.

Jerry, just like Sancho, does not enter the story until, and precisely in, Chapter 7 of Book 1. The description "honest neighbour [and] half-witted fellow" applied to him tallies exactly with Cervantes's "labrador vecino suyo, hombre de bien ... pero de muy poca sal en la

---

[43] It is worth pointing out, too, that the uncertainty that surrounds Jerry's family name (Tugwell, Tagwell, Tackwell, Tugwool, Tug-mutton) is identical with that hovering over Don Quixote's (Quijada, Quesada, Quejana, Quijano), and that the exchange of words between Jerry and Mr. Wildgoose quoted above is a fair imitation of the frequent verbal skirmishes between Sancho and Don Quixote.

mollera" (I, 7, 125), though Graves precedes his description with the hint that Jerry might be smarter than he seems at first glance ("passed amongst his...less sagacious neighbours")—this is true also of Sancho, but the fact is not stated in *Don Quixote* and only becomes apparent as the story unfolds. Jerry and Sancho both use and dismiss their malapropisms with a casual flair and sauciness which are at the same time lovable and irritating. There are some obvious differences between the two characters (their education and some details in their physical appearance), but, on the whole, they are very much alike.

There is no question about it, Jerry Tugwell, or Tagwell, or Tackwell, is an engaging character. Although Graves completely removed Cervantes's characters from their original environment and remodeled them to suit his own purposes, he successfully retained the most characteristic and appealing qualities of the original Sancho. Jerry likes to live well, to drink moderately, to talk, smoke, and sleep as often as possible, and he swears only when it is indispensable. Moreover, Graves presents Jerry to his readers in a humorous and sympathetic fashion. Jerry's simplicity and his attachment to worldly things are not abused or exaggerated. They are only complementary to his good heart, his fidelity towards his master, and his amusing behavior.

It is true that Jerry does not make great play with proverbs and does not have a mount, nor is he as well drawn as, for example, Fielding's Partridge; but, on the whole, Jerry's positive qualities outweigh his shortcomings and he is a closer imitaiton of Sancho than either Partridge or Smollett's Timothy Crabshaw.

Sancho the Governor won the praise of Henry Brooke in *The Fool of Quality*.[44] The novel is not indebted to *Don Quixote* to any appreciable degree, but in one of the sections in which the Author argues with a Friend about topics concerning his work (like Cervantes in the Prologue to Part I). Brooke says:

> But, let me turn, with reverence, to kiss the hem of the robes of the most respectable of all governors and legislators, Sancho Pansa. What judgments! what institutions! how are Minos, and Solon, and the inspired of the goddess Ægeria here eclipsed! Sancho, thou wast a peasant, thou wast illiterate, thou wast a dunce for a man, but an angel for a governor; inasmuch as,

---

[44] Chapter 4, *The Fool of Quality; or, The History of Henry Earl of Moreland*, 5 vols. (London: W. Johnston, 1766-1770). Although the title-page reads "In Four Volumes," in fact five volumes were published, I and II (1766), III (1768), IV (1769), and V (1770).

contrary to the custom of all other governors, thou didst not desire any thing, thou didst not wish for any thing, thine eye was not bent to any thing, save the good of thy people! therefore thou cou'dst not stray, thou hadst no other way to travel. Could Æsop's log have been moved to action upon the same principle, the regency of storks had not prevailed among men. How am I provoked, Pansa, when I see thee insulted! How am I grieved when I find thee deposed! Saving the realms of a certain majesty, I say, and sigh to myself, O, that the whole earth were as thine island of Barataria, and thou, Sancho, the legislator and the ruler thereof (I, 154-55).

Across the Atlantic, one of the first American novels presents the reader with a completely different evaluation of Sancho's ability to govern from that of Brooke, and with a master-servant relationship even less convincing than that of Smollett's Sir Launcelot and Timothy.

The principal characters of Hugh Henry Brackenridge's *Modern Chivalry*[45] are Captain John Farrago, a bachelor "of about fifty-three years of age, of good natural sense, and considerable reading; but in some things whimsical, owing perhaps to his greater knowledge of books than of the world" (p. 29), and Teague O'Regan, a "long-legged" (p. 47), "redheaded" (p. 54) young man with "a too great fondness for women" (p. 38). Teague "is but a simple Irishman . . . of a low education; his language being that spoken by the aborigines of his country. And if he speaks a little English, it is with the brogue on his tongue. . . . Teague can neither write nor read. He can sing a song, or whistle an Irish tune; but is totally illiterate in all things else" (p. 46).

There is no question but that Brackenridge drew inspiration from *Don Quixote* for the general plan of his novel. Both Don Quixote and Sancho are mentioned several times in connection with Captain Farrago and Teague, and there are some passages which bring to mind similar occurrences in *Don Quixote*.[46] It is soon evident, however,

---

[45] *Modern Chivalry: Containing the Adventures of Captain John Farrago and Teague O'Regan, His Servant*, edited by Lewis Gaston Leary (New Haven, Connecticut, 1965). First editions: Part I, Vols. I and II (Philadelphia, 1792), III (Pittsburgh, 1793), IV (Philadelphia, 1797), Part II, Vols. I and II (Carlisle, Pennsylvania 1804-1805). In 1815 Brackenridge republished all six volumes of *Modern Chivalry* with numerous changes and some additions. This study is concerned only with Part I (1792-1797).

[46] See, for instance, Brackenridge's belated statement that he was weaving his "history" with extracts from the original journal of Captain Farrago

that the episodic structure and the two principal characters are only a device for introducing a series of brief, disconnected disquisitions on topics ranging from government to love, duels, and the origin of the races of men.

Teague is depicted from the very beginning as an illiterate nincompoop, a coward, a scoundrel, a malicious liar, and a hypocrite. He is, nevertheless, successively on the point of becoming state representative, member of the American Philosophical Society, preacher, Indian chief, and socialite, and he is finally appointed Collector of the Excise on Whiskey by the President of the United States himself.[47] Teague feels no love or affection towards his master, and on one occasion he does not hesitate to abandon him without notice (pp. 120-52).

Captain Farrago's attitude towards Teague is also thoroughly disconcerting. He repeatedly encourages his servant to better himself. He tries to teach him how to sign his name, and goes to the extreme of hiring a ballet instructor to help Teague gain grace in his demeanor (pp. 217-24). In Volume III, Book 1, Chapter 8, Captain Farrago advises his servant on how to take care of his dress and physical appearance, and how to behave in society, as Don Quixote does with Sancho. But whenever Teague is about to rise above his station, either by getting an office or by marriage, the Captain is always the first to trip him up from behind.[48] At one point, for example, the Captain seeks the advice of a lawyer in his eagerness to punish the manager of a theatre who had horse-whipped his servant because Teague had tried to seduce the manager's wife (pp. 152-58), but later on, through his meddling, Captain Farrago causes Teague to be denied entry into a respectable home, and to be abused and horse-

---

(p. 93); Captain Farrago's suggestion to Teague that they should spend a night or two in the open, as knights-errant did (p. 106); and the humorous description of the physical charms of the mistress of a house where the travelers stay one night (p. 108).

[47] In the introduction to his edition of *Modern Chivalry* Leary notes: "Further additions [to the 1815 edition] were planned, which would see Teague O'Regan finally becoming the United States Ambassador to the Court of St. James; but Brackenridge died...without carrying them to completion" (p. 15).

[48] The only occasion on which the Captain does not interfere is when Teague is appointed Collector of the Excise on Whiskey, perhaps because it had been he who had introduced and recommended his servant to the President.

whipped by the butler of the house (pp. 251-52). It is no wonder, then, that when Teague takes up the office of Collector, master and servant separate without the least emotion or regrets. Captain Farrago immediately hires another servant, whereas Teague, like Sancho, soon finds that not everything in government is milk and honey.

Before Teague can reach his destination, he is met by a party of those from whom he is supposed to collect taxes, who strip him of his clothing, and tar and feather him without further ado. Teague manages to escape from his tormentors and climb a tree, trying to hide his nakedness and hoping to be succored by some well-meaning passer-by, but instead he is discovered by hunters who take him for a mongrel beast, a cross between an ape and a bird. They cage him and exhibit him as a scientific curiosity. Teague is held in captivity for "a year or so," and is then shipped to France to be studied by the learned Societies, but when he arrives at Nantes the revolutionary rabble takes him for a *sans culotte* and sets him free, and nothing else is known of him. The squire disappears without trace (p. 333).

The relationship between Teague and Captain Farrago is obviously similar to that betweeen Timothy and Sir Launcelot, but whereas Smollett has no quarrel with Sirt Launcelot's high-handed mistreatment of his servant, the Republican Brackenridge seems none too comfortable with the status quo, or with the newly found democracy, and he constantly both criticizes and makes excuses to justify the contradictory actions of the master, the crassness of the servant, the irresponsibility of elected officials, and the fickleness and gullibility of the people. There are, of course, fundamental differences between Timothy and Teague, and between Teague and Sancho, but it is difficult not to see Teague O'Regan as another character derived from Cervantes's Sancho.

The predominant themes that shape the general plot of *Modern Chivalry* are Teague's extreme naivety in matters of state, his relentless pursuit of preferment, and his blind confidence in his nonexistent qualifications for office, all of which remind one of Sancho.[49] His being appointed to an office and the subsequent treatment he receives at the hands of those he is supposed to "govern" bring to mind Sancho's governorship and his misadventures on the *insula* Barataria. But Brackenridge's unsympathetic and flat depiction of Teague produced an unpleasant, nondimensional character.

---

[49] Two of the later additions read: "'And, besides, [said Captain Farrago], have I not promised to do something clever towards settling you in life

Unlike Brackenridge and the English eighteenth-century novelists, English-speaking playwrights did not create new characters based on Cervantes's Sancho, but, as with Fielding's *Don Quixote in England*, they used Sancho directly in their plays. He re-entered the English stage in 1742 in James Ayres's *Sancho at Court: or, The Mock Governor*, the burlesque quality of which "is suggested by the presence among the Spanish characters of Colonel At Wit, Lord Smart, Never Out, and Lord Sparkish."[50] The same approach animates the anonymous farce *Squire Badger* (1772), and T. A. Arne's burletta *The Sot* (1775), both adapted from Fielding's earlier play.

Frederick Pilon's two-act farce *Barataria: or, Sancho Turn'd Governor*, performed at the Theatre Royal on 29 March 1785, was based on Part Two of D'Urfey's *The Comical History of Don Quixote* and retains three scenes from the original play.[51] Pilon notes in his introduction, however, that "it was found necessary to materially alter, and enrich [these scenes] with additions to give them a modern, a novel complexion. —Impressed with every veneration for the genius of Cervantes," Pilon continues, "the present writer has adhered to him as closely as the nature of dramatic writing would admit" (p. 3). But the farce has little to do with Cervantes's chapters except in the most general terms. In fact, the only judgment by Sancho retained from the original Spanish is the episode of the wronged wench who could not defend her virginity but has no trouble defending and keeping the purse Sancho had given her to atone for the seduction. None the less, Pilon's farce is not totally devoid of entertaining scenes, without falling into the lewd excesses of D'Urfey's play. For instance, on taking up office Sancho makes his ass his secretary, and tells his Recorder: "you shall do the business as his deputy" (p. 20). In another

---

hereafter, provided you will serve me faithfully in my travels? Something better than you have thought of may turn up in the course of our rambles.' Teague was moved chiefly with the last part of the address"; and, "boldness and assurance [Teague] possessed in exact proportion to his want of knowledge," *Modern Chivalry*, edited from the complete edition of 1846 by Ernest Brennecke, Jr. (New York, 1926), pp. 18 and 230. It is also interesting to note that Brackenridge changed the "great fondness for women"—unlike Sancho (Leary's edition, p. 38), to "great fondness for whiskey"—like most English Sanchos and Sancho-like characters (Brennecke's edition, p. 15).

50 Knowles, "Cervantes and English Literature," in *Cervantes Across the Centuries*, p. 285.

51 *Barataria: or, Sancho Turn'd Governor* (Dublin: Printed for Wilkinson et alii, 1785).

scene, when Sancho, who cannot keep from thinking of food all the time he is discharging his official duties, is finally taken to the dining room, he is told that his wife and daughter (who had joined him at Barataria) must eat first, and that he must be present during their meal. Sancho accepts this Baratarian custom and endures the ordeal stoically, but when it is his turn to eat and his doctor prevents him from touching any dish, Sancho goes berserk and starts throwing things about.

The Sancho of Pilon is, however, a clownish coward who refuses to defend the *insula* when its siege begins. Instead of arming himself, Sancho runs all over the stage yelling:

> This comes of nibbling at governments...where shall I fly! this way, I know, leads to the garden, and I'll steal off there and hide myself, if its only behind a gooseberry bush;...adso! I was rushing into the lion's mouth,...'tis out of the frying pan into the fire; I'll jump out of this window.... What shall I do, where shall I hide? I'll get under the table; a dogs place, and a whole skin is better than laced robes and danger (pp. 35-36).

When Sancho cannot be found after the battle, the Duke sends his underlings to look for him amongst the slain, offering a thousand crowns to whoever shows him Sancho's head. Sancho then pops his head out from under the table and says: "Then my Lord I claim the reward myself" (p. 36).

When one compares *Don Quixote in England* with *Barataria, Sancho at Court, Squire Badger,* and *The Sot,* Fielding's gracious rendering of the squire stands out at once, especially because, as is now self-evident, the stage is not the medium most fitted to do justice to Sancho's personality. The inevitably restricting nature of farces. ballets, bur-lettas, and short comedies, limits from the outset the creation and adequate treatment of a complex character.[52] Unfortunately, the stage was precisely where eighteenth-century Italian, Spanish, and French writers most frequently placed Sancho.

---

[52] Lack of depth of character was not considered a drawback by all writers of this period. Alain René Lesage, for example, considered it a desirable feature, and thought that the Sancho of Avellaneda was an excel-lent character because there are no contradictions in him; this made him "'plus original même que celui de Cervantes'" (Bardon, p. 411). The intrica-cies of the personality of Cervantes's Sancho were, for Lesage, inconsisten-cies, flaws. Lesage's defense of the apocryphal *Don Quixote* was published in 1702, and his loose translation of Avellaneda's work appeared in 1704. See also Monique Joly's "Tres autores en busca de un personaje: Cervantes,

Another unflattering characterization of Sancho for the stage appears in *Don Chisciotte in corte della duchessa*, a melodrama written by the Venetian playwright Apostolo Zeno and represented apparently on Mardi gras in 1727. Flaccomio considers that in this work Sancho is a "buffone grossolano" (p. 45), and states: "Qui non troviamo ombra di dolorose considerazioni, nemmeno umorismo troviamo in questo melodramma, chè l'umorismo richiede un pensiero; troviamo solamente il ridicolo.... Infatti i personaggi si muovono, mossi da non so quale istinto; i più artistici episodii del Cervantes sono qui trasformati in sciocche parodie" (p. 59)[53]

In Italy Sancho found more of a kindred spirit in the Sicilian writer Giovanni Meli, author of the poem *Don Chisciotti e Sanciu Panza* (1787). Meli forces Sancho to go through some traumatic experiences. At the beginning of the poem Rosinante and Sancho's beloved ass become possessed by the necromancers and Don Quixote has to kill their mounts in order to destroy his enemies; later on, Don Quixote takes Sancho for an evil magician and cuts his nose clean off his face with one slash of his sword; at the end of the poem, Sancho involuntarily becomes the indirect cause of his master's death (Flaccomio, pp. 90-98).[54] But Meli's Sancho surmounts all of these misfortunes. He is a shrewd and witty peasant, who at one point even manages to convince his master that Dulcinea's enchantment can be broken only through Don Quixote's own deeds rather than through Sancho's lashing himself. "Qui la situazione è nettamente capovolta ed è ora la volta di Sancio di impancarsi a giudice e disporre del destino suo e di quello del suo padrone" (Flaccomio, p. 113). This Sancho, Flaccomio continues, "è dotato di uno spirito profetico: egli è il poeta [Meli] stesso," and his ideas in praise of rural life "sone le

---

Avellaneda y Lesage frente a Sancho Panza," *Actas del Quinto Congreso Internacional de Hispanistas*, 2 vols. (Bordeaux, 1977), II, pp. 489-99. Joly considers that the three different Sanchos reflect in their use of folkloric material the different emphases Cervantes, Avellaneda, and Lesage give to this aspect in their works.

[53] Flaccomio finds reminiscences of Sancho's "malaugurato governo dell' isola Barattaria" in Giovanni Battista Lorenzi's *L'idolo cinese* (Palermo, 1773), p. 87.

[54] After one of Sancho's usual remarks questioning the prowess of the knight, Don Quixote engages in a senseless struggle with a crooked tree in a futile attempt to show Sancho that he has not lost his strength and can straighten up the trunk of the tree. As a consequence of this exertion, Don Quixote dies of exhaustion at the foot of the tree, and in defeat.

stesse idee che il Meli ripeterà più tardi nelle *Riflessioni* ed in certi punti le stesse parole" (pp. 118 and 119). "Sancio è l'esponente del pensiero del Meli" (p. 137). In a letter to Avolino di Paola, Meli himself explains his conception of Sancho:

> Mi lusingavo...di aver fatto comprendere nelle ingenue, però argute risposte di Sancio, che esso, abbenchè pria rozzo ed ignorante, perchè niente istruito, fosse stato dalla natura dotato di somma adeguatezza e perspicacia di mente...per mettere in assetto le sconnesse cognizioni che, in mezzo alle sciocchezze, venivangli dal padrone somministrate, di maniera che, riproducendolo a proposito, purgate dalle stravaganze, apparissero tutt' altre che quelle di pria...per indi concluderne che le stesse, stessissime cognizioni, che in un uomo di buon senso e di testa quadra formano il filosofo, od almeno uomo di giudizio, in un'altra testa...formano un pazzo.
>
> (Flaccomio, p. 122)

The tacit identification of the poet with Sancho, and his obvious approval of the aspirations he sees in him—a healthy, peaceful, and quiet life farming in the countryside and living day to day from the fruits of mother earth—are so totally opposed to the general opinion held by writers and critics of the period, that they make Meli stand out as Sancho's unquestionable flag bearer in the eighteenth century.

Spanish writers of that century were not capable of discovering in Sancho any of the virtues Meli found in the squire. Amongst the various Spanish plays of the period which were based on *Don Quixote* surprisingly few are dedicated solely to Sancho. Of the fifteen plays studied by LaGrone (pp. 43-60, and 116-18), only three dealt specifically with him, and of these two, *Ínsula Barataria: o Todo el reino es una quinta* and *Sancho Panza*, are known only by title through the catalogue of Cayetano Alberto de la Barrera y Leirado, and the other, Joseph Santos's *Las caperuzas de Sancho* (1776), does not have Sancho as its principal character. This *entremés* concerns the robbery and recovery of the five small cocked hats that Sancho ordered to be given to the prisoners kept in the Baratarian jail (II, 45, 377-78).[55] After analyzing this group of fifteen plays LaGrone concludes: "[*Don Quixote*, eighteenth-century Spanish] authors seem to have felt, is irresistible as a parody bordering on the grotesque;...Don Quixote and Sancho become consciously ridiculous puppets" (p. 61).

In eighteenth-century France, as in Italy and Spain, *Don Quixote* and Sancho had a stronger appeal for playwrights and composers

---

[55] LaGrone, pp. 44 and 53.

than for novelists, with the great majority of theatrical pieces being written before the revolutionary upheavals of the last years of the century;[56] but most of these works merely repeat one another and show little originality. Of the thirty-odd musical and literary works on Cervantine themes written for the stage between 1700 (*Mascarade de don Quichotte*) and 1789 (*Le Nouveau Don Quichotte*, opera bouffe in two acts by Boissel and Stanislas Champein), perhaps only three need to be considered here in some detail: the tragicomedy *Basile et Quitterie* (1713?),[57] the comic ballet *Don Quichotte chez la Duchesse* (1743), and the opera bouffe *Sancho Pança dans son Isle* (1762).

In *Basile et Quitterie* Gaultier depicts a well-balanced Sancho, who has the earthy weaknesses of the original character, feels a deep affection for his daughter, and shows a great attachment to his ass:

> C'est un âne, Monsieur, qui vaut son pesant d'or,
> Pour qui je sens dans l'âme une tendresse extrême;
> Que je regarde enfin comme un autre moi-même.
>
> (Bardon, p. 503)

The tender tone of this remark reminds one of Sancho at his best. The Sancho of Gaultier is also a popular philosopher who uses proverbs opportunely, and is persistent in his search for an office. He never disdains the inviting aroma of viands, nor a refreshing gulp of wine, but he never falls into the ignoble extremes of a glutton or a drunkard (Bardon, pp. 500-04).

Charles Favart's comic ballet in three acts *Don Quichotte chez la Duchesse* was presented by the Académie Royale de Musique in 1743. Its plot revolves around Altisidora's love for Don Quixote; but the Altisidora of Favart, unlike the young, playful, and mischievous maiden of Cervantes, is truly and madly in love with the knight. On two different occasions she confesses her passion to him and asks him to marry her, but Don Quixote declines on both occasions, telling her that he is totally and for ever devoted to his lady Dulcinea. After being rejected for the second time, and in a rage of jealousy, Altisidora transforms the knight into a bear and Sancho into a monkey (Act 2), but the wizard Merlin feels pity for the two heroes and returns them to their former selves in the third act. Sancho then

---

[56] Bardon mentions only one play for the years 1790-1799, Jean Guillaume Antoine Cuvelier de Trie's *L'Empire de la folie: ou La Mort et l'apothéose de Don Quichotte* (1799).

[57] Bardon gives the date 1723, but the catalogue of the Bibliothèque Nationale lists a copy of 1713.

goes to Africa, where he marries a Congolese heiress, and the abandoned Don Quixote embarks for Japan in search of Dulcinea (Bardon, pp. 634-37).[58] Favart retained the original names of Cervantes's characters and based his ballet on an episode from *Don Quixote*, but the use of witchcraft, the reciprocal forlornness of knight and squire, and the marriage of Sancho are too far removed from Cervantes's constant striving for verisimilitude and from the literary personalities of the original characters for one to regard the ballet as an extension of the Spanish novel.

The opera bouffe *Sancho Pança dans son Isle*, written by François Philidor and Antoine Poinsinet, was presented at Fontainebleau on 20 October 1762. In this work Sancho longs for the love of a young maiden, Juliette, and tries to entice her by promising her that they will marry and she will become his princess or his queen if he ever becomes a prince or a king. There is, however, one insurmountable obstacle between Sancho and his "Dulcinea"; Juliette already has a lover, Don Crispinos Alonzos Tapagino dellos Fuentes Peyros, who, upon learning of Sancho's intentions, challenges him to a duel. The two rivals meet, but they are terribly afraid of each other and end the duel after a few exchanges, with Sancho returning to his duties as governor of Barataria.

Off stage Sancho did not fare any better. The squire of an anonymous French continuation of *Don Quixote* resembles the original Sancho only on the surface.[59] He mispronounces words, uses proverbs freely, and never tires of speaking, but his overall attitude towards life bears no relation whatsoever to that of Cervantes's character (Bardon, pp. 433-34).

Another anonymous work, *Les Regrets de Sancho-Pança sur la mort de son asne: ou Dialogue de Sancho et de Don Quichotte sue le même sujet, et autres Nouvelles en vers*, published in 1714, was inspired by Sancho's love for his ass, and, as the title clearly explains, deals with the mourning of Sancho upon the death of his four-legged companion. But, somewhat

---

[58] The plots of Favart's ballet and Zeno's *Don Chisciotte in corte della duchessa* are completely different. For summaries of Zeno's melodrama see Flaccomio, pp. 50-60, and Giuseppe Carlo Rossi's "Interpretaciones cervantinas en la literatura italiana del siglo XVIII," to be published in *Actas del II Simposio sobre el P. Feijóo, 1976* (Oviedo).

[59] *Suite nouvelle et veritable de l'histoire et des avantures de l'incomparable Don Quichotte de la Manche. Traduite d'un Manuscrit Espagnol de Cide-Hamet Benengely son veritable historien.* The sixth and last volume bears the title *Histoire de Sancho Pansa, alcade de Blandanda.* This continuation appeared anonymously in Paris between 1722 and 1726 (Bardon, p. 853).

inconsistently, Sancho's grief is immediately and easily cured when Don Quixote sends him to the kitchen, knowing that there is no pain of Sancho's which cannot be mitigated with food. "Go," Don Quixote tells Sancho, "go:"

	Egayer ton [âme] chagrine Sur quelque morceau de ton goût.
SANCHO.	Mon appetit est mort à tout.
DON QUICHOTTE.	Le jambon le fera renaître.
SANCHO.	Vous êtes toûjours mon bon maître.
DON QUICHOTTE.	Le ventre ne peut se trahir.
SANCHO.	J'y vais donc pour vous obéir.

(Bardon, p. 439)

Sancho was also the model for several French servants, but the resemblance between these Sancho-like characters and Cervantes's character lies, according to Bardon, only in their fondness for proverbs, insatiable hunger, volubility, and occasional shrewdness (pp. 618-25).

In France, but not in the other European countries, Sancho was frequently used as a saritical weapon. The French critic Jean Monnet, for instance, speaking of the gullible playwright Poinsinet, says that Sancho and Poinsinet have in common the stupidity of a young goose and the malice of an ape (Bardon, p. 589). The Abbot Ferdinand Galiani, a relative of Diderot, affirms in one of his letters that Voltaire is being ironical when he praises the government of Cicero in Cilicia, and, to drive his point home, Galiani compares Cilicia to Barataria and Cicero to Sancho (Bardon, p. 546). Saint-Just makes another derogatory comparison when in his poem *Organt* he calls the playwright Denis Desessarts Sancho:

> *Organt vit là* M..., dont le talent
> Est d'écorcher [Molière] impunément,
> Et Des..., le Sancho de l'école,
> Qui croit l'Olympe assis sur son épaule.
> (Bardon, p. 725)

In his *Cours de littérature dramatique* (1819-1820) Julien Louis Geoffroy refers ironically to the playwright Philippe Fabre d'Eglantine saying: "'O législateur des nations, exterminateur des préjugés, oracle de l'humanité et de la raison, à quel point ton génie s'est-il ravalé! L'apôtre des principes éternels de l'ordre n'est plus que l'écho de Sancho Pança'" (Bardon, p. 732). Two other examples: in 1791 Bonneville, an irate citizen, rebuked the Assemblée Nationale, and angrily called Mirabeau "Sancho Pança Mirabeau" for what he considered to be a stupid decision in favor of the Prince of Condé; and on another occasion a lady addressed the following reproach to an unidentified man: "Tu fais la doucereux comme à vingt ans. Ça t'va bien, avec ton ventre à la Sancho Pança'" (Bardon, pp. 723 and 724).

On the other hand, Antoine Houdar de la Motte, Voltaire, François Gayot de Pitaval, and Jean Baptiste de Boyer, Marquis d'Argens, praise Sancho in their works. Houdar de la Motte approves of the "'prudente raison d'un Sancho'" in his *Réflexions sur la Critique* (1715); in his *Dictionnaire philosophique* (1764) Voltaire states: "'Je ne connais point de meilleur juge que Sancho Pança: cependant il ne savait pas un mot du code de l'île de Barataria.'" Pitaval in his *Causes célèbres* (1749) uses Sancho's verdicts at Barataria as examples to set the pattern for judges "pour les cas d'exception." Boyer makes repeated use of both Sancho and Don Quixote in his *Lettres juives* (first edition, The Hague. P. Paupie, 1736). At one point, he invokes Sancho and Don Quixote to help him fight journalists, especially Antoine Bruzen de la Martinière and François Aubert de la Chesnaye-Desbois, who were the main source of his woes: "'au Naïf et Inimitable Sancho Pança,'" cries Boyer, "'vrai modelle des bons et fidèles écuyers, Gouverneur de l'Ile de Barataria,'" and he entreats the squire to come with Don Quixote and succor him against "ces usurpateurs de noms, professions, titres glorieux," and together force them to stop writing (Bardon, pp. 386, 550, 608, and 540).

It is clear that seventeenth-century Frenchmen used Sancho as a made-to-order instrument either to offend, praise, downgrade, or extol the objects of their criticism, indifferent to the true personality of the squire, and only according to their specific needs. To seal Sancho's overall misfortune in France, the first edition of Jean Pierre Claris de Florian's translation of *Don Quixote* appeared in the last year of the century.[60] Florian altered the original text mercilessly, "mais, de tous les personnages, celui qui a été le plus arrangé, façonné, et gâté, c'est Sancho" (Bardon, p. 708). In his *Mélanges de philosophie, d'histoire et de littérature* (1828-1830) Charles Marie Dorimond, Abbot of Féletz, criticized Florian's presumption: "'C'est un grand tort pour un traducteur de *Don Quichotte* de gâter Sancho,'" says the Abbot, because Florian has made Sancho lose his original simplicity and naivety (Bardon, p. 714).

---

[60] *Don Quichotte de la Manche, Traduit de l'Espagnol de Michel de Cervantes par Florian* (Paris: P. Didot l'Aîné, 1799). This translation was published post-humously.

The sheer number of eighteenth-century French references to, and works inspired by *Don Quixote* analysed by Bardon is overwhelming evidence of the popularity that Cervantes's work and characters attained in that century. Just as the ocean settles as the storm approaches, however, France's interest in *Don Quixote* diminished with the coming of tempestuous times, for it is only natural for social turmoil to bring new favorites to the fore. The new spirit despised everything that reminded it of the old regime, and banished the sumptuous representations of ballets, comedies, masques, and plays that had flourished under the aegis of Louis XIV and his royal successors. Until then, Sancho's popularity in eighteenth-century France had not been altogether enviable, but with the fall of Louis XVI Sancho almost disappears from the French stage.

Sancho found a more congenial environment amongst three German writers of the same period, Friedrich Justin Bertuch, Johann Gottfried von Herder, and Friedrich Maximilian von Klinger. For Bertuch, whose German translation of *Don Quixote* appeared in 1775-1777, Sancho represented the common people. In point of fact, Ber-liked Sancho so much that the tone of his translation "is more fitting for the squire than for the knight" (Bergel, p. 317). Herder also preferred "'the quiet [!], good natured, always satisfied [!] Sancho Panza'" (Bergel, p. 314) to Don Quixote and his aristocratic attitude. In his "Reflections on World and Literature" (1803) Klinger "confronts Sancho Panza, as governor, with the rulers he had known; [and] the comparison is entirely in Sancho Panza's favor" (Bergel, p. 315). Finally, Frederick II, King of Prussia, praises Sancho's judgments in a letter to Voltaire (1766):

> Sancho Pança était un grand jurisconsulte; il gouvernait sagement son île de Barataria. Il serait à souhaiter que les présidiaux eussent toujours sa belle sentence sous les yeux; ils respecteraient au moins davantage la vie des malheureux, s'ils se rappellaient qu'il vaut mieux sauver un coupable que de perdre un innocent.
>
> (Bardon, p. 568)

Thus, the Age of Enlightenment continued the critical trend set by the previous century and split Sancho's personality in two alien halves: one half, a laughable buffoon, the other, a wise judge. And the farcical nature and tone of the great majority of works inspired by *Don Quixote* in seventeenth- and eighteenth-century Europe clearly show that Cervantes's novel was considered primarily a humorous, a burlesque work, and that most writers did not in the least hesitate to use and stress in their works only the grotesque and ridiculous idiosyncracies of Don Quixote and Sancho.[61] Hence, squire and knight gradually became ideal stock characters in the hands of European playwrights, who used them in the same fashion as they used the cuckold, the miser, the drunkard, and the blustering Spanish soldier.

Sancho was better understood and treated by eighteenth-century novelists, especially English novelists such as Fielding and Graves, who were able to re-create and vitalize Sancho through the sympathetic depiction of their own characters modeled after Cervantes's squire. Eighteenth-century England was, without a doubt, the country that best appreciated and put to use Sancho's literary possibilities; but even there Fielding and Graves were the exceptions rather than the rule, as in their own countries were Meli in Italy, and Bertuch, Herder, and Klinger in Germany. "To most other contemporary critics," says Bergel, "Sancho Panza is a grotesque and coarse figure. The Opinion of [Georg Christoph] Lichtenberg is typical: 'Sancho Panza is a person whose only concerns are money and food,' [and this] is also the way in which the novels imitating *Don Quixote* present [him]" (p. 316). True, Florian's 1799 translation of *Don Quixote* closed the century with a more elaborate and a more refined Sancho than previous translations, but it fails to do justice to Cervantes's original character because the squire's own personality all but disappears amongst the added frills of characterization.

---

[61] See also Fidelino de Sousa Figueiredo's "O thema do *Quixote* na litteratura portuguesa do seculo XVIII," *Revista de Filología Española*, 7 (1920), 47-56. Figueiredo gives a summary of Antonio José da Silva's play *Vida do grande D. Quixote de la Mancha e do gordo Sancho Pança* (1733), and notes that Silva's approach to Don Quixote "consistiu em seleccionar episodios para os reproduzir com a indispensavel condensação, e buscar suggestões para as amplificar exaggerando o comico cervantino até ao baixo burlesco. Assim amplia e carrega as côres da scena da partida de Sancho, o qual deixa por testamento uma extravagante peça dum gosto muito contestavel e que attinge o tom obsceno" (p. 52). In "Don Quijote en el teatro portugués del siglo XVIII," *Anales Cervantinos*, 3 (1953), 349-52, José Ares Montes mentions an anonymous *entremés* entitled *O grande governador de Ilha dos Lagartos* (1774), and concludes that it is in fact a rehashing of scenes 4 and 5 of Silva's earlier play.

PLATE 4 The speech on the Golden Age
by J. Vanderbank (London: J. and R. Tonson, 1738)
    Courtesy of the British Library, Cerv.319, vol. 1, facing p. 76

PLATE 5 Ginés steals Sancho's ass
by Brévière (Milan: Andrea Ubicini, 1841)
        Courtesy of the British Library, Cerv.312, vol. 2, p. 39

✣ 3 ✥

From Unwelcome Shadow to Individual

> ¿Qué me importa lo que Cervantes quiso o no
> quiso poner allí y lo que realmente puso? Lo
> vivo es lo que yo allí descubro, pusiéralo o no
> Cervantes, lo que yo allí pongo y sobrepongo
> y sotopongo, y lo que ponemos allí todos.
>
> MIGUEL DE UNAMUNO
> *Del sentimiento trágico de la vida*
> "Conclusión"

HE DIFFERING VIEWS of Sancho that began appearing in the Age of Enlightenment were clearly a step forward towards the realization and recognition that he is a far more complex character than had been thought until then; but the good opinion that, amongst others, Fielding, Meli, Gaultier, and Bertuch had of him well-nigh disappeared under the rising tide of Romantic criticism that began swelling at the end of the century. This drastic reversal was due chiefly to the tendency of critics to envisage Sancho and Don Quixote symbolically as representing simple, contradictory elements rather than as complex and independent literary characters.

Although Bardon considers that with the publication of Jean-Jacques Rousseau's *La Nouvelle Héloïse* "et avec la sensibilité de Rousseau, s'inaugure dès 1761 le romantisme sympathique à don Quichotte" (p. 634), it was perhaps the Swiss scholar Johann Jakob Bodmer who was the first to see "Cervantes as a conscious artist;... particularly [for] the way in which [he] develops the contrast between Don Quixote and Sancho" (Bergel, p. 313). But the main influence that led the German Romantics into viewing Don Quixote

and Sancho as incarnations of contrasting and irreconcilable prin-
ciples was the philosophical theories of Johann Christoph Friedrich
von Schiller concerning the relationship between pairs of opposites
(finite-infinite, idea-reality, naïve-sentimental, Greek-modern). Following this line of thought, Friedrich Wilhelm Joseph von Schelling,
Novalis, Adam Heinrich Müller, and the brothers August Wilhelm
and Friedrich von Schlegel considered that the knight and the squire
were the antipodal elements of the dualities ideal-real, dream-reality,
mind-body, poetic-realistic, and romantic-prosaic (Bergel, p. 321-23),
Sancho being, of course, the real, the reality, the body, the realistic,
and the prosaic.[62] These dualities were echoed in Spain by Antonio
Alcalá Galiano, and in France by Jean Charles Léonard Simonde de
Sismondi, the second of whom tersely stated that "l'invention fon-
damentale de Don Quichotte, c'est le contraste éternel entre l'esprit
poétique et celui de la prose.'"[63]

    In England, Samuel Taylor Coleridge accepted the theory that
each value exists only in relation to its opposite, to which it is
completely bound, and applied it to Cervantes's characters. In 1818,
in one of his lectures, Coleridge stated the following:

> [Don Quixote] becomes a substantial living allegory, or personi-
> fication of the reason and the moral sense, divested of the
> judgment and the understanding. Sancho is the converse. He is
> the common sense without reason or imagination;...put him
> and his master together, and they form a perfect intellect; but
> they are separated and without cement; and hence each having
> a need of the other for its own completeness, each has at times
> a mastery over the other.[64]

For Coleridge, Sancho and don Quixote are, too, the "cheater and the
cheated" (p. 103), and share no middle ground. Coleridge perceptively

---

[62] See also Franco Meregalli's "Cervantes nella critica romantica tedesca,"
Annali di Ca'Foscari, 11 (1972), 381-95, and Anthony J. Close's monograph *The
Romantic Approach to "Don Quixote": A Critical History of the Romantic Tradition in
"Quixote" Criticism* (Cambridge, 1978), especially Chapter 2.

[63] Franco Meregalli, "La critica cervantina dell'ottocento in Francia e in
Spagna," *Anales Cervantinos*, 15 (1976), 121-48, at pp. 125 and 133. Meregalli
notes that in the seventeenth century, "sul terreno propriamente critico, la
Spagna aveva seguito docilmente i moduli prevalenti in Europa, e special-
mente in Francia" (p. 132).

[64] "Lecture viii: Don Quixote: Cervantes," in *Coleridge's Miscellaneous Criticism*, edited by Thomas Middleton Raysor (London, 1936), p. 102. Coleridge
delivered this lecture on 20 February 1818. For the fundamental "weakness,
incoherence and indistinctness" of Coleridge's philosophical thought see René

notes the interdependence of knight and squire, but there are patent weaknesses in his cognizance of the characters. He considers that Don Quixote and Sancho are opposite absolutes, each representing a different kind of "sense," but by depriving Don Quixote ("reason and the moral sense") of "judgment" and "understanding," and Sancho ("common sense") of "reason" and "imagination," Coleridge carries his generalization too far. This sort of all-exclusive proposition is untenable with respect to *Don Quixote* because it does not do justice to the complexities of Cervantes's novel.

Charles Lamb was basically of the same opinion as Coleridge. For him "the image of the high-souled, high-intelligenced Quixote (the errant Star of Knighthood, made more tender by eclipse) has never presented itself divested from the unhallowed accompaniment of a Sancho."[65] Then Lamb proceeds to write a lengthy panegyric of Don Quixote at the expense of both Cervantes and Sancho. He considers *Don Quixote*, Part II, inferior to Part I, and says:

> In the First Adventures, even, it needed all the art of the most consummate artist in the Book way that the world hath yet seen, to keep up in the mind of the reader the heroic attributes of the character without relaxing; so as absolutely [sic] that they shall suffer no alloy from the debasing fellowship of the clown [Sancho]. If it ever obtrudes itself as a disharmony, are we inclined to laugh; or not, rather, to indulge a contrary emotion? —Cervantes, stung perchance by the relish with which *his* Reading Public had received the fooleries of the man, more to their palates than the generosities of the master, in the sequel let his pen run riot, lost the harmony and the balance, and [sacrificed] a great idea to the taste of his contemporaries,...he abandoned his Knight, and has fairly set up the Squire for his hero. For what else has he unsealed the eyes of Sancho? and why, instead of that twilight state of semi-insanity, (the madness at second-hand—the contagion, caught from a stronger

Wellek's "Samuel Taylor Coleridge and Kant," in *Immanuel Kant in England 1793-1838* (Princeton, 1931), pp. 65-135; the quotation is from p. 68. In "S. T. Coleridge: His Theory of Knowledge," *Transactions of the Wisconsin Academy of Sciences, Arts and Letters*, 48 (1959), 221-32, at p. 223, Joan Larsen has noted that the difficulty "in Coleridge's use of language is not only to be found in the mental leap the reader must make between what is rationally argued and what is emotionally felt through poetic image, but also in Coleridge's practice of using similar or identical imagery to describe separate categories of thought processes."

[65] "Barrenness of the Imaginative Faculty in the Production of Modern Art," in *The Life, Letters and Writings of Charles Lamb*, edited by Percy Hetherington Fitzgerald (London: E. Moxon and Co., 1876), IV, p. 99.

mind infected—that war between native cunning and hereditary deference, with which he has hitherto accompanied his master —two for a pair [almost],) does he substitute a downright Knave, with open eyes, for his own ends only following a confessed Madman (pp. 101-02).

And the renowned English art critic John Ruskin says in the first volume of *Modern Painters* (1843) that only the "lowest mind would find in [*Don Quixote*] perpetual and brutish amusement in the misfortunes of the knight, and perpetual pleasure in sympathy with the squire" (Knowles 1947, p. 289).

Few nineteenth-century writers were able to resist the general current and take a firm stand against the bitter Romantic criticism of Sancho. He received some praise from Prosper Mérimée (1826), Juan Valera (1864)—who objected to the application of the prose-poetry duality to Don Quixote and Sancho (Meregalli 1976, pp. 125 and 137)—Louis Simon Auger (1825), and Jules Gabriel Janin (1835)— who thought that Sancho was a successful character and an indispensable counterpart of Don Quixote (LaGrone, p. 64). But out of the handful of defenders of Sancho the only critic who compared the knight and squire at length was the Abbot of Féletz in his *Mélanges de philosophie, d'histoire et de littérature* (1828). He studied in detail the virtues and weaknesses of Cervantes's characters and concluded that they are not a pair of opposites. Bardon paraphrases his account of Sancho's personality:

> Sancho nous est, lui aussi, fort bien rendu. Il nous amuse de ses proverbes, nous séduit par l'attachement qu'il montre à son maître, par la tendresse qu'il montre à son âne. Comme il est vrai, à son tour, et bien humain, avec les contradictions de sa nature, avec 'son *demi bon-sens* . . . qui lui fait voir les folies de don Quichotte',—avec 'sa *demi-folie* qui lui fait néanmoins toujours espérer cette *maudite isle près de la mer!* ce qui ne l'empêche pas de demander prudemment des *gages*, quitte à *rabattre l'île sur ses gages,* quand elle viendra'. . . . Admirons justement en lui ce mélange de bon sens et de folie, de propos sérieux et bouffons, de bonnes et de mauvaises qualités, de naïveté et de finesse! Sancho est homme, un pauvre homme comme nous, et nous sourions de nous retrouver en cette image comique de nous-mêmes (pp. 794-95).

The Abbot of Féletz accurately perceived that Don Quixote's squire is not a simple character, that he has both weaknesses and virtues, imagination and common sense; but the Romantic interpretation of Sancho was so intensely and persistently proclaimed that it left its mark in most criticism of this period. In another monograph Bardon quotes or paraphrases the unflattering opinions of Sancho expressed by some contemporaries of the Abbot of Féletz:[66] Victor Hugo (Sancho "arrive comme Silène,—dieu nouveau monté sur un âne, sur l'Ane, symbole de l'Ignorance") (p. 260), Théophile Gautier (Sancho is "*'l'homme positif, la raison vulgaire à côté de la noble folie,'*" "*'la raison prosaïque, le gros bon sens à côté de l'enthousiasme et de la poésie,'*" "Sancho Pança et don Quichotte s'opposent l'un à l'autre par la nature intime, par les tendances de tout l'être; et ils s'opposent ainsi dans le livre entier") (pp. 271, 272, and 275), and Auguste Vacquerie ("L'antithèse se marque au physique comme au moral. L'un raide, haut dressé sur son Rossinante, habite la nue; l'autre, corpulent et appesanti sur son grison, semble attiré vers le sol qu'il touche presque de ses larges pieds") (p. 276). These sweeping condemnations of Sancho, coupled with the stereotyped image of the squire inherited from the stage of the previous century, greatly influenced contemporary playwrights in the depiction of their Sancho-like characters. The French theatre of the Napoleonic era is indeed the genre which best exemplifies contemporary thought about Sancho.

Three plays should be mentioned in this connection: first, Nicolas Brazier's *Rodomont: ou le Petit Dom Quichotte* (1807), whose two principal characters, Rodomont and his servant Médor, are, according to Bardon, the "stupide Sancho d'un stupide don Quichotte" (p. 779), second, the melodrama in three acts *Bédeno: ou le Sancho de Bisnagar*, co-authored by Goldmann and Jean Aude, presented at the Théâtre de l'Ambigu Comique on 6 October 1807, and last, *Sancho dans l'Isle de Barataria*, a *pantomime bouffonne* by Cuvelier de Trie, first staged in 1816 at the Théâtre du Cirque Olympique. It would be repetitious to summarize here the plots of these works; suffice it to say that they present Sancho again as he had been previously portrayed by earlier French playwrights, a stupid buffoon incapable of any higher thoughts; see Bardon, pp. 776-79.

Sancho received very much the same treatment from the pens of contemporary Spanish playwrights. LaGrone studies forty-four nineteenth-century plays based on *Don Quixote* (Pérez Capo lists fifty-four), of which only five use Sancho as their principal character.

---

[66] "*Don Quichotte* en France: L'Interprétation romantique," *Les Lettres Romanes*, 3 (1949), 263-82. For Stendhal's opinion see Jean Jacques Achille Bertrand's "Génesis de la concepción romántica de Don Quijote en Francia: Segunda parte," *Anales Cervantinos*, 4 (1954), 41-76, p. 43. For a reference to Sancho and Barataria by Napoleon, see *Grand Dictionnaire Universel du XIXe Siècle*, (Paris, 1866-1890), II, p. 201.

These plays are: *Sancho Panza en su ínsula* (anonymous *sainete*, c. 1800), José Maqueda's play in one act *Sancho Panza en su gobierno* (1812), Luis Mariano de Larra y Wetoret's *La ínsula Barataria* (*zarzuela*, 1864), Juan Molas y Casas's *Sancho Panza* (*capricho cómico*, 1881), and *El gran Sancho Panza* (anonymous *zarzuela*, c. 1900). Of the five only *Sancho Panza en su gobierno* portrays Sancho with some accuracy, the other four farces evince the usual exploitation of Sancho's shortcomings and his mishaps in Barataria. LaGrone finds the anonymous *Sancho Panza en su ínsula* representative of the way in which material from *Don Quixote* can be converted into modern slapstick, and his summary of the plot clearly shows the tendency of playwrights to distort the image of the squire:

> According to the new scheme of things, Sancho Panza, who was intoxicated the night before, finds himself transformed as if by magic into the governor of Barataria. Though he objects to the ceremonies, he takes a liking to one of his subjects, who overwhelm him with their welcome, that is, Julieta, a seamstress; but she happens to be the girl friend of a bully soldier, who smashes Sancho's nose, once the governor is induced to fight. The doctor is of no help; he merely puts Sancho on a stricter diet. A letter is received from Don Quixote, but neither the governor, his secretary, his archivist, nor his doctor knows how to read. Sancho watches a magnificent meal disappear before his very eyes. When his subjects come to arm him for the encounter with some approaching invaders, they find him under the table, consuming the remnants of the meal that were overlooked by the doctor. Sancho resigns his governorship; the Duke explains that it was all a joke; and Sancho wonders who actually has been the victim, he or the others.
>
> (LaGrone, pp. 76-77)

Six non-Cervantine elements of the plot can be pointed out: Sancho's drunkenness, his sudden transformation into governor of Barataria, his infatuation with Julieta, his fight with the soldier and the bloodying of his nose, his cowardice and gluttony when Barataria is under seige, and, lastly, the Duke's confessing to him that the whole episode was merely a jest (thus undercutting the great personal sacrifice that Sancho makes in Cervantes's novel when he resigns his office of his own accord). These additions, however, leave no doubt about the literary source of the *sainete*: *Sancho Panza en su ínsula* is a poor imitation of Poinsinet's opera bouffe *Sancho Pança dans son Isle* (1762); see Chapter 2, p. 44.

This group of French and Spanish plays and the sample of critical exegeses cited above could be supplemented by hundreds of allusions and references to Sancho in the various monographs dealing with the fortunes of *Don Quixote* in nineteenth-century Europe, showing that during this period almost every European writer or critic of any stature mentioned or commented on Sancho at one time or another. It is startling to discover, therefore, how little attention Russian writers paid to him. Ludmilla Buketoff Turkevich has noted that "the character of Sancho Panza held surprisingly little appeal for the Russians," concluding that "perhaps the only clear-cut Russian example of [the master-servant] relationship is to be found in [Aleksandr Nicolaievich] Ostrovski's drama *The Forest*" (1870; first staged in 1871).[67] The principal characters are the impetuous and idealistic Gennadi Neschastlivtsev, the hero of the play, and his servant Arkashka Schastlivtsev. Arkashka "is simple, good-natured, witty, modest in ambitions, keenly sensitive to the exigencies of life, and he possesses a marvelous ability to use what little he has to the greatest personal advantage" (Turkevich, p. 131). But if there is only one Sancho-like character in Tsarist Russia, he and his master did not escape the prevalent tendency of writers to compare them and set them apart as opposites.

Apparently the first Russian critic to analyze in depth the personality of Sancho was Dmitri Sergeievich Merejkovski in his "Don Kikhot i Sancho," published in *Severny Viestnik*, in 1889. According to Constantin Nicolaievich Derjavin, "este análisis minucioso de todas sus palabras y todos sus actos muestra la figura del fiel escudero de don Quijote como representante del pueblo, como una encarnación del realismo práctico, como un Mefistófeles ridículo al lado de su Fausto tragicómico."[68]

For Ivan Sergeievich Turgenev also, Sancho was a symbol of the common people, and Don Quixote a symbol of the aristocracy. From Turgenev's point of view Sancho becomes a docile, blindfolded moujik, whose natural destiny is simply to follow and pay homage to his superior:

> [Sancho's attachment to his master is a common] peculiarity of the masses—in the tendency towards happy and honest blindness, in the propensity for disinterested enthusiasm, and in the scorn of daily bread.... A great, universally historical peculiarity!... The mass always ends up by following, believing implicitly those persons whom it had formerly jeered, whom it damned and persecuted, but who, undaunted by its persecutions and

---

[67] *Cervantes in Russia* (Princeton, 1950), p. 224.

[68] "La crítica cervantina en Rusia," *Boletín de la Real Academia de la Historia*, 94 (1929), 215-38, at p. 226.

even by its damnations, mindless of its laughter, go unswerv-
ingly forward, with their eyes fixed upon their goal. They seek,
they fall, they rise, and finally find.[69]

The poet Iakov Petrovich Polonski, on the other hand, was not
interested in the social significance of Sancho, but he was disturbed
by what he considered the presence of two different Sanchos in
Cervantes's novel. In a letter written in the second half of the
nineteenth century, Polonski says:

> [I] prefer a pure, unadulterated poetic motif or image. I was
> unpleasantly puzzled, I remember, by Sancho Panza's wise
> speeches in Cervantes' *Don Quixote*, where he too, for some
> reason, went into the mountains and almost became a governor.
> Whence comes this sudden administrative sagacity?
>
> (Turkevich, p. 82)

Polonski, like Lamb, could not accept the eddies, backwaters, and
rapids of Sancho's complex personality. He would have liked a
smooth, pellucid, and constant current, the simple, obedient serf of
Turgenev, a servant never seeking to rise, or capable of rising, to his
master's level. Polonski's opinion shows, none the less, a critical
awareness almost non-existent in Turgenev's sweeping generalization. A similarly all-embracing theory can be found in V. Karelin's
introduction to his translation of *Don Quixote* (St. Petersburg, 1866),
where Sancho and Don Quixote are still being subjected to the
contrastive approach prevalent amongst the Romantics. Derjavin
suggests that in his introduction Karelin "es el primero en definir y
caracterizar el *quijotismo* como un hecho psicológico propio no sólo de
los hombres aislados, sino también de los círculos sociales en ciertos
momentos de su vida política" (p. 221). And Turkevich notes that for
Karelin, Don Quixote is "typified by a total renunciation of the
sensual ['I,' and]...in contrast to this form of human behavior...
there stands a form of conduct completely devoted to the sensual
interests of the individual, as exemplified by Sancho. Sancho's own 'I'
is the only thing that matters to him; all else is of no account....
Between these two poles...lies the mass of mankind" (p. 86). It was
also Karelin who coined the term "Sanchism" to designate the, in his
view, self-serving and down-to-earth attitude of the squire.

Unlike Turgenev and Polonski, Fedor Mikhailovich Dostoievski
was not critical of Sancho. He describes knight and squire in one of
his diary entries for September 1877:

---

[69] From "Hamlet i Don Kikhot" (1860); quoted by Turkevich, p. 109.

Don Quixote [is]...the most magnanimous of all knights on
earth, the simplest in soul and one of the greatest men in
heart,...[and Sancho,] his faithful armor-bearer...—the personification of common sense, prudence, cunning, the golden
mean—chances to become a friend and fellow-traveller of the
insanest man on earth;—precisely he, and no other! He deceives
Don Quixote continually; he cheats him like a child, and at the
same time he fully believes in his great mind; he is tenderly
fascinated by the greatness of his heart; he also gives full
credence to the fantastic dreams of the valiant Knight, and not
once does he doubt that the latter finally will conquer the
island![70]

Here Dostoievski is, like Coleridge, mixing what "is rationally argued" with what "is emotionally felt through poetic image" (see
footnote 64), but although he comes near the trap unconsciously laid
by the Romantics—Don Quixote is "the most magnanimous of all
knights" and Sancho is "the personification of common sense"—he
avoids falling in it by immediately entering into a more balanced and
accurate description of the idiosyncrasies of both characters.

From the opinions of these four Russian writers, and from the
other evidence that has been accumulating, one could already draw
the inference that novelists (Fielding, Graves, Dostoievski) are more
likely than playwrights, poets, or critics to discover, understand, and
capture in their works the polyfacetic personality of Sancho. And it
was precisely two novelists, Juan Montalvo and Charles Dickens,
who created the best two nineteenth-century interpretations of the
squire.

Most studies of Dickens either do not mention Cervantes or *Don
Quixote* at all, or if they do, it is only in vague references and without
entering into any detail. Whether or not *The Pickwick Papers* is indebted
to *Don Quixote* has been a bone of contention for some time. Fitzmaurice-Kelly has no qualms about stating that Mr. Pickwick's manservant, Sam Weller, is a "Cockney variant of Sancho" (p. 28).
Dominic Bevan Wyndham Lewis disagrees with this view:

Having tipped a respectful beaver to the master Dickens one
may be excused for failing to perceive the parallel sometimes
proclaimed between *The Pickwick Papers* and its acknowledged
model. Save that Pickwick develops from a buffoon into a
paladin, and that his relationship with Weller blossoms into a
bond something like that existing between Sancho Panza and

[70] *The Diary of a Writer*, translated by Boris Leo Brasol (New York, 1954),
pp. 835-36.

his master,... these two deathless works have nothing in common but a picaresque plot.[71]

But Cervantes's influence on *The Pickwick Papers* can in fact be detected
not only in the overall sequence and nature of the events, but also in
more subtle details.

Dickens was acquainted with Cervantes at an early age both
directly through reading *Don Quixote* and indirectly through the works
of Fielding and Smollett:

> [His] *childhood years in Chatham were a happy time.... He was too busy
> roaming the lower town and the clanging dockyard, exulting in his rapid
> progress at school, and gulping down great draughts of* Tom Jones,
> Peregrine Pickle, Roderick Random, Don Quixote, The Vicar of
> Wakefield, The Arabian Nights, *and* Robinson Crusoe, *which he
> had found in a little back room in the house.*[72]

Dickens does not mention either Cervantes or *Don Quixote* in *The
Pickwick Papers*, and yet there are some similarities between the two
novels which suggest that at the very least he must have been aware
of the parallels between his plot and characters and those of Cervantes. Three features that are common to both works are the
semblance of historicity given to the narration (readers are repeatedly
told that the stories were taken from original manuscript sources),
the careful search by the authors for further information and their
temporary failure to discover it (cf. Chapters 8, 9 and 52 in *Don*

---

[71] *The Shadow of Cervantes* (New York, 1962), p. 42. Lewis's slack use of the
term "picaresque" is regrettable, as is his failure to realize that the two
aspects he refers to as links between *Don Quixote* and the *The Pickwick Papers* are
of pivotal importance and make undeniable the relationship between the tow
novels. Alexander Welsh's "Waverly, Pickwick, and Don Quixote," *Nineteenth-
century Fiction*, 22 (1967-1968), pp. 19-30, and Gale's "Cervantes' Influence on
Dickens, with Comparative Emphasis on *Don Quijote* and *Pickwick Papers*,"
Anales Cervantinos, 12 (1973), 135-56, are two very disappointing studies,
especially the latter, which contains only the patently obvious and the
irrelevant. Gale states that "the most basic similarity... is that both are
novels" (p. 143), that "both are written in the third person singular," and that
"both novels are in the picaresque tradition" (p. 144), and these similarities
are discussed at length; for Sancho and Sam Weller see pp. 148-49 and 152. I
have been unable to consult J. L. Skinner's "Changing Interpretations of *Don
Quixote* from *Hudibras* to *Pickwick* (unpublished dissertation, Cambridge, 1973),
or to read Horst Wagner's "Zur Frage der Erzähleinschübe im *Don Quijote* und
in den *Pickwick Papers*," *Arcadia*, 9 (1974), 1-22.

[72] *The Heart of Charles Dickens: As Revealed in His Letters to Angela Burdett-Coutts*,
edited by Edgar Johnson (New York, 1952), p. 5.

Quixote, Part I, and the beginning of Chapters 4 and 13 in *The Pickwick Papers),* and the interpolation into the main text of extraneous stories (Chapters 13-14, 33-35, 39-41, and 51 in *Don Quixote,* Part I; Chapters 3, 6, 11, 14, 17, 21, 29, 36, and 49 in *The Pickwick Papers).* It is worth emphasizing also that Mr. Pickwick and Sam reappear in Dickens's weekly serial *Master Humphrey's Clock* (1840), just as Don Quixote and Sancho do in Part II.[73] Master Humphrey says: "I remarked [to Mr. Pickwick] that I had read his adventures very often,... [and] I condoled with him upon the various libels on his character which had found their way into print. Mister Pickwick...added that no doubt I was acquainted with Cervantes's introduction to the second part of Don Quixote [sic], and that it fully expressed his sentiments on the subject" (pp. 365-66). And Mr. Weller, Senior, introduces Sam to Master Humphrey in the following fashion: "My son Samivel, sir, as you may have read on in *history"* (p. 394; my italics).

Furthermore, following his initial intention of giving to his readers "diverting characters,"[74] Dickens created a ridiculous, pear-shaped, naive gentleman, who goes searching for adventures in his mid-fifties; compare *Don Quixote,* "Frisaba la edad de nuestro hidalgo con los cincuenta años" (I, 1, 71). Mr. Samuel Pickwick is not an old man playing knights and dragons like Don Quixote, of course, but his chastity, his fights for justice and truth, his absurd misadventures, his love for his servant, and his desire to do all possible good are unmistakably quixotic. The fact that in other respects Mr. Pickwick and Don Quixote are dissimilar—Mr. Pickwick is of medium-height, plump, bald, with a benevolent countenance; he is well-off, wears circular spectacles, and dresses just like his friends and numerous of his contemporaries—does not affect the argument.

Like Don Quixote's, Mr. Pickwick's personality seems to change as the novel progresses. Dickens attempts to explain and justify these changes in his Preface:

> It has been observed of Mr. Pickwick, that there is a decided change in his character, as these pages proceed, and that he becomes more good and more sensible. I do not think this change will appear forced or unnatural to my readers, if they will reflect that in real life the peculiarities and oddities of a man

[73] "The Mystery of Edwin Drood and Master Humphrey's Clock," Charles Dickens Centennial Edition, Edito-Services S. A., Geneva, n.d.

[74] *The Posthumous Papers of the Pickwick Club* (Oxford, 1964), Preface, p. x. The first installment of the series was published on 31 March 1836, and the first edition of *The Pickwick Papers* in book form appeared in 1837.

who has anything whimsical about him, generally impress us
first, and that it is not until we are better acquainted with him
that we usually begin to look below these superficial traits, and
to know the better part of him (p. xii).[75]

But in truth it is not the character who changes.It is Dickens's more
sympathetic descriptions of Mr. Pickwick's personality and deeds
which turn the pompous, clownish founder of the Pickwick Club of
Chapter 1 into the cheerful, respectable, understanding, and admirable Mr. Pickwick of the last chapters of the novel. Mr. Pickwick
becomes more attractive to the reader because Dickens "appeals to
the domestic feeling of his readers, and endeavours to show vice in
its worst colours, while he strives to supply virtue with the most
lovely tints, in order that he may inculcate morality by rendering the
one disgusting and the other attractive."[76]

More important to this study are the numerous points of similarity between Dickens's and Cervantes's servants, all the more striking
because in other respects the characters are distinct and individual.

Sam Weller, like Sancho, was not part of the original plan and
appears only after Mr. Pickwick has already returned from his first
sally:

> 'Sam!'
> 'Hallo,' replied the man with the white hat.
> 'Number twenty-two wants his boots.'
> 'Ask number twenty-two, wether he'll have 'em now, or
> wait till he gets 'em,' was the reply.
> 'Come, don't be a fool, Sam,' said the girl, coaxingly, 'the
> gentleman wants his boots directly.'
> 'Well, you *are* a nice young 'ooman for a musical party, you
> are,' said the boot-cleaner (10, 119).

---

[75] It is worth noting that Dickens's self-defense and attack on his critics
sound in some respects like Cervantes's in his Prologue to *Don Quixote*, Part II;
see especially p. x of Dickens's Preface.

[76] Rafael J. De Cordova, "The *Don Quixote* of Cervantes," *The Knickerbocker*,
38 (1851), 190. However, De Cordova continues, "the only work of Dickens
which may be said to be without this claim to praise is 'Pickwick,' which is
merely a recital of ludicrous adventures ironically expressed." But one must
disagree with him. The Dickensian characteristic he mentions is only in-
cipient at this stage, but it is none the less present in *The Pickwick Papers*
(witness Mr. Edmunds and "poor" Mrs. Edmunds in the interpolated story
"The Convict's Return"), and helps explain the radical changes Mr. Pickwick
apparently underwent.

In such a casual manner does the reader first take notice of Sam, as he is discharging his duties at the White Hart Inn. Sam is short and slim, and on that momentous occasion he "was habited in a coarse-striped waistcoat, with black calico sleeves, and blue glass buttons; drab breeches and leggings. A bright red handkerchief was wound in a very loose and unstudied style round his neck, and an old white hat was carelessly thrown on one side of his head" (p. 118). There is little else in the way of description, and it is up to the reader's imagination to complete the physiognomy of the character. Nor is there any hint in the text of why, how, or exactly when Mr. Pickwick comes upon the idea of employing Sam as his servant. Sam's precise age is never disclosed, but he must be on the threshold of his twenties when Mr. Pickwick calls him to his apartments in Goswell Street and offers him twelve pounds a year, two suits, and room and board to attend upon him (12, 155). Sam accepts Mr. Pickwick's offer on the spot, and that very evening he is already at work taking care of Mr. Pickwick's baggage.[77]

Sam derives great pleasure from talking, and his conversation is indefatigable, entertaining, and full of witty retorts:

> 'Pretty busy, eh?' said [Mr. Wardle's legal adviser to Sam].
> 'Oh, werry well, sir,' replied Sam, 'we shan't be bankrupts, and we shan't make our fort'ns. We eats our biled mutton without capers, and don't care for horse-radish wen ve can get beef.'
> 'Ah,' said the little man, 'you're a wag, a'nt you?'
> 'My eldest brother was troubled with that complaint,' said Sam; 'it may be catching—I used to sleep with him.'
> 'This is a curious old house of yours,' said the little man, looking round him.
> 'If you'd sent word you was a coming, we'd ha' had it repaired;' replied the imperturbable Sam (10, 124).

He constantly meddles in other people's conversations, either interjecting a brief, droll anecdote, or offering his practical, common-sense advice without having been asked for it:

---

[77] Dickens probably decided to give Sam a major role in the narrative when Alfred Jingle, Esq., alias "the stranger," alias "the Spanish traveller," alias "Captain Fitz-Marshall," took himself out of the story by showing his true character when he accepted 120 pounds sterling to forfeit his intention of marrying Mr. Wardle's sister Rachael (Chapter 10). Until then it had been he who had enlivened and added piquancy to the story with his continuous, telegraphic conversation, his contagious good humor, and his impudence (Jingle reappears briefly in Chapters 15, 25, 42, 45, 47, and 53).

'I'll tell you what I shall do, to get up my shooting again,' said Mr. Winkle,...'I'll put a stuffed partridge on the top of a post, and practise at it, beginning at a short distance, and lengthening it by degrees. I understand it's capital practice.'

'I know a gen'l'man, sir,' said Mr. Weller, 'as did that, and begun at two yards; but he never tried it on agin; for he blowed the bird right clean away at the first fire, and nobody ever seed a feather on him arterwards.'

'Sam,' said Mr. Pickwick.

'Sir,' replied Mr. Weller.

'Have the goodness to reserve your anecdotes till they are called for.'

'Cert'nly, sir.'

Here Mr. Weller winked the eye which was not concealed by the beer-can he was raising to his lips with such exquisiteness, that the two boys went into spontaneous convulsions, and even the long man condescended to smile (19, 256).

Sam frequently clinches his commentaries with an apt and humorous saying of his own invention: "out vith it, as the father said to the child, wen he swallowed a farden" (12, 154); "Now, gen'l'm'n, 'fall on,' as the English said to the French when they fixed bagginets" (19, 255); "why, I think he's the wictim o' connubiality, as Blue Beard's domestic chaplain said, with a tear of pity, ven he buried him' (20, 273); "if this don't beat cockfightin', nothin' never vill, as the Lord Mayor said, ven the chief secretary o' state proposed his missis's health arter dinner" (39, 549). He does not, however, string such remarks together.

Sam speaks with a heavy Cockney accent, mispronounces words, and uses malapropisms throughout the story, but although no one corrects him, he does not hesitate to correct other people:

'I only know that so it is. It's a reg'lation of natur—a dispensary, as your poor mother-in-law used to say.'

'A dispensation,' said Sam, correcting the old gentleman.

'Wery good, Samivel, a dispensation, if you like it better,' returned Mr. Weller, [senior]; 'I call it a dispensary, and it's alvays writ up so, at the places vere they gives you physic for nothin' in your own bottles; that's all' (52, 736).

It is difficult to be certain to what extent Sam is a glutton, firstly, because his needs are well provided for and seldom does one hear him complaining of an empty stomach, and secondly, because Mr. Pickwick is a hearty eater himself, and he is the first to understand that eating and drinking are two aspects of life which cannot be overlooked:

'Now, Sam,' said Mr. Pickwick, 'the first thing to be done is
to—'
'Order dinner, sir,' interposed Mr. Weller. 'It's wery late, sir.'
'Ah, so it is,' said Mr. Pickwick, looking at his watch. 'You
are right, Sam' (16, 211).

In fact, all the characters of *The Pickwick Papers* are fond of food and
drink, and most of them spend a large part of their lives at the table.
One good thing can be said of Sam in this respect: he never gets
drunk, he always "[regales] himself with moderation at the nearest
tavern" (39, 550). There is a passage where he is shown "dispelling all
the feverish remains of the previous evening's conviviality" with a
"halfpenny shower-bath" (16, 212), and he seems to be familiar with
the most recondite details of every London tavern, but he holds his
liquor well and is never caught in a state of intoxication, something
which cannot be said of Mr. Pickwick and his innumerable friends.

Sam becomes attached to Mr. Pickwick from the very first moment he enters his service, and his devotion towards his master
increases with the passing of time and attains admirable degrees of
self-sacrifice, loyalty, and perseverance. On the famous occasion,
when Mr. Pickwick is unjustly put into the debtors' prison for
stubbornly refusing to pay the legal expenses of the suit brought
against him for breach of promise, Sam would willingly renounce his
freedom to continue serving his master in jail. When Mr. Pickwick
orders him to leave the place at once, Sam obeys him, but finds a way
to return and stay with his master. He goes out and incurs a debt,
refuses to pay it, and is immediately taken to prison, where he
remains attending on Mr. Pickwick until he recovers his freedom.
This episode in *The Pickwick Papers* reminds one of a similar event in
Don Quixote: the knight is being taken back to his village "enchanted"
inside a cage, and Sancho tells him: "sería bien que vuestra merced
probase a salir desta cárcel, que yo me obligo con todo mi poder a
facilitarlo, y aun a sacarle della, . . . y si no nos sucediese bien, tiempo
nos queda para volvernos a la jaula, en la cual prometo, a ley de buen
y leal escudero, de encerrarme juntamente con vuestra merced" (I, 49,
576). Like Sancho, Sam demonstrates his attachment to his master in
many other instances, but the passages just quoted are representative
of the extent to which both would go to protect their masters.

Another of Sam's commendable qualities is his valor. When compared with Sancho, Sam is the personification of courage itself, but
one should take into consideration that he is a young, well-built lad
with all the impulsiveness and strength of youth. Only on a few
occasions does the reader have the opportunity to see him in full

action. Many a time he is ready to take a more active part in Mr. Pickwick's affairs, but common sense and his master's stern orders to refrain from taking any part in the skirmishes hold him back. In Chapter 50, Mr. Pickwick is taken to prison and suffers an impudent visual inspection by some of the jailers:

> Mr. Pickwick winced a good deal under the operation, and appeared to sit very uneasily in his chair; but he made no remark to anybody while it was being performed, not even to Sam, who reclined upon the back of the chair, reflecting, partly on the situation of his master, and partly on the great satisfaction it would have afforded him to make a fierce assault upon all the turnkeys there assembled, one after the other, if it were lawful and peaceable so to do (pp. 571-72).

Only once does he tell a lie: " 'Why, how did you come here?' said Mary. . . . 'O'course I came to look arter you, my darlin',' replied Mr. Weller; for once permitting his passion to get the better of his veracity" (39, 548). At times his curiosity is stronger than he is, and he is not above peeping through keyholes when his interests are at stake:

> 'Call a hackney-coach there, directly, and bring this lady's bill, d'ye hear—d'ye hear?'
> 'Cert'nly, sir,' replied Sam, who had answered Wardle's violent ringing of the bell with a degree of celerity which must have appeared marvellous to anybody who didn't know that his eye had been applied to the outside of the keyhole during the whole interview (10, 127).

Usually, however, he is able to control himself and his curiosity.

His origins are humble, his state in life is low, and although he has somehow learned to write, his writing is as picturesque as his speech—because he "never had occasion to spell [his surname] more than once or twice in [his] life, [he] spells it with a 'V' " (34, 483)—but all these disadvantages do not dishearten him in the least:

> 'When I wos first pitched neck and crop into the world, to play at leap-frog with its troubles,' replied Sam, 'I wos a carrier's boy at startin': then a vagginer's, then a helper, then a boots. Now I'm a gen'l'm'n's servant. I shall be a gen'l'm'n myself one of these days, perhaps, with a pipe in my mouth, and a summer-house in the back garden. Who knows? I shouldn't be surprised, for one.'
> 'You are quite a philosopher, Sam,' said Mr. Pickwick. (16, 209).

And in his own steadfast, unassuming way, Sam goes on dreaming of advancing his prospects in life,although, as with Sancho and his governorship, not if that means that he has to abandon his master. When in Chapter 56 Mr. Pickwick actually suggests to Sam that he should marry his sweetheart Mary, leave Mr. Pickwick's service, and begin earning "an independent livelihood" for himself and his future family, adding that he is "proud and happy to make [Sam's] future prospects in life [his] grateful and peculiar care" (p. 789), Sam stubbornly refuses to hear another word on the subject. Two years later, however, upon the death of Mr. Pickwick's old housekeeper, he promotes "Mary to the situation, on condition of her marrying Mr. Weller at once, which she did without a murmur" (57, 801), and thus Sam settles comfortably into a married life in Mr. Pickwick's house at Dulwich, which no doubt will become Sam's dreamed-of *insula* on the death of the heirless Mr. Pickwick.

Unlike Sancho, Sam does not need or have a mount (because Mr. Pickwick travels by stagecoach), nor are his youth and bachelor status characteristic of Sancho either, but these are temporary circumstances which go with his comparative youth. On the other hand, it has been seen that Sam answers back to his master and allows himself some liberties which one would not expect from a well-bred servant, that he corrects other people's malapropisms, that he does not lack courage, that his meddling does not always encounter a favorable response from his master, that his common sense and station in life do not prevent him from dreaming of becoming a gentleman or hoping for an *insula* with a "summer-house in the back garden," that he punctuates his speeches with humorous sayings and constantly mispronounces words, that he has a moving attachment to Mr. Pickwick "which nothing but death will terminate" (57, 801), that he is curious, entertaining, very talkative, and that he has a healthy appetite and matching taste for liquor without being a glutton or ever becoming inebriated. These similarities between Sam Weller and Cervantes's character do seem to suggest that Sancho played some part in the modelling of Mr. Pickwick's faithful companion. The fact that Dickens does not once mention Cervantes, his characters, or *Don Quixote*, should not lead critics astray. It is to some degree understandable that the young Dickens of four-and-twenty was reluctant to share with any one else the remarkable success his series had already achieved by the fifth installment. In point of fact, in his Preface to the first edition of *The Pickwick Papers* in book form, Dickens refutes his detractors who had intimated that the original idea for the story was not his by entering into a lengthy explanation of when and how the series was conceived, and he categorically states that the original idea for the characters and setting was his (see pp. x-xii). But this is beside the point. Like its printed predecessors, *Tom Jones* and *The Spiritual Quixote*, *The Pickwick Papers* is a thoroughly original, thoroughly enjoyable novel, and the literary influences one can descry in the text, whether or not Dickens acknowledged them, provide merely the structural skeleton of the edifice, not the building itself. And this is also true of the quixotic Mr. Samuel Pickwick and his Cockney squire Sam Weller.

Dickens took Sancho and altered him substantially, playing up his good parts and playing down his weaknesses, but without refining him, or making him unrecognizable; and Sam's popularity amongst scullions, publicans, cooks, coachmen, and especially young and pretty chambermaids, is a tribute to Dickens's sympathetic depiction of his character.

Sancho fared well, too, across the Atlantic in a South American novel purporting to supply additional information on the exploits of Don Quixote and Sancho. In *Capítulos que se le olvidaron a Cervantes* (1895) the Ecuadorian essayist Juan Montalvo narrates some adventures that, according to him, befell knight and squire within the time span of Cervantes's Part II.

The Sancho of Montalvo has all the traits of the original character, but Montalvo overemphasizes the squire's fondness for proverbs, his tendency to use malapropisms, the annoyance that these habits of Sancho cause in Don Quixote, and the knight's pedantic insistence on correcting him.[78] These aspects of Cervantes's novel become so dominant in *Capítulos que se le olvidaron a Cervantes* that Don Quixote begins to talk in proverbs, and Sancho begins to reply with his master's casuistry:

---

[78] *Capítulos que se le olvidaron a Cervantes: Ensayo de imitación de un libro inimitable,* edited by Gonzalo Zaldumbide (Mexico City, 1972), there are seventeen instances of malapropisms: requesito-requisito (14, 103), paragarfio-parágrafo (15, 106), esprucu-escrúpulo (18, 114), pataratas-cataratas (19, 115), pantasmas-fantasmas (19, 118), sorbidad-sobriedad, mihuelos-[diminutive of *míos*] (37, 172), ingüente-ungüento (39, 176), palafrenes-paladines (39, 177), conflicto-convicto (45, 193), acioma-axioma (46, 197), rudimentos-elementos (48, 203), alfaina-alfana (50, 211), piorverbio-proverbio (57, 228), pórlogo-prólogo (59, 234), arnaconismos-anacronismos (59, 235), seso, sexo (60, 236). For instances of pedantic corrections see Chapter 37, 171-72, and Chapter 45.

—¿Pero qué es esto de echar refranes a dos manos, como quien traspala trigo? El bobo que es callado, por sesudo es reputado; llévate de esta regla. —No es regla, sino refrán, contestó Sancho (37, 172).

—Durillo soy para ese negocio, tornó Sancho a decir; pero fuera peor que no tuviera en donde [recibir los azotes]: y vuesa merced sabe el acioma de «más da el duro que el desnudo». —A trueque de no dejarte pasar el *acioma*, dejaré pasar esta falta a nuestro contrato. El que acabas de proferir no es acioma ni axioma, sino refrán mondo y lirondo (46, 197).

Don Quixote realizes what is happening to him, and he finally tells Sancho: "pásame tu sandez, pásame tu pusilanimidad, pásame tu bellaquería, pásame todo; pero no me comuniques esta sarna perruna que te infesta, con nombre de refranes" (37, 172).

Sancho's hunger is also never forgotten for long, and Montalvo treats it with the indulgent and understanding tone of Cervantes:

El alma se le iba a Sancho tras aquel humillo [de puchero]: hubiera querido verse ya mano a mano con la cazuela, aun cuando ella no prometiera tanto como las bodas de Camacho (3, 70)

Rocinante y el rucio, aderezados ya, estaban a la puerta del castillo, y Sancho Panza averiguándose con las alforjas, las cuales, gracias a doña Engracia, las tenía rebosando de pollos, cecina, bizcocho y otras curiosidades muy del gusto de ese buen escudero. No había para él ocupación más grata que la de acomodarlas, ni rato más alegre que el de abrirlas. De gula, no comía, pero no le desagradaba mojar un mendrugo en un caldero de gallinas; y en viniéndole a la mano un tercio de capón, daba tan buena cuenta de él, que no había cuándo porfiar que lo concluyera (44, 189).

This nineteenth-century version of Sancho is still able to fall asleep instantaneously, even under the most adverse circumstances, although on one occasion he actually wakes up without Don Quixote's prodding:

Sancho...cogió el sueño de tan buena gana, que se llevó la noche hasta cuando los pajaritos empezaban a llenar de música la frondosidad de los árboles.... Aquí fue donde Sancho Panza abrió los ojos, por la primera vez sin que su amo le despertase, y en un largo, escandaloso desperezo se puso a cantar unas como seguidillas picarescas (46, 198).

Montalvo's Sancho is afraid of what he cannot see—the dragging of chains, the hair-raising wailing of veiled maidens, the mysterious noises that crawl out of the woods at night—but he does not fear the tangible, and he proves his courage on several occasions. When he alone is receiving the blows, Sancho just crouches and covers his body as well as possible, but when his master is in danger, or is being abused by his foes, Sancho forgets all precautions and pounces on the enemy without another thought:

> Aquí estaban [Don Quijote y Sancho] de la disquisición, cuando cayó allí arrebatadamente el hombre a quien Don Quijote había vencido una hora antes; y, echándose sobre él sin andarse en razones de ninguna especie, le hubiera quitado la vida ahorcándole entre sus dedos de fierro, si Sancho no arremetiera con el belitre, y de tan buena guisa, que a pocas vueltas le tenía debajo.... Sintiéndose lleno de fuerza y brío Sancho, se alzó en un pronto, cogió la lanza, y le dio tal mano de palos al caído, que le dejó por muerto (5, 77-78).

> Brandabrisio cogió a su vez por el pescuezo a Don Quijote, y poniéndole zancadilla le obligó a soltar presa y dio con él en el suelo. Viendo Sancho cómo tiraban a matar a su señor, embistió con el enemigo, y menudeó tan bonito sobre ellos, que los puso como nuevos con más de seis mojicones en las narices (37, 170).

Thus, Sancho manifests his affection for his master not only in a passive manner, but by defending him actively and taking on his shoulders what in most cases was destined for Don Quixote's. He shows a more blatant disrespect for his master, his deeds, and his lady Dulcinea than Cervantes's character, but he more than compensates for his impertinence with a firm and sincere love for the knight. Moreover, this disrespect can be blamed mainly on Sancho's inability to remain silent for long rather than on real insolence, and is nothing an opportune blow from Don Quixote's lance would not instantly cure.

The Sancho of Montalvo talks at length and with the consummate ability of a statesman about the imaginary affairs of the kingdom he would rule one day, and wisely advises a widow eager to get married on matters pertaining to married life (Chapters 26 and 27). He is forever bringing into his conversation with Don Quixote, and complaining about, the abuses he suffered at the hands of those who tossed him at the inn and the Yanguesian carriers. More frequently than not, Sancho's complaints encounter a cool reception, but sometimes they anger the knight and develop irate arguments, which soon disperse like a summer storm, and master and squire continue their ramble in perfect harmony, until another heavy cloud begins to form and they enact the scene all over again. On one occasion Don Quixote is so tired of listening to Sancho's grievances that he threatens to send him back to their village for good, but the good-natured Sancho, "viendo que en efecto su señor ni por asomos venía a ser culpable de su última aventura, echó por el atajo confesando en buenos términos el motivo de su impaciencia, y dijo cómo le había salido la lengua de madre sin voluntad ni intención que mereciesen el trepe con que acababa de ser castigado" (31, 152).

The sequence of events that take place in *Capítulos que se le olvidaron a Cervantes* are apparently occurring after the knight and squire have already left the ducal palace for the second time and are on their way back to their village (i.e. between Chapters 71 and 72 of Part II), creating numerous inconsistencies in relation to Cervantes's novel. Some examples of these inconsistencies: Don Quixote breaks his word given to the knight of the Blanca Luna that he would not do battle for a year (II, 64, 534) engaging in several battles and entering a tournament (in Chapter 56 he even fights Sansón Carrasco again and defeats him). In Chapter 44 Sancho shows that he loves his ass above everything:

> el rucio es mi hermano de leche, juntos hemos crecido, juntos hemos vivido, juntos hemos de morir. No porque ayer fui gobernador y mañana he de ser conde, me he de poner a repudiar a mi compañero. Con mi rucio me entierren, señores (p. 190).

But earlier in the book he had vented his fury on the innocent animal—"maldiciéndolo todo en este mundo, cerró con el rucio a mojicones, como si él hubiera tenido la culpa" (31, 151)—something that never happens in *Don Quixote*. And in Chapter 25 another character implies that Don Quixote's adventure with the lions is already in print, when in fact it takes place in Part II (Chapter 17), not in Part I, which was the only Part printed before Don Quixote's death:

> [mi capellán] no ha leído sin duda la historia de vuesa merced, y no sabe que el señor Don Quijote se llama *el caballero de los Leones* (p. 135).

On the whole, however, Montalvo tried to keep in line with Cervantes's story and structure (there are numerous references to Cide Hamete) without repeating episodes or copying his style outright. Montalvo was aware, of course, that he was perpetrating an offense of lèse-majesté in the eyes of Cervantes's admirers and was worried by his daring, as is shown by his fifty-nine-page explanatory prologue, his "Comentario" at the close of Chapter 46, his attack on the spurious *Don Quixote* of Avellaneda, his reiterated statements that he is not trying to improve on, or even imitate Cervantes, and his reluctance to have his work published in his lifetime—the novel appeared posthumously. Montalvo's fears were, no doubt, justified within the contex of his times and milieu, because the publication of *Capítulos que se le olvidaron a Cervantes* would have given fresh ammunition to his political and literary enemies, who would have made sport of him, accusing him of trying both to emulate and correct Cervantes, and pointing out where, in their opinion, he had failed. Artistically speaking, Montalvo did not need to worry, because, although his overall style and language cannot be compared even remotely with those of Cervantes, he was none the less able to copy Cervantes in some short passages, and he captured the personalities of Don Quixote and Sancho and the fine points of their complex relationship as no one before him had. Montalvo recognized and exploited throughout his novel the "if-you-don't-tell-I-won't-tell" element of innocent complicity that binds master and squire together, their gradual adaptation to one another and to new or changing circumstances, and their sincere need of and love for the other. Moreover, by emphasizing the good traits of Sancho, Montalvo created, as Dickens had done before him, an amiable character, not as original as Sam Weller, it is true, but one who does honor to his model.[79]

With Sam Weller and the Ecuadorian squire of Montalvo the rehabilitation of Sancho had begun anew. Dickens and Montalvo rescued him from the lopsided intellectual fantasies of the Romantic critics and their followers and from the poor theatrical imitations of the period, thus recovering with them the momentum he had received at the pens of Fielding and Graves. Although already in the

---

[79] In his article "La más afortunada imitación del *Quijote*," *Hispania*, 9 (1926), 275-83, Manuel Pedro González disagrees with this evaluation of Montalvo's work: "Grande es la distancia que media entre 'El Caballero de los Leones' y la caricatura de Montalvo; pero más lamentable aún es el resultado obtenido con Sancho.... Aquella sutil divisoria que tan hábilmente entendió Cervantes entre amo y mozo, parece haber desaparecido en los *Capítulos* y así vemos que Sancho, triplicadas ahora sus malas cualidades, sin pizca de respeto por el ideal de su amo, hace fisga constante de sus caballerías con una sorna y malicia de la que el marido de Teresa Cascajo era incapaz. Su lenguaje es, con frecuencia irrespetuoso y descomedido, careciendo desde luego, de aquella suprema gracia que en Cervantes nos deleita (p. 282).

eighteenth century the interpretation of Cervantes's novel had begun
to pass, imperceptibly at first but irretrievably, from the hands of the
creative writers to those of the literary critics, it was the nineteenth
century which would set the pattern and the emphasis that the
appreciation of *Don Quixote* would follow in our century. The tenden-
tious Romantic interpretation which had all-too-successfully separated master and squire and isolated them at opposite poles, with Don
Quixote receiving all the praise and Sancho only derogatory remarks,
did not disappear when the Romantic theories which had given rise
to this polarization were discredited. This interpretation continued
permeating *Don Quixote* criticism, as Anthony Close has convincingly
argued in his *Romantic Approach to "Don Quixote"*, but under different
disguises.

One cannot leave the nineteenth century, however, without men-
tioning one of the best and certainly the best known illustrators of
Don Quixote, Paul Gustave Doré. On 1st January 1864 appeared on the
market an illustrated edition of Louis Viardot's French translation of
Don Quixote containing three hundred seventy drawings by Doré
engraved by H. Pisan (Paris: L. Hachette, 1863).[80] This is, without a
doubt, one of the most beautiful and elegant editions of *Don Quixote*
ever printed. Doré masterfully captured in his drawings all the heroic
and legendary atmosphere of the romances of chivalry and depicted
the every-day life of the Spain of his time with an eye for detail that
no one has surpassed.[81] The long, thin, Grecoesque figure of Don
Quixote drawn by Doré stands out in all its nobility and idealism in
the midst of the natural grandeur of the Sierra Morena, and,
whether fighting windmills or wineskins, amongst goatherds or
noblemen, hanging from his wrist or addressing the company gathered at the inn, he is always indisputably the center of attention.
Sancho, in contrast, is a fat rustic with a week-old beard, or a dark
ogre from an oriental fairy tale. He is seen in the very first plate
almost literally melting on his ass, his face a shapeless and grotesque
ball.

[80] Doré's drawings have been reproduced in several other nineteenth-
and twentieth-century editions of *Don Quixote*.

[81] In preparation for his illustrations for *Don Quixote* Doré traveled ex-
tensively in Spain in 1862 in the company of Jean Charles Davillier, and he
returned to Paris with numerous sketches, some of which were published in
1862 and 1863 together with an account of their trip; see Bertrand's "Génesis
de la concepción romántica de Don Quijote en Francia," *Anales Cervantinos*, 3
(1953), 1-41, especially pp. 31-34, and Miguel Romera-Navarro's *Interpretación
pictórica del "Quijote" por Doré* (Madrid, 1946).

Doré's engravings and the splendid editions of *Don Quixote* printed in nineteenth-century Europe are proof that Cervantes's novel was by then widely recognized as a classic, and his rendering of the Knight of the Sad Countenance clearly shows that Don Quixote had become a Romantic symbol, a heroic and idealistic figure whose laughable misadventures had been turned into mythical feats. Doré's depiction of Sancho show, on the other hand, that the squire was still regarded by the great majority of critics, writers, and artists of the period as the despicable buffoon and greedy villager of previous centuries, as a symbol of everything the Romantics considered ignoble, base, or earthy.

In 1614 Avellaneda gave readers a Sancho who is a liar, a drunkard, a glutton, and an unfaithful servant. At the beginning of the eighteenth century Peter Anthony Motteux noted in the Preface to his English translation of *Don Quixote* (London: Samuel Buckley, 1700-1712) that "any man of half the Squire's wit may read in this single character all the mean, slavish, and ungenerous Spirit of the Vulgar in all Countries and all Ages: sordid Avarice, sneaking Pity, a natural Inclination to Knavery, and a superstitious Devotion. The whole Multitude in little."[82] And at the close of the nineteenth century Henry Dwight Sedgwick, Jr. stated that "one loves [Sancho] as one loves a dog;...the shag-haired little villain, *nullius filius*, who barks at your guests, and will gnaw a drumstick in my lady's chamber unless he be prevented."[83] Almost three hundred years of imitations and criticism had clearly done only little to improve the general opinion of Sancho.

[82] Quoted by Arthur Efron, "Satire Denied: A Critical History of English and American *Don Quixote* Criticism" (unpublished dissertation, University of Washington, 1964), p. 59.

[83] "Don Quixote," *Atlantic Monthly,* 77 (1896), 256-64, at p. 263.

PLATE 6 Sancho's awakening
by Brévière (Milan: Andrea Ubicini, 1841)
          Courtesy of the British Library, Cerv.312, vol. 2, p. 40

PLATE 7 Sancho and his ass
by J. Heredia (Mexico City: Masse y Decaen, 1842)
      Courtesy of the British Library, 12489.l.18, vol. 1, facing p. 38

4

Sancho in the Age
of the Professional Critic

> Pray, Sir [Critic], in all the reading which you
> have ever read, did you ever read such a book
> as Locke's Essay upon the Human Understand-
> ing?—Don't answer me rashly— because many,
> I know, quote the book, who have not read
> it—and many have read it who understand it
> not.
>
> LAURENCE STERN, *Tristram Shandy*,
> Book 2, Chapter 2

 VERY CERVANTIST HAS AT ONE TIME or another said
something about Sancho, and many twentieth-
century Hispanists, Comparatists, and specialists in other literatures and in other related and
unrelated disciplines think it their right and
their duty to make a stab at *Don Quixote* whether
or not they have read it. Frequently, then, critics and writers are merely citing commonplaces
and basing their theories not on the text of *Don Quixote* itself, but on
what other critics have said before them. The same arguments are
repeated *ad nauseam*. Both specialists and non-specialists have created
around Sancho what Salvador de Madariaga, writing about Don
Quixote, called an "ideósfera," the phenomenon resulting from each
new generation's adding its own interpretation to the already thick
intellectual atmosphere that envelops the character.[84] This chapter,
therefore, will consider mainly those works directly concerned with

---

[84] *Guía del lector del "Quijote": ensayo psicológico sobre el "Quijote"* (Bilbao, 1926),
pp. 111-12.

Sancho, and those which are either representative of a specific critical
trend or dwell on the master-squire relationship.

When the Romantics used Don Quixote and Sancho as symbols
for contrasting attitudes (aristocratic-popular), literary antonyms
(poetry-prose), entelechies (soul-body), or abstract concepts (romantic-prosaic), their contribution to the exegesis of Cervantes's characters was not, of course, totally novel. Before 1658 John Cleveland
(1613-1658) had already likened to them two differing human activities:

> The Truth is, the Soldier and the Gentle-
> man are like *Don Quixot* and *Sancha Pancha*,
> one fights at all adventures to purchas
> the other the Government of the Island.[85]

But the romantics carried to extremes this tendency to reduce the
complex personalities of master and squire to simple absolutes, and
critics still very much under their influence continue their approach.
Miragist critics wish to find, and as a result see, hidden meanings
where in fact none exist. The following quotations from Rudolph
Schevill, Arthur Machen, Helmut Hatzfeld, and Max Daireaux make
the point:

> As life invariably restores a balance between extremes, so the
> idealism of the . . . knight unwittingly finds a corrective lens in
> the squire who is destitute of any imagination or vision. . . . The
> contrast is naturally bound to endure through their entire
> association, because of the irreconcilable contradiction which
> exists not only between the two minds of Don Quixote and
> Sancho, but, by the essence of life itself, between our body and
> spirit, our demerits and virtues, our illusions and achievements.[86]

> The eternal moral . . . of *Don Quixote* is the strife between tem-
> poral and eternal, between the soul and the body, between
> things spiritual and things corporal, between ecstasy and the
> common life, . . . there is a perpetual jar, you are continually
> confronted by the great antinomy of life, . . . the perpetual trag-
> edy of life itself, symbolized.[87]

[85] "The Characters of a Country Committeeman," *The Works of Mr. John
Cleveland* (London: R. Holt, 1687), p. 74; as quoted by Knowles in his
unpublished dissertation, p. 61.

[86] Schevill, *Master Spirits of Literature: Cervantes* (London, 1919), p. 216.

[87] Machen, *Hieroglyphics: A Note upon Ecstasy in Literature* (New York, 1923), p.
66.

Aquel que quiera entender el *Quijote* como obra de arte tiene, en primer lugar, que ver claro cuál es su asunto, que no es otro que la descripción del eterno conflicto entre el Idealismo (Don Quijote) y el Materialismo (Sancho, el Mundo).... Don Quijote y Sancho Panza, en su manifiesta oposición, ponen ante los ojos una eterna antítesis llevada hasta los más mínimos pormenores.[88]

Don Quichotte sur Rossinnante et Sancho sur son âne, l'un derrière l'autre se profilant et s'entretenant de mésaventures passées et des merveilleuses aventures qui les attendent, don Quichotte en escomptant la gloire et Sancho le profit, et tous deux poursuivent cet éternel dialogue qui oppose l'âme éprise d'idéal au corps uniquement soucieux des nécessités immédiates de la matière et pourtant entraîné par la chimère.[89]

Curiously enough, the authors expect their readers to accept such statements as if they were the Gospel, and some critics swallow them with relish although, both authors and critics would require textual critics to qualify their less sweeping and far more verifiable findings with cautionary phrases such as "in my opinion," "in all likelihood," and "perhaps." But as the Abbot of Féletz had shown a century earlier, a careful comparison of the two characters is sufficient to evince the untenability of these theories. After studying the personalities of master and squire, Paolo Savj-López concludes that

---

[88] Hatzfeld, *El "Quijote" como obra de arte del lenguaje*, translated by M. C. de I. (Madrid, 1949), p. 9; first edition: Leipzig-Berlin, 1927. See also pp. 39-45.

[89] Daireaux, *Cervantès* (Paris, 1948), p. 216. For Don Quixote and Sancho as a class-struggle antithesis see Francisco María Tubino's "¿Necesita el *Quijote* comentarios?" in *Cervantes y el "Quijote": estudios críticos* (Madrid, 1872), pp. 197-218; Tomás Carreras y Artau's *La filosofía del derecho en el "Quijote"* (Madrid, 1903); Vladimir Maksimovich Friche's "Shekspir i Servantes," *Sovremenny Mir*, 4 (1916), 110-23; Anatoli Vasilevich Lunacharski's *Istoria zapadnoyevropeiskoi literatury* (Moscow, 1924); and Cesare de Lollis's *Cervantes reazionario e altri scritti d'ispanistica*, edited by Silvio Pellegrini (Florence, 1947), pp. 83-87. For Tubino and Carreras y Artau see Close, 1978, pp. 105-06 and 123-24; for Friche and Lunacharski see Turkevich, pp. 202-06. Ramón León Máinez, *Cervantes y su época*, Jerez de la Frontera, 1901, considers that "Don Qujote es un caballero nobilísimo, sobrio, ilustrado, á quien le duele la corrupción de costumbres, el rebajamiento del antiguo carácter español, la fastuosidad de las clases elevadas y las ambiciones de todas [las clases sociales]," (p. 428). "Sancho Panza simboliza al pueblo rudo, metalizado de sus tiempos; para él no había más que una felicidad, una gloria: la de comer, beber, dormir, enriquecerse, y trabajar poco. También significa la clase media, infatuada entonces, y contaminada por el vicio del lujo y de la ambición, y por adquirir pingües cargos y títulos á ejemplo de las clases elevadas y poderosas," (p. 429).

Tanto lontano era Sancio, nell'intendimento del suo creatore, dall'unità alquanto rigida d'un significato simbolico, e tanto era vana nella critica l'affannosa ricerca di quel simbolo!...E le due figure che per secoli sono apparse alla critica in violento contrasto, si toccano in realtà sotto molti rispetti.[90]

None the less, symbolic interpretations of the relationsip between Don Quixote and Sancho continue to dominate present-day criticism. Alvaro Fernández Suárez, for one, thinks that "Sancho representa, al lado de Don Quijote, el papel de la madre sustentadora, madre vital, la que defiende siempre el sentido de la savia. Sancho fué, en la común vida de aventuras, la madre de Don Quijote-niño-espíritu."[91] But we owe to Edward Fitz-Gerald Brenan, the modern critic fondest of this sort of comparison, the most original pair of opposites of this century.

But perphaps the relationship between the pair may best after all be compared to that most intimate of partnerships, marriage. The long dialogue between them that takes up the principal part

[90] *Cervantes* (Naples, 1913), p. 94. See also Emile Gebhart's *De Panurge à Sancho Pança: Mélanges de Littérature européenne* (Paris, 1911), especially pp. 235 and 257-58. In his *Mensonge romantique et vérité romanesque* (Paris, 1961), René Noel Girard, also, states that the Romantic interpretation of *Don Quixote* is too simplistic: "Lorsqu'il est avec Don Quichotte, Sancho compose, à lui seul, cet indispensable décor rationnel—c'est là ce qui le rend si méprisable aux yeux des romantiques—mais, dès qu'il passe au premier plan, l'écuyer devient l'exception qui se détache, une fois de plus, sur le bon sens collectif. C'est alors le désir métaphysique de Sancho qui fait l'objet de la révélation" (p. 147); "L'opposition entre Don Quichotte l'*idéaliste* et le *réaliste* Sancho...est réelle mais secondaire; elle ne doit pas nous faire oublier les analogies entre les deux personnages" (p. 13); but he still accepts the existence of the ideal-real dichotomy. Like Girard, Friedrich Schürr seems not to have made up his mind, as the following contradictory excerpt shows: "Con razón se han interpretado las dos figuras como símbolos, como antítesis de idealismo y realismo, alma y cuerpo, espíritu y materia, etc. [here Schürr shows approval of the symbolic interpretation]; son símbolos poéticos y no alegorías o personificaciones imaginadas como tales por Cervantes [they are the product of Cervantes's imagination]. Porque tienen tantos rasgos del poeta, Don Quijote y Sancho no son abstracciones [is Schürr now showing disapproval of the symbolic interpretation?] vestidas posteriormente de indumentos, sino hombres de carne y hueso" [they are not the product of Cervantes's imagination, they are human beings?], "Cervantes y el romanticismo," *Anales Cervantinos*, 1 (1951), 56. And Gale even now (1973) considers that "Don Quixote and Sancho supplement one another.... They are [a pair], each individually representing an [opposing] view of life and it is only when the men are seen together that they are seen in their true perspective" (p. 148).

[91] *Los mitos del "Quijote"* (Madrid, 1953), p. 143.

of the book suggests, in a more ceremonious key, the familiar dialogue of married couples. It is made up of the same inconclusive wranglings, the same recriminations and *tu quoques*, the same fixed recollections and examples dragged out again and again from the past to clinch an argument.... Just as in married life, every disagreement leads back to some classic precedent or "You said so-and-so."...Don Quixote plays the part of the unmitigated male and Sancho that of the semi-dependent female. Hence the long story of Sancho's fidelities and infidelities .... How true to life, too, it is that, as the spiritual potency of the male declines, the female should rise and spread herself and dominate! Through almost the whole of the second part it is Sancho who is the leading figure, and in the last chapters we see him, in spite of his touching devotion to his master, getting ready for a prosperous widowhood. The knight dies as all men die, when—sane, empty, deflated—he has fulfilled his role of impregnator. In this capacity one might say that Sancho symbolizes the passive and feminine world, which requires heroes and men of ideas to fertilize it.[92]

Another farfetched interpretation of the Don Quixote-Sancho relationship was proposed by Manuel Durán in the Pomona College Symposium on "Cervantes and the Renaissance" (November, 1978):

La panza de Sancho evoca la de los grotescos demonios de las ánforas corintias.... El papel de Sancho consiste en ofrecer un constante contraste, una continua parodia crítica a las altas aspiraciones quijotescas, en la misma forma en que las parodias medievales...contrastan y en cierto modo corrigen las elevadas aspiraciones de la Iglesia medieval. Sancho representa a Don Carnal, en empeñado diálogo ante la Cuaresma ascética del caballero andante (p. 82).... Es Sancho Panza el que representa la influencia siempre latente pero casi siempre oculta de las tradiciones carnavalescas, Sancho con su vientre rotundo, su

---

[92] *The Literature of the Spanish People: From Roman Times to the Present Day*, 2nd ed. (Cambridge, 1965), pp. 183-84; first edition, 1951. Brenan's symbolic interpretation has recently been given some authority by being put in the mouth of Cervantes himself: "[Cervantes] said, I often think of [Don Quixote and Sancho] as a married couple, especially in this second book I'm writing, ...because each needs the other to confirm his identity and actions. Male and female attributes flicker and fluctuate between them and they talk all the time," Robin Chapman, *The Duchess's Diary* (London, 1980), pp. 31-32. My colleague Marian G. R. Coope brought this short novel to my attention.

amor a la comida, sus necesidades fisiológicas insoslayables, sus disparates lingüísticos, su risa robusta y prolongada.[93]

Durán has defeated in the process the arduous progress that Sancho had made through hundreds of years of imitations and criticism by returning him to the role of laughable buffoon he had been forced to play in previous centuries.

But one of the most strongly worded and more sustained of the numerous critical assaults that have been leveled at Sancho comes from Close.[94] Disconcertingly putting the cart before the horse, Close begins his article with his conclusions:

> The essence of Sancho Panza's character is comic *simpleza* or *necedad*.... The aim of this article is to show that his wisdom in Part II corresponds to that of the simpleton-fool.... Vestigially throughout the novel and palpably in the episodes in the Duke's palace, Sancho exhibits the jester's typical attributes of conduct. Both in his comicality and in his wisdom, he implicitly pertains to the species of innocent court-fool celebrated in Erasmus's *The Praise of Folly* (p. 344)....If Sancho is in some sense mentally deficient, then his wisdom...ought to be regarded as being the inspired perspicacity of the madman or the fool (p. 345).

Close then proceeds to argue his case by showing the many similarities he finds between the manner in which Sancho acts and is treated and mistreated in *Don Quixote*, Part II, and the behavior of, and common pranks played on, historical and fictional jesters and court-fools of the period. Numerous inconsistencies, however, creep into his argument: "Simpleton Sancho has a more restricted range of wit than the clever *gracioso*.... His diffuse and inconsequential recitals of [proverbs] are primarily an aspect of his comic artlessness" (p. 350).[95]

---

[93] "El *Quijote* a través del prisma de Mikhail Bakhtine: carnaval, disfraces, escatología y locura," *Cervantes and the Renaissance*, edited by Michael D. McGaha (Easton, Pennsylvania, 1980), p. 85. For Bakhtine see also J. M. Pelorson, "Le Discours des armes et des 'lettres' et l'épisode de Barataria," *Les Langues Néo-Latines*, 69 (1975), 56-57, footnote 12. See also Augustin Redondo, "Tradición carnavalesca y creación literaria: del personaje de Sancho Panza al episodio de la ínsula Barataria en el *Quijote*," *Bulletin Hispanique*, 80 (1978), 39-70.

[94] "Sancho Panza: Wise Fool," *Modern Language Review*, 68 (1973), 344-57.

[95] Close's opinion on Sancho's stringing together of proverbs echoes Edward C. Riley's statement in that respect: "Sancho has the inborn wit and wisdom of the peasant but lacks formal education. A symptom of the former is his remarkable facility in proverbs, while his ill-judged use of them reflects the latter. In other words, he is in this respect well endowed by nature but

And yet, "Sancho has more wit and a wider spectrum of personality-traits than the stock literary embodiment of the simpleton" (p. 375). "[He] can cite proverbs both as a form of verbal foolery and in order to substantiate his judicious reflections.... [His] wise remarks generally have a religious or moralistic character" (pp. 350-51). Is it really possible to have a character who is a mentally deficient, artless simpleton with a restricted range of wit and a tendency to inconsequential recitals of proverbs also sustaining judicious reflections which are charged with religious and moralistic content, and having more wit and a wider spectrum of personality-traits than the stock literary embodiment of the simpleton? Close also makes the following comparison: the "saintly imbecile" hero of Lope's play *El rústico del cielo* has, "besides stupidity,... various traits characteristic of the stage-*bobo*—laziness, greed, illiteracy—and is therefore in several respects comparable with Sancho Panza" (p. 353). The pendulum apparently has completed a full swing, and we are once again back with the Sancho of Avellaneda. But Close adds:

> Sancho never is or becomes a paragon of saintliness. Yet his failings are venial; his ingenuousness is basically without malice; and his generosity and moral sense can earn him such epithets as *bueno, cristiano, discreto,* and *sincero.* His wisdom can therefore justifiably be likened to that of the holy innocent or saintly fool (p. 355).

Close's vacilating vision of Sancho clearly shows that the squire is too complex a character to be pigeonholed, as Close himself acknowledges in the last paragraph of his article (p. 355). But at the same time this paragraph seems to contradict most of what was stated earlier, leaving the reader with the uneasy feeling that throughout the article Sancho has been called all sorts of insulting names without any serious justification. Why call him, either directly or by association, *necio, bobo,* natural fool, jester, mentally deficient, simple-minded, stupid, forgetful, impertinent, cowardly, artless, lazy, greedy, imbecile, illiterate, vulgar, and so on, without proving the textual validity of all these accusations? Surely, it is impossible for a well-drawn character to be all that and, also, have moral sense and be wise,

---

lacks art.... Don Quixote on occasion evinces a certain irritated admiration, but he is usually critical. The point of his criticism, which is simply an echo of those writers from Quintilian to Mal Lara who warned against the abuse of *sententiae* and *refranes,* is that they should be used aptly and in moderation," *Cervantes's Theory of the Novel* (Oxford, 1964), pp. 69-70; first published in 1962.

generous, *bueno, cristiano, discreto,* and *sincero* (see Chapter 5 of this study). Close's interpretation clearly shows the difficulties that arise when one reads the text of *Don Quixote* on two totally different levels simultaneously, literal-realistic ("in Sancho's own words") and symbolic ("Sancho represents"). More surprising, however, from the pen of the author of *The Romantic Approach to "Don Quixote",* are the Romantic overtones of the following statement: "the squire...represents, in opposition to his master, all that is down-to-earth and fallibly human" (p. 357).

Another symbolic interpretation of Sancho is that of Lucio Pabón Núñez:[96]

> [Sancho] no es el símbolo del materialismo y la estulticia sino de las altas virtudes del idealista y muy despierto pueblo español (p. 553).... Bastaría el relieve de cristiano viejo, de buen ciudadano y de venerable padre de familia...para hacer de éste un símbolo de la cimera calidad del alma popular de España (pp. 561-62).... Es el símbolo del pueblo español, con todas sus estelares virtudes históricas y sus humanísimos defectos.... [Y] por más que [Sancho] aprenda como el mejor de los discípulos de todas las universidades de los libros y de la vida, continuará como símbolo perfecto del pueblo de cuyas entrañas brotó (p. 579).

One should regard these types of allegorical and symbolical interpretations of *Don Quixote* and its characters more as coruscations enriching literary fiction than as contributions to literary criticism. These sorts of theories have, none the less, found propitious soil in which to grow and multiply in the open fields of non-specialists and Comparatists,[97] but they have lost some of their appeal. Madariaga,

---

[96] "Sancho o la exaltación del pueblo español," *Cuadernos Hispanoamericanos,* 58 (1964), 541-80. See also Manuel Socorro's *La ínsula de Sancho en el reino de Don Quijote* (Las Palmas, 1947; cover 1948), especially pp. 5 and 12.

[97] For other sweeping or idiosyncratic interpretations of Sancho's character, his relationship with his master, or *Don Quixote* as a whole see: Part 2, Chapter 1 of Georg Szegedi Lukács's *Teoría de la novela,* translated from the French by Juan José Sebreli (Barcelona, 1971), pp. 103-20 (first edition, *Die Theorie des Romans,* Berlin, 1920); Van Meter Ames, *Aesthetics of the Novel* (Chicago, 1928), pp. 125-27; Thomas Mann, "Voyage with *Don Quixote*," in his *Essays of Three Decades,* translated by Helen Tracy Lowe-Porter (New York, 1948), pp. 429-64 (Mann wrote this particular essay in 1934); Nikos Kazantzakis, "On Entering Spain," in his *Spain* (New York, 1963), pp. 15-22 (first edition, Athens, 1957); Michel Foucault, *Les Mots et les choses: Une archéologie des sciences humaines* (Mayenne, 1966), pp. 60-64, and 222-24; Siegfried Kracauer, *History: The Last Things before the Last* (Oxford, 1969), pp. 216-17 (Kracauer

Américo Castro, Dmitri Konstanovich Petrov, and Hipólito R. Romero Flores, for example, disagree with the critics who see Don Quixote and Sancho as opposites or as symbols. Madariaga notes disapprovingly that "la tradición superficial ha reducido [la] maravillosa trama psicológica [del *Quijote*] a una línea melódica de elemental sencillez. Don Quijote es un caballero valiente e idealista. Sancho es un bellaco positivo y cobarde" (p. 132). Castro affirms that the master-squire relationship "is not a question of the opposition of idealism and materialism, but rather, of the projective will of Don Quixote and the receptive will of Sancho.... [Don Quixote] drives his world over the routes that he has previously traced,... [Sancho] adjusts his receptive mode of life to the exigencies which he encounters, be they material or ideal."[98]

For his part, Petrov wrote: "The Spanish peasant and the nobleman, the servant and the master—here is the explanation of the supposed allegory of the novel. Cervantes did not plan any antitheses or contrasts, he merely portrayed in poetry what lived together in life."[99] Petrov's opinion was shared by his compatriot Shepelevich: "if one cannot consider Don Quixote as an unadulterated idealist, nei-

---

quotes also a remark by Franz Kafka concerning Sancho, p. 217); George Stafford Gale, "Don Nixon's Sancho Panza?" review of Henry Kissinger's *The White House Years*, in the *Spectator*, 243 (24 November, 1979), 17-18. For psychological analyses of the personalities of Sancho and Don Quixote see Helen Deutsch, "Don Quijote und Donquijotismo," *Almanach der Psychoanalyse*, 10 (1935), 151-60; Walter Blumenfeld, "Don Quijote y Sancho Panza como tipos psicológicos," *Revista de las Indias*, 2nd series, No. 38 (1942), 338-68; and Harry W. Hilborn, "Lo subconsciente en la psicología de Sancho Panza," *Studia Iberica, Festschrift für Hans Flasche* (Bern-Munich, 1973), pp. 267-80. Drake's summaries of the first two articles read in part: "Sancho also has some resemblance to the castrated father figure. But Sancho has a maternal side; he seems to be the author's humorous mockery of motherhood," (Deutsch; Drake, I, 96); "Psychological types may be divided into two categories: 1. the *plesioclinos*, the Sancho Panzas, who are interested in things close at hand in time or space; 2. the *teleclinos*, the Don Quijotes, who are concerned with matters far off in time or space.... [Although] the Knight and the Squire are two different types at the beginning of Cervantes' novel, at the end of the story the *plesioclino* Sancho assumes the attitude of a *teleclino*" (Blumenfeld; Drake, II, 29).

[98] "Incarnation in *Don Quixote*," in *Cervantes Across the Centuries*, p. 150.

[99] Review of vol. II (1903) of Lev Yulianovich Shepelevich's *"Don Kikhot" Servantesa, Zhizn Servantesa i yego proizvedenia* (St. Petersburg, 1901-1903), in *Zhurnal Ministerstva Narodago Prosveschenia* (1904), p. 179; quoted by Turkevich, p. 169.

ther can one regard Sancho as his antithesis—the representative of the bourgeois attitude towards life. Fascinating as such a contrast would have been, Cervantes did not exploit it. Sancho is not opposite from, but similar to, his master."[100]

And Romero Flores has stated the following: "Hay que desechar ese tópico de Sancho 'mera contrafigura' del Ingenioso Hidalgo, que es la inveterada opinión sustentada por el vulgo e incluso por gran parte de la crítica cervantina."[101]

Moreover, the great majority of critics now comment on the development that Sancho's character seems to undergo as the novel progresses. This development had already been pointed out in the nineteenth century, but it was thanks to Miguel de Unamuno's highly subjective interpretation of Cervantes's novel that it began attracting the attention of critics.[102] Sancho's greediness, says Unamuno,

> no dejaba de tener, aun sin él saberlo, su fondo de ambición, ambición que creciendo en el escudero a costa de la codicia, hizo que la sed de oro se le transformase al cabo en sed de fama (p. 52).... Sancho vivía, sentía, obraba y esperaba bajo el encanto de un poder extraño que le dirigía y llevaba contra lo que veía y entendía, y...su vida toda fué una lenta entrega de sí mismo a ese poder de la fe quijotesca y quijotizante (pp. 151-52).

Unamuno felt, it hardly needs saying, a great affection for both Don Quixote and Sancho, In his book, he constantly prods the squire to change his ways, to believe in, and imitate his master; and whenever Sancho does or says something that meets with the approval of Unamuno, he immediately showers the squire with praise, encouragement, and exclamation marks.

After Unamuno's sensitive and in numerous respects accurate, though idiosyncratic, exegesis of *Don Quixote*, countless critics have called their readers's attention to this aspect of Cervantes's characterization of Sancho. Friche, for example, notes that "as the plot develops, Sancho grows spiritually and becomes increasingly wise" (Turkevich, p. 204); Madariaga thinks that ."la estrella de Don Quijote

---

[100] "Trekhsotletie *Don Kikhota* Servantesa," *Vestnik Yevropy*, 223 (1905), 328-40; paraphrased by Turkevich, p. 170.

[101] *Biografía de Sancho Panza, filósofo de la sensatez* (Barcelona, 1952), pp. 17-18.

[102] *Vida de Don Quijote y Sancho según Miguel de Cervantes Saavedra, explicada y comentada por Miguel de Unamuno*, 6th Austral edition (Buenos Aires, 1945); first published in 1905.

influye sobre la de Sancho, y en virtud de esa ley de atracción vemos cómo nuestro ambicioso en concreto va poco a poco sintiendo el señuelo de satisfacciones menos materiales" (p. 154); William James Entwistle, too, notes that Sancho "is not static,...and in the last agony it is Sancho who believes in the possibility of ranging hills and dales in shepherd-dress, making an endless eclogue from life";[103] Ramón Menéndez Pidal emphasizes Sancho's amelioration as shown in his use of popular sayings and *romances*: "Sancho el de los refranes es [en la Segunda Parte], a veces, Sancho el de los romances.... Sancho se mejora y purifica";[104] for his part, Brenan states that "as the book progresses [Don Quixote and Sancho] are constantly affecting and even invading one another. The simple contrast between them with which it started breaks down,...[and] this leads to moments in which they almost appear to have changed places" (p. 182); and even Schevill and Hatzfeld put their symbolic interpretations temporarily aside to note the importance that Sancho's education under Don Quixote has in the novel: when Sancho "first begins his quest of adventures [he] is merely a peasant and swineherd, much bewildered at seeing himself taken out of his realistic world and plunged into an imaginary life of romance,...[but he takes] on an unusual polish through constant contact with the well read Don Quixote" (Schevill, pp. 253 and 266), and, "la educación de Sancho... completa la aureola de la pura humanidad de su amo, y...poco a poco alumbra en el cobarde, egoísta, vulgar y necio aldeano un servidor agradecido, ilustrado y un amigo" (Hatzfeld, p. 13). Like Schevill and Hatzfeld, Victor Rudolph Bernhardt Oelschläger and Fernando Sainz see Sancho's Quixotification as an educational process. Oelschläger considers that the depiction of this process was perhaps the most important reason why Cervantes wrote his novel:[105]

> The all-pervasive purpose of Cervantes in writing *Don Quijote*, judging by abundant internal evidence, was probably to portray the epic of life *as it is* and *as it ought to be*, and to demonstrate that the gap between these two extremes can be bridged to a large extent by a democratic educational process of raising and improving the spiritual and cultural level of the common people .... The gradual indoctrination of Sancho is enacted so deftly throughout the story and the dramatic results are climaxed so

103 *Cervantes 1547-1616* (Oxford, 1940), p. 133.

104 *De Cervantes y Lope de Vega* (Buenos Aires, 1940), pp. 42-43.

105 "Sancho's Zest for the Quest," *Hispania*, 35 (1952), 18-24.

movingly at the end as to make this a plausible interpretation of his message (p. 18).... He was personifying the ever-present deterrents to educational progress and improvement: ignorance, short-sightedness, intolerance, incompetence, envy, pettiness, insincerity, and indifference. These are the enchanters who make Quijote's Quest a real challenge.... Furthermore, our attention is repeatedly called to Sancho's precocious cultural progress, certainly one of Cervantes' major interests—if not his key objective—in the story.... Only in this perspective can we appreciate the full implications of the spiritual and intellectual "Quixotization" of Sancho (p. 19).... Very early he develops a sophomoric pride in his gradual acquisition of knowledge and, very humanly,...loves to display his own culture before those who know less than he. After all, Sancho is actually attending the University of Life and his grades are well above average" (p. 22). "[But] only at the end of his Senior Year, at Commencement time, when he is about to lose his major professor and be forced to start his independent career, does the light begin to dawn.... [His earlier] hesitations are more naturally and psychologically explainable as the growing pains of Sancho's educational "Quixotization" (p. 20).... The gifted Sanchos of the masses will always repay and justify the efforts expended upon them to broaden their horizon, to ennoble their perspective, to elevate their aspirations indefinitely to achieve and improve (p. 24).

Whether or not one agrees with this narrow and markedly donnish interpretation of Cervantes's aims in *Don Quixote*, Oelschläger's article must be seen as a refinement of, and a clear improvement on, Sainz's earlier note on the subject:[106]

[El programa de Don Quijote] no comprendía la educación de los escuderos; es decir, de los Sanchos; y sin embargo, cuando el caballero de la Mancha realizó la más grande y verdadera de las aventuras, la de morirse, lo único que había logrado era achicar un poco el vientre de Sancho y agrandarle considerablemente el cerebro y el corazón;...en la lucha contra la ignorancia, la malicia, la socarronería, el egoísmo y el realismo grosero de su acompañante, Don Quijote alcanzó una estupenda victoria.... La cátedra duraba desde el amanecer hasta que a Sancho se le cerraban los ojos y los oídos (p. 363).... [Y] aquel hombre achaparrado y sucio, que salió de su pueblo cargado de mendrugos y cebollas, vuelve a su aldea de mala gana,...dispuesto a continuar con su amo la tarea de ennoblecer el mundo (p. 365).

[106] "Don Quijote educador de Sancho," *Hispania*, 34 (1951), 363-65.

There can be little doubt that there is indeed some process of characterization in *Don Quixote*, but it is also palpably clear that critics are by no means certain how to define it or explain it. In 1950, for instance, Dámaso Alonso revised the theory of Unamuno, Madariaga, and Giovanni Papini on the linear and progressive ascent of Sancho's Quixotification, stating that this theory is too simplistic an explanation of Sancho's personality because it does not take into consideration those passages in which the squire appears to regress and behaves just as he did in the earlier chapters:[107]

> Sancho ha de titubear entre picaresca e idealidad a lo largo de todo el libro.... Porque lo característico del alma de Sancho es que en ella el movimiento de ilusión y desilusión se reproduce ondulatoriamente a través de todas las páginas de la obra (p. 59).... Cervantes ha pintado el alma de Sancho sin prisa y sin preocuparse del orden mismo de las pinceladas (p. 62).

The truth is that Unamuno, Madariaga, and Papini do indeed notice and point out the ups and downs of Sancho's progress through the pages of Cervantes's novel, but their main emphasis is on showing the overall, final amelioration he has attained by the end of the story rather than the intermediate stages of the process, which are what interest Dámaso Alonso most.

More recently, Eduardo Urbina has also questioned the accuracy of the simple Quixotification theory.[108] It is worth quoting his conclusions:

> [Ya en la primera mitad de la Primera Parte del *Quijote*] Sancho se ha mostrado simple, temeroso, crédulo e ingenuo. Ha dudado y ha creído. Ha huido y ha luchado. Ha golpeado y ha recibido golpes. Ha sufrido y ha gozado. Ha mentido y ha sido engañado. Ha reído y ha llorado. Ha perdido y ha ganado. En definitiva, Sancho es ya, al final del capítulo veintisiete, un ser complejo, enriquecido por las experiencias sufridas pero todavía, fiel a su naturaleza, paradójico en el reconocimiento de sus dudas e ilusiones (p. 125).... Vemos que no es necesario esperar al final

---

[107] "Sancho-Quijote, Sancho-Sancho," *Homenaje a Cervantes*, (Valencia, 1950), II, 53-63. For Papini see "Don Chisciotte dell'inganno," *La Voce*, 8 (1916), 193-205, especially pp. 196-97; and "Cervantes" in his *Stroncature*, 5th edition (Florence, 1920), pp. 347-57, especially pp. 353-56; first published in 1916.

[108] "Sancho Panza 'escudero sin par': parodia y creación en *Don Quijote* (1605, 1615)" (unpublished dissertation, University of California at Berkeley, 1979).

del segundo *Quijote*, o aducir la 'quijotización' del escudero, presumiblemente allí llevada a cabo, para afirmar la existencia de un Sancho bien acabado...al concluirse el *Quijote* de 1605 (p. 136).

A similar conclusion can be inferred from Amado Alonso's article "Las prevaricaciones idiomáticas de Sancho."[109] In this article Amado Alonso considers all the malapropisms and semantic blunders that Sancho commits in *Don Quixote* and determines that they do not have any satirical purpose (p. 13), but rather are just another element of Cervantes's comical depiction of his character. He calls the reader's attention to the fact that several other Cervantine characters also use malapropisms (the niece, the housekeeper, the innkeeper, and Pedro, the goatherd, in *Don Quixote*; la Repolida in the *Entremés del rufián viudo*; Panduro in the *Entremés de la elección de los alcaldes de Daganzo*; Monipodio, la Cariharta, Maniferro, and Chiquiznaque in *Rinconete y Cortadillo*). This aspect of Cervantes's writings evinces, Amado Alonso continues, the preoccupation with proper, correct, and elegant speech so characteristic of the Renaissance. Sancho is an excellent example of the process of refinement that was taking place then. To begin with, he resents Don Quixote's insistence on correcting him and rejects outright the *hablar polido* that is being imposed on him; later on, he admits and accepts the existence of a higher linguistic stratum; finally, he himself becomes an advocate of the movement by correcting Teresa's malapropisms. Amado Alonso, therefore, sees a three-stage progressive amelioration, but the evidence he cites corresponding to these three stages does not follow the chronological order— (1) II, 7 and 9, (2) I, 19, 25, and 30; II, 7 and 35, and (3) II, 5. Thus, if we accept the theory of the Quixotification of Sancho as propounded by Amado Alonso, we also have to acknowledge the fact that this process was already complete by Chapter 5 of Part II, where the conversation between Sancho and his wife referred to by Amado Alonso takes place.

A study which might have thrown light on numerous aspects of Sancho's personality is Romero Flores's *Biografía de Sancho Panza*, but this lengthy monograph does not add anything new to Sancho criticism. It is just a rehashing of previous theories with a misguided insistence on seeing Sancho and Don Quixote as reflections of Cervantes's dual personality:

---

[109] *Nueva Revista de Filología Hispánica*, 2 (1948), 1-20. See also Joly, "Ainsi parlait Sancho Pança," *Les Langues Néo-Latines*, 69 (1975), 3-37. This article does not study Sancho's speech or language proper, but rather his use of *"lapsus"* (barbarisms, wordplays, and colloquialisms), proverbs, and what Joly misleadingly calls *"sermons"*; see Appendix 18, items 3, 10-12, 14, 21, and 26.

Las fantasías del Ingenioso Hidalgo están siempre refrenadas por las invocaciones realistas de Sancho Panza, y nada mejor que este dualismo para representar el alma de Cervantes, ... [quien] es Don Quijote y Sancho a la vez (pp. 52-53).[110]

By identifying Cervantes with both characters Romero Flores thinks himself safe to engage in theorizing about Cervantes's life, with the characteristic inconsistencies of this sort of criticism—a character acts or speaks for its author whenever it says something that supports the critic's theory, but it conveniently does not when what it does or says does not fit the proposed critical frame. According to Romero Flores, the idealistic Cervantes of the turn of the century (when presumably *Don Quixote*, Part I was being written) becomes by progressive Sanchification the realistic Cervantes of his last years:

Resulta bien claro advertir cómo Cervantes, antiguo quijotófilo, va emparejando cada vez más con Sancho y haciéndole responsable de sus juicios (p. 253).

And thus, what was supposed to be Sancho's "biography" becomes, in effect, a romanticized account of Cervantes's life, with Cervantes and Don Quixote dominating over one half of the book. The study of Sancho's personality proper does not begin until page 107, and in its midst there is a section entitled "Sanchificación de Don Quijote" (pp. 209-28). Even the twenty-four photographs chosen to accompany the study have little or nothing to do with Sancho. Moreover, the sections dealing with Sancho merely expand on and repeat what earlier studies had already shown. This book is, in fact, a hodgepodge of ideas and methods of approach taken principally from Unamuno's *Vida de Don Quijote y Sancho*, José Ortega y Gasset's *Meditaciones del "Quijote"*, and folk theories advanced by Menéndez Pidal, but lacking the scholarship and organization of Menéndez Pidal, the sense of synthesis and profound vision of Ortega y Gasset, and the sensibility and contagious enthusiasm of Unamuno.

What Romero Flores is incapable of doing in three hundred-odd pages of his *Biografía de Sancho Panza*, Federico Sánchez y Escribano, Dorothy Tharpe, Teresa Aveleyra Arroyo de Anda, and Charles

---

[110] John Aiken Moore, too, in "The Idealism of Sancho Panza," *Hispania*, 41 (1958), 73-76, subscribes to this theory: "Sancho was a manifestation of Cervantes himself to a degree only little below that of Don Quixote. Cervantes was always a Don Quixote. In his finer moments, he was a Sancho also," p. 74.

Vincent Aubrun each accomplished in a few pages.[111] Sánchez Escribano considers that Sancho is "la configuración exacta de todos los
villanos, vivos y muertos y por nacer";[112] but in order to present an
unencumbered picture of Sancho as a "vivo ejemplar de una clase
social," he centers his study on only those characteristics of Sancho
which fit this preconceived image of the squire, thus intentionally
disregarding those traits of Sancho and passages in *Don Quixote* which
show Cervantes's character as a distinct individual. Tharpe pieces
together a character profile of Sancho from what the squire says
about himself in *Don Quixote*.[113] Aveleyra describes Sancho's social
status, work, figure, personality, and family ties in the first four pages
of her study, dedicating the remainder to elucidating the Sanchification of Don Quixote (a process she considers of paramount importance, pp. 5-7), and the friendship between Don Quixote and Sancho,
the one thing, in her opinion, that keeps master and squire together
through thick and thin.[114]

Aubrun's interests are similar: Sancho's personality, background,
and physical appearance, and the relationship between him and Don
Quixote.[115] For Aubrun Sancho is both a comical character expressly
created to make people laugh with his name and figure and a peasant
who makes palpable to us the difficulties that impoverished Spanish
farm hands and their families were facing in those years. He sees the
relationship between Don Quixote and Sancho, not as a friendship,
but as the result of two differing socio-economic points of view
getting together. Perhaps the principal motive for Sancho to enter
the service of Don Quixote, writes Aubrun, is that he cannot live on
the products of his small parcel of land. "Il se loue comme ouvrier
agricole" (p. 20); but Don Quixote sees the arrangement under a
completely different light. For him, his spoken offer to his neighbor

---

[111] See also Pabón Núñez, pp. 555-77; and Marco Fidel Suárez, "Sancho
Panza," in *Cervantes en Colombia*, edited by Eduardo Caballero Calderón (Madrid, 1948), especially pp. 223-32.

[112] "Sancho Panza y su cultura popular," *Asomante*, 3 (1948), 33-40, at p.
33.

[113] "The 'Education' of Sancho as Seen in His Personal References,"
Modern Language Journal, 45 (1961), 244-48.

[114] "Un hombre llamado Sancho Panza," *Nueva Revista de Filología Hispánica*,
22 (1973), 1-16.

[115] "Sancho Panza, paysan pour de rire, paysan pour de vrai," *Revista
Canadiense de Estudios Hispánicos*, 1 (1976), 16-29.

and Sancho's acquiescence seal a traditional feudal contract between a lord and his vassal, entitling Sancho to receive protection, sustenance, and grants of lands, honors, and titles from the knight, but no salary. Sancho regards it as a civil contract between a master and a servant for room and board, and fixed wages, a contract which should be put in writing and legalized. Aubrun then comments in great detail on the numerous arguments that arise between Sancho and Don Quixote because of this initial misunderstanding, and shows how Sancho cunningly manages to allot himself a daily salary and, at the same time, to reap the benefits to which he is entitled under the feudal compact. Aubrun concludes that there are two Sanchos in *Don Quixote*:

> Le Sancho couard, goulu et malicieux, c'est le paysan pour de rire. Le Sancho, homme de bien, bon père et bon époux, avec ses failles et ses vertus, ses contradictions et ses humeurs, c'est une certaine image du paysan pour de vrai (p. 26).

Franklin Oakes Brantley, Moore, and Raymond Smith Willis have written also on Sancho's family ties, his reasons for following Don Quixote, and his socio-economic status. In "Sancho's Ascent into the Spheres," Brantley has noted that Sancho "is a poor man who has a wife and two children to support, and...[he] does make it clear repeatedly that his reason for following Don Quijote is to find a bonanza somewhere,...so that he and his family can escape from poverty and enjoy the life of the wealthy."[116] Moore states that, in addition to being an idealist thirsting for adventure, Sancho is looking after his interests: "the seeds...of idealism [are] firmly centered in Sancho's basic nature (p. 73);...[but] he would answer, yes, if anyone should offer him a better life.... Furthermore, we might ask, 'What does he have to lose?' If he stays at home he faces drought, disease, and many other uncertainties. Perhaps worst of all, he faces the monotony of life in Argamasilla" (p. 74). Willis sees also freedom, "the freedom to live and not merely exist," as the main reason behind Sancho's decision to follow Don Quixote: "this freedom is its own justification and it does not even require the support of the promise of an island";[117] but he asks his readers to "picture Sancho a little younger than Don Quixote," and, in direct opposition to Aubrun and Brantley, as "a man of substance and property, a little farm at least.

116 *Hispania*, 53 (1970), 37-45, at p. 38.

117 "Sancho Panza: Prototype for the Modern Novel," *Hispanic Review*, 37 (1969), 207-27, at p. 217.

Poor he may have been, but not destitute, witness his donkey, his well-filled saddle bags and wine skin, when he finally set out. Especially observe his corpulent figure: starving men don't grow fat. So he was no miserable wretch, grasping at any straw.... His life was moderately comfortable and secure. He is not one of society's dispossessed" (pp. 214 and 216).

Of these monographs, the studies by Aveleyra and Aubrun are probably two of the best and most useful articles on Sancho. They are concise and give a clear and accurate picture of the squire's personality. Unavoidably, they repeat much of what had been said earlier, but bring this information together in one article and introduce some common sense and careful textual reading into an otherwise chaotic world of idiosyncratic and textually unsupportable exegeses.

Aveleyra and Aubrun consider Sancho as one of the elements of the master-squire relationship, something which I have avoided as much as possible in my own monographs on Sancho. My article "Sancho's Fabrications: A Mirror of the Development of His Imagination," and my note "Playing Chess in Don Quixote," [118] consider two aspects of Sancho's use of his own resources and wit, because Don Quixote could not have taught Sancho to lie and to argue logically in the short period of time (approximately six months) they spent together.[119] Don Quixote's contribution to Sancho's way of responding to different circumstances is as a catalizer rather than a teacher or originator. In my first article I studied the three most important lies that Sancho tells in Don Quixote: 1) he makes up the everyday happenings of a village to avoid being scolded by his master for returning without having delivered Don Quixote's letter to Dulcinea (I, 31, 382-86), 2) he convinces Don Quixote that three peasant girls are

---

[118] *Hispanic Review*, 38 (1970), 174-82.; and *Romance Notes*, 22 (1981), 202-07.

[119] Murillo has convincingly demonstrated 1) that there is no correlation between the time span covered by the historical dates given, directly or indirectly, in *Don Quixote* (1589-1614), the fictional duration of Don Quixote's adventures (approximately seven months—Part I, two months; one month interval between the Parts; and Part II, four months), and the mythical, winterless year of perpetual spring and recurrent summer in which the action takes place (Part I, July-September; Part II, April-August), and 2) that the limitations imposed by this mythical year and the fact that The Captive's Tale (I, Chapters 39 to 41) was not written within the sequential order of the other episodes explain and justify these chronological discrepancies; *The Golden Dial: Temporal Configuration in "Don Quijote"* (Oxford, 1975), see especially pp. 33-66.

Dulcinea and her ladies in waiting (II, 10, 107-13), and 3) he tells the Duchess a fairy tale based on his imaginary, aerial trip on Clavileño (II, 41, 353-54). These three fabrications are very important because they have serious repercussions throughout the novel, and because they show how Sancho responds always in a similar manner to circumstances which are beyond his control. "Playing Chess in *Don Quixote*" deals with Sancho's ability to dispute logically with his master, outmanoeuvre his Jesuitic argumentations, and drive his point home. These two monographs corroborate once again the fact that Sancho is, as Samuel Butler put it three centuries ago, "much more wise and Politique [than] his Master with all his Study'd, and acquir'd Abilities."[120]

Perhaps the only two present-day critics who consider that Sancho is a deformed and ignoble peasant from beginning to end are Willis and Francisco Maldonado de Guevara. Willis thinks that the squire remains "to the end, gross, grotesque, and limited in intelligence, though not in native wit. He [is] still in essence the buffoon" (p. 227), and Maldonado de Guevara states that after resigning his governorship Sancho can continue his past life, "puede seguir pensando en otras ínsulas y seguir siendo el mismo, es decir lo mismo."[121] But Willis and Maldonado de Guevara are merely confirming the central fact that the quixotification process, whether accepted as such, revised, questioned, or denied, has become *el caballito de batalla* of twentieth-century Sancho criticism. Almost all other aspects of Sancho's personality have become subservient to this overriding process of Quixotification. This shift of critical interest is clearly seen in the treatment of the episode of Sancho's governorship.

As a whole, in the seventeenth, eighteenth, and nineteenth centuries plays and critical comments which considered this episode dealt with it in isolation, outside the frame of reference of *Don Quixote*, and detached from the rest of the action. Because of this tendency, Sancho's personality was frequently split into two totally alien halves: a gross and vulgar peasant and a wise and exemplary governor. The twentieth century has revised this obviously drastic and crude dichotomy. The various approaches to the problem of integrating Sancho's governorship with the other apparently contradictory aspects of his character can be sorted out into three main groups.

---

120 *Characters and Passages from Note-Books*, see above, footnote 11.

121 "Apuntes para la fijación de las estructuras esenciales en el *Quijote*," *Anales Cervantinos*, 1 (1951), 159-231, at p. 201.

The first and most numerous group is made up of those critics who attribute Sancho's exemplary discharge of the office of governor of Barataria to the piecemeal amelioration of his personality, his progressive Quixotification, and the advice that Don Quixote gives him before he takes up office.[122] Unamuno and Madariaga, amongst many others, are, as has been seen, staunch supporters of this point of view.

A second group of critics consider that there are two Sanchos (rather than one split in half), the Sancho of Part I and the Sancho of Part II; this theory is of course, only a dressed-up, more refined version of the old misconception. Joaquín Casalduero, Savj-López, Romero Flores, Leif Sletsjöe, Brantley, and Pelorson belong in this group:

> In 1605, Don Quixote and Sancho neither opposed nor complemented each other; the two figures were the same, what changed was their dimension, when one figure is put in relation with the other a new whole is formed. In 1615, this interplay of two different autonomous measurements forming one whole no

---

[122] For Don Quixote's advice to Sancho see Peter Frank de Andrea, "El 'gobierno de la ínsula Barataria', Speculum Principis cervantino," Filosofía y Letras, 13, No. 26 (1947), 241-57, and Donald William Bleznick, "Don Quijote's Advice to Governor Sancho Panza," Hispania, 40 (1957), 62-65. These two critics are chiefly concerned with the sources of Don Quixote's advice to his squire, but they tacitly accept that Sancho was influenced by these rules of conduct and applied them during his brief stay at Barataria. De Andrea considers that Sancho "es la cabal encarnación del Gobernador Cristiano de Juan Márquez .... [La visión de Cervantes] del ars gubernandi [tiene un fondo cabalmente eticista], porque el gobierno de la ínsula tiende a reflejar el concepto popular del gobernante, [las ideas reinantes en su tiempo], contrariamente a la mayoría de las otras publicaciones de la época que propenden a ser reverberaciones del pensamiento erudito" (p. 243). Bleznick notes that "in his governorship Sancho demonstrated his inherent sincerity and honesty linked with perspicacity and sharp-wittedness. He viewed the problems of his domain realistically. In addition, his intimate conversance with the psychology of his subjects aided immeasurably in his decisions" (p. 64). Brantley disagrees, noting that Don Quixote's advice "is as useless as it is gratuitous" (p. 43). He considers that Sancho's exemplary behavior during his governorship arises from a decision consequent on his trip on Clavileño and made on the night immediately following: "Sancho's remarkable change of character occurs directly as a consequence of the Clavileño trick.... Possibly it was that night when he was alone in his room that the Squire had his moment of profound seriousness, when he shaped his meditation and reached his resolution [to abandon all greed]" (pp. 39 and 43). The gist of this theory had already been proposed by Oelschläger (pp. 21-22).

longer exists. On the other hand, is emphasized their mutual dependence which makes more evident the different quality of the two figures; on the other, they continuously struggle to separate and there arrives a moment in which they must separate, that moment when Don Quixote believes himself, for the first time, a true knight, and Sancho, a true governor.[123]

Nella seconda parte...è Sancio che prende il sopravvento: ma un altro Sancio, trasformato per la necessaria varietà della narrazione. Così i Sancio sono due.... La seconda parte è il romanzo di Sancio (Savj-López, pp. 92-93).

El pastor de puercos adocenado y simplón que sale a las páginas en 1605, sin otro designio que hacer y decir lo que cuadra a un tipo de su condición, en 1615, al cabo de los años, resurge con unos caracteres y una significación distintos de los que tuviera a la hora de la primera salida (Romero Flores, p. 233).

La [figura] del escudero no experimenta una evolución lenta del comienzo de la novela de 1605 al fin de la de 1615. En el medio hay un eslabón que falta. Hay ruptura, y precisamente entre las dos partes de la gran novela (p. 92). La pintura que ha hecho de Sancho su gran creador no está falta de incorrecciones o, al menos, de incoherencias (p. 91).... Cervantes necesitó de un escudero,... y no lo creó de un solo tirón. Fue añadiendo trazos, y tal vez es por ello por lo que la figura de Sancho no nos convence,... pero no será posible explicar de este modo la existencia de DOS SANCHOS (pp. 97-98).... ¿Dónde está esta ruptura o divisoria entre los dos Sanchos? Está precisamente entre la primera y la segunda parte; por tanto, entre 1605 y 1615 (p. 99).[124]

Don Quijote and Sancho evince no change of character in Part One;...in Part Two, on the other hand, they are portrayed as

---

[123] Casalduero, "The Composition of Don Quixote," in Cervantes Across the Centuries, pp. 92-93.

[124] Sletsjöe, Sancho Panza, hombre de bien (Madrid, 1961). Edmund de Chasca disagrees with Sletsjöe's theory, stating that "Cervantes plasmó a Sancho como personaje complejo desde el principio mismo de su creación, no hay diferencia fundamental entre el Sancho de 1605 y el Sancho de 1615," "Sancho-Sanchuelo, Sancho-Sancho, Sancho-Sanchísimo," in Estudios literarios de hispanistas norteamericanos dedicados a Helmut Hatzfeld con motivo de su 80 aniversario (Barcelona, 1974), pp. 73-86, at p. 79. In his article de Chasca studies briefly some of the squire's characteristics, paying special attention to three sentences spoken by him: "desfaga ese agravio y enderece ese tuerto, matando a ese hideputa" (I, 29, 363), "cada uno es hijo de sus obras" (I, 47, 563), and "debajo de ser hombre puedo venir a ser papa" (I, 47, 563); see pp. 80-81 and 83-84.

evolving through experience into new personalities: Quijote gradually regains his sanity while Sancho grows into a wiser and better man.... [Sancho's] growth in the second part... involves a spiritual victory, a personal triumph over unwholesome tendencies. The precise moment of this victory, the moment when by an act of will Sancho abandons earthly ambition and dedicates himself to the higher reality, is not protrayed in the novel.... [It] occurs [between 1605 and 1615] while he is absent from the reader's view (Brantley, p. 37).

Le Sancho qui disait "Regardez, ce sont des moulins" n'est pas le Sancho de Barataria, qui, comme transfiguré, perce les ruses les plus subtiles, tend les pièges les plus adroits.... Le juge ne connaît pas de la réalité tangible, mais de la réalité humaine des pensées et des calculs secrets; d'un réel qu'il faut construire, sur lequel on peut se tromper, ou être trompé (Pelorson, p. 53).

Finally, there are those critics who see Sancho's governorship in function of a larger, more comprehensive denominator. Urbina, Joly, John Jay Allen, Pelorson, again, and Redondo can represent this group. Urbina considers Sancho's presence in a continuation of his parodic function:

Los juicios de Sancho como gobernador no deben de ser tenidos como desquite o afirmación de la discreción ganada junto a don Quijote y, menos aún, como consecuencia de sus consejos. Son, más propiamente, afirmación de su natural discreto y socarrón y, en segundo término, extensión de la parodia del escudero (p. 200).... [Y] lo que le une a [don Quijote] no es su fidelidad, ya que atiende primero a su interés, sino su presencia obligada en la parodia (1979, p. 205).

Joly detects in the Baratarian chapters a heavily ironical tone, in keeping with Cervantes's depiction of Sancho as a folk character imbued with common sense, but incapable of discharging any weightier office adequately. To prove her point, Joly quotes a passage from Chapter 66 of Part II, in which, after Sancho has advised a group of peasants on how to ensure that the two contestants, one fat and one thin, have equal chances of winning a race, one of the peasants makes the following remark:

—Si el criado es tan discreto, ¡cuál debe de ser el amo! Yo apostaré que si van a estudiar a Salamanca, que a un tris han de venir a ser alcaldes de corte; que todo es burla, sino estudiar y más estudiar, y tener favor y ventura; y cuando menos se piensa el hombre, se halla con una vara en la mano o con una mitra en la cabeza (p. 544).

And she concludes that the farmer is making master and squire the butt of his irony:

Palabras cargadas de una ironía nada tierna, que—entre otras cosas—claramente apuntan al trastorno mental que lleva a confundir una habilidad que sólo alcanza a resolver adivinanzas de tipo tradicional con la que han de tener los hombres llamados a ejercer los más altos cargos. Tan extravagante confusión de valores sólo es concebible en la perspectiva carnavalesca de un gobierno mentiroso y de corta duración, o sólo cabe en el magín de un rústico burdo e ignorante (p. 499).

Allen, however, reaches the opposite conclusion. In his opinion, the peasant is praising both Sancho and Don Quixote, evincing the completely different reactions that master and squire arouse at the beginning of Part I and at the close of Part II.[125] Allen is correct in seeing the peasant's remark as praising Don Quixote and Sancho, because the peasants do not know who they are, nor does the knight engage in any antics, nor does Sancho come out with any of his exaggerations or humorous remarks. Therefore, there is no cause for derision. Sancho has solved the peasants' problem, and they simply praise his good sense.

For Allen, Sancho's governorship is but one step in the progressive amelioration that Cervantes's characters undergo in the novel. He traces some parallels between the careers of Sancho and Don Quixote, noting that in Part I the following weaknesses are characteristic of both: excessive self-confidence, serious lack of self-knowledge, and blindness to the unbridgeable chasm that lies between their stations in life and those to which they aspire. But as the story unfolds, Allen concludes, these failings are slowly replaced by a more moderate self-confidence, deeper knowledge of the self, and the realization and acceptance of their shortcomings, these developments culminating in final confession and repentance at the end of the novel:

[But] the epiphany does not include Sancho; on the contrary, though it is he who articulates the statement which makes explicit the implicit process of self-mastery as victory, his own situation represents a comic reduction of Don Quijote's self-discovery, since he is unable to assimilate fully the lessons of the governorship. It is precisely the bogus lashings alluded to in the

---

125 "The Governorship of Sancho and Don Quijote's Chivalric Career," *Revista Hispánica Moderna*, 38 (1974-1975), 141-52, at p. 148.

epiphany scene [II, 72, 580] which constitute the sign of Sancho's backsliding into greed, and thus of his inability to follow
his master on the plane of transcendence,...and the common
notion of Sancho as Don Quijote's disciple at the end of the
novel, ready to carry forward his master's quixotic quest, is
simply incompatible with the text. It would nevertheless be ill-
advised to judge Sancho too harshly, for he survived his moment of recognition. One cannot live in the rarefied atmosphere
of transcendence, for to live is to err. Which is why Don Quijote
must die at the moment of maximum lucidity (p. 152).

In his conclusion Allen moves away from the Quixotification theory,
but by seeing Don Quixote in opposition to Sancho, as a heroic and
admirable figure, he nearly falls into the clutches of the Romantic
interpretation.

Pelorson and Redondo, for their parts, interpret the episode of
Barataria as an extension of Cervantes's veiled attack on the *letrados*
and the venality of contemporary Spanish justice:

[Il] est vrai que les juristes étaient souvent les premiers à se
plaindre de corruptions dans leur milieu. Mais tout en recon-
naissant l'écart entre les principes et les pratiques, ils tendaient
souvent à tirer personnellement leur épingle du jeu, par des
tirades de vertueuse indignation, ou de moralisme grandilo-
quent. Au lieu de montrer directement la vénalité d'un juge,
Cervantès a eu le trait de génie de montrer un rustre, réalisant
le plus simplement du monde un idéal présenté dans de doctes
livres comme très difficile (Pelorson, p. 52)...Il y aurait donc
une parodie des *Letrados* dans le *Quichotte*, parodie moins remar-
quée que les autres (celle des romans de chevalerie, celle des
romances), peut-être parce qu'elle est moins digne d'intérêt, en
effet, (dans la mesure où elle ne se rattache pas directement au
thème central du déclin), également parce qu'elle n'est pas tout à
fait sur le même plan (p. 54).

Al ejercer su gobierno [Sancho] ha sido un modelo de diligencia,
conciencia y rectitud. Su actividad gubernamental es una lección
de moral política. Se ha lucido particularmente como juez: sus
sentencias han sido rápidas e intachables mientras que la justicia
oficial es larga, venial y viciosa.... Frente a tan lamentable
situación, resplandece el íntegro gobierno y la deslumbrante
justicia de Sancho, quien no hace más que aplicar la doctrina
evangélica ("con Cristo en la memoria"). ¿No querrá decir Cervantes—que tanto tuvo que quejarse del gobierno y de la justicia
de su España—que para ser buen gobernador y buen juez
(primera obligación del que gobierna) más importa ser *verdadero*
cristiano que no gran letrado o capitán? El perfecto gobernante,

¿no será el que tiene la ley de Jesús impresa en el corazón, un gobernante tal como lo pinta Erasmo en su *Institutio principis christiani?* Por ello puede ilustrar mejor estos preceptos el "tonto" Sancho Panza, el cristiano sincero y sin letras, el pacífico representante de la verdad popular, de la uténtica verdad (Redondo, pp. 68-69).[126]

When we look beyond the specific areas of interest already described, the difficulties of trying to summarize what twentieth-century critics think about Sancho are all too obvious. The mixtures of praise, scorn, or praise and scorn, that he receives from critics are such, and the contradictions we find even within the same monograph are so blatant, that it is impossible to see the true Sancho amongst the scores of distorted and incomplete images of him being reflected in this critical house of mirrors. On the one hand, Menéndez Pidal tells us that the squire is "de corazón pobre y bondadoso, de ánimo fiel, que duda de todo y lo cree todo, y en donde brota abundante la discreción por entre la dura corteza de la socarronería, alcanzando la más zahorí sabiduría popular en juicios comparables a los de Salomón y a los de Don Pedro el Cruel" (*De Cervantes y Lope de Vega*, p. 43), Efron disagrees, considering that "Sancho's governorship is certainly not the unquestionably exemplary thing it is assumed to be. Perhaps the ability of a common man to become a governor blinds normally perceptive critics to any possible defects in Sancho's arbitrary lawmaking, and to his own blindness to any fault in one of his subjects who had kept a young daughter confined to the house for a decade" ("Satire Denied," p. 14). B. A. Krzhevski assures us that Sancho "is not a good-for-nothing peasant, but a man endowed by nature with a good heart and common sense";[127] Madariaga is certain that Sancho, "lejos de ser cobarde, se manifiesta como un hombre viril,... [pero] está dispuesto a luchar sólo cuando hay razón para ello, es decir

---

[126] See also de Andrea, pp. 254-55. Sletsjöe considers that the Baratarian episode is a socio-political satire: "Estoy de acuerdo con Morel-Fatio en que la historia del gobierno de Sancho es una sátira política, no con dirección al Estado o al Rey, sino que el punto de mira ha sido más dilatado y más general. Se me antoja que su crítica va dirigida contra la gente acomodada que se burlaba de los pobres" (p. 102); for Alfred Paul Victor Morel-Fatio see "Social and Historical Background," in *Cervantes Across the Centuries*, pp. 101-27.

[127] Paraphrased by Turkevich, p. 211, from "*Don Kikhot* na fone ispanskoi literatury XVI-XVII st.," in the edition of *Don Quixote* published by the Russian Academy, *Khitroumny idalgo Don Kikhot Lamanchski*, (Moscow, 1929), I, pp. xxxix-lxxix.

causa" (*Guía del lector*, pp. 135 and 137). Aubrun finds a comical contrast between Sancho's poverty and his big stomach, "Sancho le journalier devait être maigre comme un clou. Son embonpoint, c'est pour de rire" ("Sancho Panza," p. 18), but Willis notes, by contrast, that the squire is "a man of substance and property.... Observe his corpulent figure: starving men don't grow fat" ("Sancho Panza: Prototype," p. 214). Fitzmaurice-Kelly is equally sure that Sancho goes with Don Quixote "as a foil to heroism," and that he is the "embodiment of calculating cowardice, malicious humour, and prosaic common sense," and a "slower-witted, vulgar, practical person" ("Cervantes in England," p. 15). Waldo David Frank, for his part, notes that "as the tale grows, poor Sancho is more and more enmired in confusion. He is in danger of madness, losing his distinction between the world of shapes and this world of ideas in which Don Quixote rides";[128] Pavel Ivanovich Novitski writes that "Don Quixote despises the dull and platitudinous mentality of churls like Sancho Panza, who believe the transfiguration of the universe to be but madness and arrant nonsense and can see only the inns and the pigsties."[129] Close does not hesitate to call Sancho "vulgar simpleton," "simpleton," and "irremediably fallible" on the only four occasions in which he qualifies the squire's name in his *The Romantic Approach to "Don Quixote"* (pp. 17, 20, 198, and 241). Bardon compares Beaumarchais, the French playwright, to Sancho, noting that like the squire Beaumarchais has "l'esprit de ruse, l'absence de scrupules, le goût du bien-être, l'amour de l'argent, l'attachement à ses intérêts" (*"Don Quichotte" en France*, p. 683).

I realize that some of these quotations might not do full justice to the perhaps less simplistic opinion critics have about Sancho, but their purpose here is merely to underline again, if it needs underlining, how little critics are in accord when it comes to appraising Sancho's personality.

When we come to the literary influence of Sancho in this century we fare little better. The tercentenary of the publication of *Don Quixote*, Part I (1605), caused a rush of critical and literary works based on or inspired by Cervantes's novel. At least three Spanish plays that deal with Sancho appeared in those years: M. Calandrelli's *Sancho en la ínsula Barataria* (1904), Magín Morera y Galicia's *Un*

---

[128] "The Career of the Hero," in *Cervantes Across the Centuries*, p. 186.

[129] "Thematic Design," in *Cervantes Across the Centuries*, p. 242.

desgobernado gobernador (1905), and Perier's *La ínsula Barataria* (1905).[130] Sancho is also the subject of three Brazilian poems contributed by Filinto de Almeida (two sonnets) and Joaquim de Araujo (a short poem) to the volume *Discursos pronunciados na sessão commemorativa do tricentenario da publicação do D. Quixote* (Rio de Janeiro, 1905).[131] "Os sonetos perfiguram um dialogo em que Sancho Pança, de regresso, confessa a sua desillusão profunda," writes Fidelino de Sousa Figueiredo, "[e] o conteúdo do poemeto 'Visões do Quixote' é um novo quadro do contraste do idealismo desinteressado e chimerico de Quixote com o commodismo egoistico de Sancho" (p. 168). But as the titles of the Spanish plays and the summaries of Figueiredo indicate, these works merely repeat what earlier writers had already exhausted.[132]

There have also, of course, been numerous film, radio, musical, and T.V. adaptations of *Don Quixote*, all necessarily reducing the length of the work and inevitably interpreting Cervantes's novel and his characters in different ways. The trade in paintings, prints, statues, and cartoons depicting Sancho and his master has continued unabated. Here, however, I shall limit myself to discussing only those literary works which are of some importance to this study.

Jean Camp wrote a French continuation to *Don Quixote* with Sancho playing the principal role (*Sancho*, Paris, 1933). At the beginning of the story, Camp spins his tale by borrowing short passages from *Don Quixote* and setting into them his own version of the Cervantine episodes. He also introduces numerous factual changes.

For instance, he changes Sanchico's name to Toribio, increases the number of Sancho's children to three—Toribio (ten years old), Sanchica (eight), and Juanita (four)—and accepts Argamasilla de Alba as Sancho's hometown. For Camp Sancho is still the stereotyped character of previous centuries:

> [Sancho] aime l'argent, la terre, la table comme un pauvre homme qui n'a jamais eu dix écus à la fois, dix arpents de friche, la pâtée à sa suffisance. Il est sale comme Labre, ignorant comme son roussin, bête et laid comme personne (p. 10).... De sa main

[130] Mentioned by LaGrone, p. 95-97.

[131] See Fidelino de Sousa Figueiredo, "O thema do *Quixote* na litteratura portuguesa do seculo XIX," *Revista de Filología Española*, 8 (1921), 161-69.

[132] I have not been able to read José Abaurre y Mesa's *Historia de varios sucesos ocurridos en la aldea después de la muerte del ingenioso hidalgo don Quijote de la Mancha* (Madrid, 1901).

velue il s'évente en mâchonnant une bulbe d'oignon. Béat, congestionné, somnolent, il s'aveulit délice (p. 35).

After the death of his master Camp's Sancho begins to change. First he becomes the village storyteller:

Quand le soleil brûle droit les sillons, du côté d'Alcazar, il voit poindre genêts ou mules. Ce sont des visites pour lui, des curieux, des savants, voir des incrédules qui veulent écouter ses exploits de sa bouche (pp. 72-73).... Sancho est l'auteur à la mode. Il faut bien qu'on en paie les belles histoires.... L'auditoire glousse à l'entendre, échange des regards de complicité aux beaux passages, et s'exclame aux récits pathétiques.
—Ami Sancho, contez-nous donc encore!
Sancho sourit, râcle sa barbe, plisse ses rides. Mais les gobelets se remplissent, la mousse déborde des cruches, les onces reluisent aux doigts (p. 74).

Sancho's spreading fame reaches the ears of an idealistic Franciscan friar, "frère Serapio,...un sain François de la Table ronde" (p. 84). Brother Serapio arrives at Sancho's village and asks the squire to join him in a "Nouvelle Croisade" to rescue Dulcinea, who had fallen into the hands of African heretics. Sancho accepts Brother Serapio as his new master and begins preparations for the "crusade." Soon, an army of the poor, old, sick, deformed, and mutilated begins to grow around the pair, and, when the town cannot stand them any longer, they set off for Africa. Their trip and tribulations can be summarized as follows: as they begin their adventure their army is joined by groups of gentlemen and knights of the old religious, military orders wanting to take part in their crusade; but this happy state of affairs does not last for long. Pillaging, crime, and murdering take over, defections start occurring, towns close their doors when the "pilgrims" approach. Then, Sancho, in a moment of weakness, makes love to one of the prostitutes that follow them. He immediately repents, and, to expiate his sin, makes public confession and asks to be punished. He is whipped and then allowed to continue his pilgrimage. After many sufferings, they arrive at the coast, but by the time they are ready to embark for Africa, a full one third of their followers have abandoned them, and, to Sancho's distress, he has to leave his ass behind because there is no room on board. Even worse, the elements are against them and the boats are wrecked on the treacherous African coast. Of the mere twenty or twenty-five pilgrims who survive the crossing several die on their first day in the desert. Finally, Sancho becomes delirious, abandons the other survivors, dies of hunger and thirst, and is eaten by a hyena.

The plot is so far-fetched, and Camp's depiction of Sancho's personality so unlike the original, that it is impossible to accept *Sancho* as a genuine continuation of Cervantes's novel.

Another work of fiction that fails to throw any useful light on Sancho's character is José Larraz López's *¡Don Quijancho, maestro! (Biografía fabulosa)* (Madrid, 1961). The Don Quijancho of the title of this ill-conceived and artistically worthless *novelón* is Roberto Núñez de los Godos Hasparren, the offspring of an ambitious and unlucky Spanish politician and a well-to-do French beauty. Roberto becomes an eccentric professor of metaphysics at the Estudio de Segovia. He subsequently loses touch with reality, fancies himself a twentieth-century descendant of Don Quixote, and resigns his position at the Estudio. After making a fool of himself on numerous occasions, he is interned in a French sanatorium. He recovers his senses in France, adopts the name of Quijancho, writes letters to his ex-colleagues explaining his theories on Cervantes's novel and proposing what he considers should have been the denouement of the story (see Chapter 20), wins the main prize of the Madrid Christmas lottery, and dies in a stupid car accident.[133]

Another false scent comes from John Fowles's novel *The French Lieutenant's Woman* (Boston, 1969). In it Fowles compares one of his own characters, Sam Farrow, Charles's servant, with Dickens's Sam Weller and Sancho.

> Sam was some ten years [Charles's] junior; too young to be a good manservant and besides, absentminded, contentious, vain, fancying himself sharp; too fond of drolling and idling.... Of course to us any Cockney servant called Sam evokes immediately the immortal Weller; and it was certainly from that background that this Sam had emerged (p. 50).... He had a very sharp sense of clothes style... and he spent most of his wages on keeping in fashion (pp. 50-51).... Charles knew very well that [Sam] was also partly a companion—his Sancho Panza, the

[133] After reading Jo Anne Engelbert's article "A Sancho for Saint Francis," *Hispania*, 46 (1963), 287-89, I read for the third time Kazantzakis's beautiful novel *Saint Francis*, translated by P. A. Bien (New York, 1962). I still fail to see any similarities between Sancho and Brother Leo. Engelbert tells us that "Leo plays as many parts as Sancho...as he enacts his many roles as companion, defender, servant, brother, cook, confidant, confessor, disciple, acolyte, and nurse" (p. 287); but it is not what the characters do that is important (most real and fictional servants play most of these roles in various degrees at one time or another), but how they do it. Moreover, the personalities of Sancho and Brother Leo are completely dissimilar, and, in my opinion, there are no other grounds of comparison.

low comedy that supported his spiritual worship of Ernestina-Dorothea [!]. He kept Sam, in short, because he was frequently amused by him; not because there were not better "machines" to be found.... The difference between Sam Weller and Sam Farrow...was this: the first was happy with his role, the second suffered it (p. 52).... Sam could, did give the appearance, in some back taproom, of knowing all there was to know about city life—and then some.... But deep down inside, it was another story. There he was a timid and uncertain person (p. 140).... His ambition was very simple: he wanted to be a haberdasher (p. 141).

From this description of Sam Farrow it is obvious that his net resemblance to either Sam Weller or Sancho amounts to nought, a fact that is brought into sharp relief when he abandons and betrays his master for a pretty maid and a more secure and comfortable position (Chapters 51-54).

Another servant, however, named Sam continues the exemplary tradition of his more faithful predecessors. Sam Gamgee is not of the race of men. He is a hobbit, one of the various mythical Tolkienian races of people.[134] His physical appearance conforms in all respects to that of his congeners. He is very short, thick-set, quick of hearing, sharp-eyed, and nimble and deft in his movements. Also, like most hobbits, he eats six substantial meals a day and is extremely fond of birthday parties. He is practical, and extremely curious. And it is precisely his inquisitiveness which gets him involved in the great mission to destroy the magic Ring of Power that has come into his master's possession, and thus permanently check the forces of Evil that are threatening to extend their influence over the whole world.

Sam is caught eavesdropping as his master Frodo and Gandalf the great wizard discuss the Ring. Gandalf is justifiably furious, so Sam, like Sancho in a similar situation, decides to play dumb:

'Eavesdropping, sir? I don't follow you, begging your pardon. There ain't no eaves at Bag End, and that's a fact' (I, 72).

Gandalf calls him a fool and threatens to turn him "into a spotted toad and fill the garden full of grass-snakes," but he changes his mind and tells Sam:

'I have thought of something better than that. Something to shut your mouth, and punish you properly for listening. You shall go away with Mr. Frodo!'

---

[134] John Ronald Reuel Tolkien, *The Lord of the Rings*, 3 vols. (Boston: second Houghton Mifflin Company edition, 1967); first edition, London, 1954-1955. All future references are to the 1967 edition by volume and page.

'Me, sir!" cried Sam, springing up like a dog invited for a walk. 'Me go and see Elves and all! Hooray!' he shouted, and then burst into tears (I, 73).

Sam, like Sancho, has got his way.

Sam is Frodo's gardener, and his initial role at Frodo's side is that of a servant rather than a helper or a companion; but things soon begin to change, and by the end of Book 1, just after Sam has sung an old tune, Frodo says:

'I am learning a lot about Sam Gamgee on this journey. First he was a conspirator [his prying into Frodo's affairs], now he's a jester. He'll end up by becoming a wizard—or a warrior!' (I, 220)

Frodo's words are, of course, prophetic, and Sam becomes Frodo's "dearest friend," Samwise (II, 252), Samwise son of Hamfast (II, 266), Master Samwise (II, 270), good Samwise (II, 285), a warrior who fights and defeats the monstrous spider Shelob (II, 337-39), the bearer of Sting (the magic sword), the phial of Galadriel, and the Ring itself (II, 342-52; III, 1-188). Finally he is plain Sam again, the ever faithful servant and gardener of Mr. Frodo.[135] but the Sam of the close of the novel is no longer the same merely practical, common-sense, inquisitive hobbit of the previous year. When he and his master were nearing the end of their quest, "as hope died in Sam, or seemed to die, it was turned to a new strength. Sam's plain hobbit-face grew stern, almost grim, as the will hardened in him, and he felt through all his limbs a thrill, as if he was turning into some creature of stone and steel that neither despair nor weariness nor endless barren miles could subdue. With a new sense of responsibility he brought his eyes back to the ground near at hand, studying the next move" (III, 211). And, thus, Sam becomes savior, guide, provider, protector, comforter, and the only source of energy that keeps his master on the move until their task has been fulfilled. When Sam returns to his village, still in the service of Frodo, he now finds himself regarded as a legendary hero. He repairs the destruction made in the woods of his beloved land with the miraculous help of the magic soil given to him by the elf Queen, and having completed this mission as gardener he settles down to a long life of peace, love, prosperity, and honors. He marries his sweetheart and both move in with Frodo, who predicts that they will have many children and that

---

[135] Throughout the last Book (III, 173-311) Sam is referred to as Master Samwise, and as Samwise on only four occasions (pp. 177, 229, 254, and 308).

Sam will become Mayor. When his master goes off with the elves to the Havens, where he will have eternal life, Sam inherits Frodo's large and beautiful home.

This conclusion is similar to that of *The Pickwick Papers*, and Sam Gamgee's touching devotion to Frodo resembles more closely that of Sam Weller for Mr. Pickwick than Sancho's attachment to Don Quixote, but in most other respects the characters of Tolkien and Cervantes are alike.

Sam, being a hobbit, is not what we would call a good-looking fellow, regardless of how attractive he might be in his sweetheart's eyes. He is the only character to use proverbs and sayings consistently, though sporadically: "apples for walking, and a pipe for sitting" (I, 192), "*it's the job that's never started as takes longest to finish*, as my old [father] used to say" (I, 376), "*news from Bree*, and not *sure as Shiretalk*, as the sayings go" (II, 255), "*handsome is as handsome does* we say" (II, 289), "*where there's life there's hope*, as my [father] used to say; *and need of vittles*, as he mostways used to add" (II, 309), "it comes home to you, as they say" (III, 297), "they're a bit too grand for daily wear and tear, as you might say" (III, 306); and he knows ballads and songs of old lore (I, 197-98, 219-20; II, 254-55). He has a baggage-pony, Bill, which he loves and cares for. For instance, when Bill has to be left to pick his own way home alone, "Sam stood sullenly by the pony and returned no answer. Bill, seeming to understand well what was going on, nuzzled up to him, putting his nose to Sam's ear. Sam burst into tears, and fumbled with the straps" (I, 317); and when the howling of wolves made Bill start in fear Sam sprang "to his side and whispered softly to him" (I, 321); but moments later Bill escaped terrorized: "Sam leaped after him, and then hearing Frodo's cry he ran back again, weeping and cursing.... 'Poor old Bill!' he said in a choking voice.... 'I had to choose, Mr. Frodo. I had to come with you'" (I, 322); and when upon his return Sam learned that the pony had come back home safely he "would not go to bed until he had visited Bill in his stable" (III, 274).

Sam weeps on numerous occasions, out of pain, emotion, fright, sadness, or happiness; he is afraid of the unknown; and his devotion to, and care for, his master parallel in many instances those of a lover for his beloved; but he is neither unmanly nor a coward and, when necessary, he shows his worth. He saves his master's life at the risk of his own many a time, and repeatedly shows that he has as much courage and common-sense wisdom as any of the other members of the Company.

He loves to eat well and often, to drink beer, to rest frequently, and to spend the night under a roof and by the warm and reassuring fire of a friendly hearth; but throughout most of their quest he suffers stoutly from heat and freezing winds, rain and snow, hunger and thirst, sleepless nights on guard and in the open, lack of rest, and tired limbs. Fortunately, once Sam lays himself down to rest he immediately falls asleep notwithstanding the hardness of the bed or the nearness of peril: "Sam slept through the night in deep content, if logs are contented" (I, 139); they "tried to go to sleep. But weary as they were only Sam found that easy to do" (I, 358); " 'Once I do get to sleep,' said Sam, 'I shall go on sleeping, whether I roll off or no,'... [and he] was snoring...long before [Frodo] closed his eyes" (I, 359); "putting away all fears [Sam] cast himself into a deep untroubled sleep" (III, 199).

Also like Sancho, Sam misses his family and village. His humor shows in his not infrequent sallies (when a member of the Company says that a cliff-wall offers shelter Sam mutters, " 'If this is shelter, then one wall and no roof make a house' " [I, 303]; see also above his answer to Gandalf) and his imitation of Gollum's speech:

> 'Hi! Gollum!' said Sam. 'Where are you going? Hunting? Well, see here, old noser, you don't like our food, and I'd not be sorry for a change myself. Your new motto's *always ready to help*. Could you find anything fit for a hungry hobbit?'
> 'Yes, perhaps, yes,' said Gollum. 'Sméagol always helps, if they asks—if they asks nicely.'
> 'Right!' said Sam. 'I does ask. And if that isn't nice enough, I begs' (II, 260).

As the story unfolds, Sam becomes bolder and does not hesitate to take the initiative on occasions. In the following extract he addresses some strangers before his master has had the opportunity to open his mouth:

> 'We have not found what we sought,' said one [Man]. 'But what have we found?'
> 'Not Orcs,' said another.
> 'Elves?' said a third, doubtfully.
> 'Nay! Not Elves,' said the fourth, the tallest, and as it appeared the chief among them. 'Elves do not walk in Ithilien in these days. And Elves are wondrous fair to look upon, or so 'tis said.'
> 'Meaning we're not, I take you,' said Sam. 'Thank you kindly. And when you've finished discussing us, perhaps you'll say who *you* are, and why you can't let two tired travellers rest' (II, 265).

But perhaps one episode in *The Lord of the Rings* best reflects the similarities between Frodo's helper and Don Quixote's squire. In Chapter 10 of Book 4, Sam suddenly finds himself the unwilling possessor of the coveted, all-powerful Ring (II, 342), and immediately the curse of the Ring hangs heavily on him:

> Already the Ring tempted him, gnawing at his will and reason. Wild fantasies arose in his mind; and he saw Samwise the Strong, Hero of the Age, striding with a flaming sword across the darkened land, and armies flocking to his call as he marched to the overthrow of Barad-dûr. And then all the clouds rolled away, and the white sun shone, and at his command the vale of Gorgoroth became a garden of flowers and trees and brought forth fruit. He had only to put on the Ring and claim it for his own, and all this could be. In that hour of trial it was the love of his master that helped most to hold him firm; but also deep down in him lived still unconquered his plain hobbit-sense: he knew in the core of his heart that he was not large enough to bear such a burden, even if such visions were not a mere cheat to betray him. The one small garden of a free gardener was all his need and due, not a garden swollen to a realm; his own hands to use, not the hands of others to command (III, 177).

And when he finds his master alive Sam voluntarily confesses that he has the Ring, even though Frodo already considers it lost or in the hands of the Enemy.

> 'I took it, Mr. Frodo, begging your pardon. And I've kept it safe. It's round my neck now, and a terrible burden it is, too.' Sam fumbled for the Ring and its chain. 'But I suppose you must take it back.' Now it had come to it, Sam felt reluctant to give up the Ring and burden his master with it again (III, 188).

Whether reluctantly or not, Sam returns the Ring to Frodo of his own accord, and the mighty Samwise son of Hamfast, the Ring-bearer hobbit, reverts to being, by his own choosing, the humble Sam Gamgee, Frodo's gardener, servant, and helper. How very much like Sancho and his governorship! There are fundamental differences between the two episodes, of course. The humorous overtones that characterize the episode of the *ínsula* Barataria are nowhere to be found in the epic seriousness of Tolkien's chapters. The dangers that Sam must face alone and the risks in possession of the Ring are all too real, whereas Sancho's governorship and the siege of Barataria are mere farces orchestrated by the bored and idle Duke and Duchess, although of course for Sancho his sudden and unexpected aggrandizement and the perils are as real and immediate as those of Sam. After the mock siege of Barataria, Cervantes writes:

> Vistióse, en fin [Sancho], y... se fue a la caballeriza, siguiéndole todos los que allí se hallaban, y llegándose al rucio, le abrazó y le dio un beso de paz en la frente, y no sin lágrimas en los ojos, le dijo:
> —Venid vos acá, compañero mío y amigo mío,... después que os dejé y me subí sobre las torres de la ambición y de la soberbia, se me han entrado por el alma adentro mil miserias, mil trabajos y cuatro mil desasosiegos.... Yo no nací para ser gobernador, ni para defender ínsulas ni ciudades de los enemigos que quisieren acometerlas. Mejor se me entiende a mí de arar y cavar, podar y ensarmentar las viñas, que de dar leyes ni de defender provincias ni reinos.
> ... Abrazáronle todos, y él, llorando, abrazó a todos, y los dejó admirados, así de sus razones como de su determinación tan resoluta y tan discreta (II, 53, 443-46).

The purposeful behavior of Sancho and Sam in, respectively, the episode of the *ínsula* Barataria and the chapters "The Choices of Master Samwise" and "The Tower of Cirith Ungol," their no-nonsense sense of duty and their determination to carry on and get the job done, their realization and acceptance of the fact that they were not made to fly at those heights, their spontaneous and graceful renunciation of their "offices," the briefness of their tenure, and their willing return to their proper roles as servants and helpers of their masters exactly parallel each other. The nobility of their conduct does not go unnoticed or unrewarded. Both Sam and Sancho keep a token of their triumph over greed and the temptation of power, Sancho the two hundred gold coins given to him by the Duke, Sam the magic sword, Sting. And both return to their families and villages to continue tilling the soil, one a gardener, the other a farmer.

Sam never complains about his master or blames him for their misadventures, he can read and write, and he is not presumptuous, argumentative, or disrespectful; but Sancho and Sam coincide in so many other aspects of their personalities and circumstances that it is impossible not to consider them akin. Neither Sancho nor Sam has an imposing figure, nor are they good-looking; both cry easily when overwhelmed by emotion; they are curious and have an adventurous spirit; they usually get away with what they want by playing dumb; they like to eat substantially, drink their fill when possible, be comfortable, and sleep under a roof, but they are not gluttons, drunks, or lazy; they interlard their speeches with humorous sallies, proverbs, and sayings; they become bolder as the story unravels; they find themselves propelled suddenly and unexpectedly into high office, but they use power wisely, overcome all temptations, and willingly and of their own accord resume their original role by the side of their masters; they love, respect, fight for, and defend their masters, and they help and encourage them to continue their quests; they each have a peaceful and lovable mount and they show great affection towards them; they work on and live from the soil; they love and miss their families and their villages; and, at the conclusion of their adventures, both can sit by the fireside at home to entertain and awe their wives, children, neighbors, and friends with the wondrous tales of knights and giants, trophies won and magic potions, princesses and magicians, sumptuous banquets and days of hunger and thirst, bandits, foes, and friendly folks, beds with silk sheets and nights spent lying on the hard ground, triumphs and defeats.

And in this manner we can finally and distinctly perceive the true image of Sancho reflected by the magic looking glass of Tolkienian lore. To be sure, we see an ennobled and magnified Sancho, but myth is the distilled essencence of every-day life. What scores of twentieth-century critics could not make whole and palpable was given immediacy and substance by one contemporary novelist.

PLATE 8 Sancho trying to visit his master
by P. G. Doré (Leipzig: Verlag von Th. Knaur, 1893)
Courtesy of the British Library, Cerv.347, vol. 2, p. 7

PLATE 9 Sancho in the battle of Barataria
by P. G. Doré (Leipzig: Verlag von Th. Knaur, 1893)
    Courtesy of the British Library, Cerv.347, vol. 2, facing p. 278

✣ 5 ✤

Cervantes's Sancho

> Aquí quedarás, colgada desta espetera y deste
> hilo de alambre, ni sé si bien cortada o mal
> tajada péñola mía, adonde vivirás luengos si-
> glos, si presuntuosos y malandrines historia-
> dores no te descuelgan para profanarte.
> *Don Quixote* (II, 74, 592)

N THE FOLLOWING PAGES I shall be using the materials collected in the Appendixes. The Appendixes are not intended to be exhaustive, because to make them so one would have to quote *Don Quixote* at length and almost in its entirety, and one would also have to repeat those passages which deal with two or more traits of Sancho in all the appropriate appendixes. Repetitions are still unavoidable, but to keep them to a minimum and to use as few quotations as possible I shall, wherever I can, simply give within parentheses cross-references by Appendix (Roman type) and passage (*italics*).

The Panzas are, in Cervantes's fictional world, a family of honest (3,17) Spanish peasants, whose old-Christian roots are repeatedly emphasized by Sancho (3, 6; 18, 5, 8, 9). They are well known in their ancestral village (3, 10), located in the plains of Castile near El Toboso (3, 5), having had at some time in the past amongst their members two famous wine tasters (3, 13). Two other worthy relatives of Sancho are his grandmother, whose down-to-earth and practical common sense appeals to him (3, 14), and an abbot, uncle to Sancho's children (3, 8), though his exact family relationship to Sancho is never made clear.

Sancho is happily married to Teresa Cascajo (3, 7, 16, 27),[136]

---

[136] There is some confusion concerning Teresa's correct name. In Part I she is referred to as Juana (or Mari) Gutiérrez, but in Part II she is consistently called Teresa Panza and Teresa Cascajo.·

although their happiness is occasionally tempered by mild quarrels, off-hand, unkind words, or some impatient outburst of anger (3, 15). They have two children, Sanchico and Mari Sancha, or Sanchica, whom Sancho loves dearly and has constantly in his thoughts (3, 7, 9, 11, 20, 24, 26, 28). They, in their turn, feel a great affection for him, a fact that is vividly conveyed in Cervantes's description of how Sanchica and her mother receive and take Sancho home upon his return from his second sally with Don Quixote (3, 29). There is some personal interest in Teresa's and Sanchica's affection on this occasion ("preguntóle [Sanchica] si traía algo"), but there is no doubt that their feelings are sincere.

Sancho's wife, although in her early forties, is of a strong and sinewy constitution (3, 22). Her only defect, according to Sancho, is jealousy (3, 15, 16). But Teresa's fears are probably unfounded. Sancho boasts twice about the totally different reception Altisidora's amorous entreaties and advances would have met with had she fallen in love with him rather than with Don Quixote (24, 4, 6), but earlier statements and Sancho's behavior throughout the story clearly show that he, like the proverbial dog, barks a lot but does not bite (24, 1, 3, 5).

Sancho's children are both in their teens. Sanchico is fifteen; little is said about him, except that his parents hope to see him enter the church with the help of his uncle the abbot (3, 8). Sanchica is probably a year younger or older than her brother (3, 12, 21), good looking (3, 26), tall, strong, and with all the freshness of an April morning (3, 12). She is apparently anxious to marry (3, 8), though her parents disagree on the social status of her husband-to-be. Teresa favors a neighbor's son, Lope Tocho (II, 5, 75); Sancho, for his part, would marry her into the nobility or the higher bourgeoisie (3, 9, 20).

There is very little in the way of description of Sancho's own figure. Cervantes tells us that in Cide Hamete's manuscript he appears drawn as a short individual with a big stomach and long legs. Hence Cervantes concludes, the two *sobrenombres* "Panza" and "Zancas" that Cide Hamete used in his manuscript must be descriptive nicknames (13, 1). But Cervantes's assumption is incorrect, at least in the case of "Panza," because Panza is a family surname, not a nickname (3, 10, 18, 19, 23); and the soubriquet "Zancas" and Sancho's presumably long legs are never again mentioned in the printed text. There is no doubt, however, that Sancho is short and stout, that he has a swarthy complexion, and sports a thick and usually unkempt beard (13, 2, 3, 7-12). Although we never learn Sancho's exact age, we can assume that he was probably in his mid-forties (cf. Teresa's age, above).

Sancho's humble origins are made patently clear throughout the story. He is an uneducated (14, *1-13*) peasant, of low birth, who has labored all his life, first as a swineherd (1, *11*), then successively as a gooseherd (1, *11*), goatherd (1, *14, 15*), farmhand (1, *7*), and farmer (1, *1-3, 6, 8, 9, 12, 16*), a background of which he is proud, never hiding or denying it (3, *19*). He is also proud of having been *muñidor* of a religious congregation (1, *5*), *prioste* in his town (1, *13*), and latterly governor of Barataria. He and his family are poor (2, *1, 2, 5-7*), but he owns an ass (2, *3, 7*; 5, *1-25*), and either owns a small plot of land or works it for someone else (1, *6*). However, to everyone's delight, Sancho and his family unexpectedly find themselves much better off thanks first to the gold coins found in Cardenio's valise, then to those later given to Sancho by the Duke, and finally to Don Quixote's generous legacy to his squire (2, *8*; 16, *5, 17, 21-23*).

Sancho is a devout Roman Catholic of old-Christian extraction. His firm and sincere belief in God, the Virgin Mary, and the Saints is unquestionable, as is his respect for the clergy. He apparently attends services regularly, listens attentively to sermons, and tries to apply the teachings of the church in his daily life (18, *1-3, 5, 6, 8-14, 16, 18-26*).

He likes wine and misses no occasion to put his *bota* to the test, but he never gets drunk because wine has on him the salutary effect of putting him to sleep before he reaches a state of intoxication (7, *5, 10*; see also Sancho's own defense against the charge that he is a sot, 7, *12, 17*). He also likes to eat, naturally, but, once again, he eats without abusing his food or making himself sick. His eating habits and manners are of course unrefined, as he himself points out in Part I (11, *154*). Cervantes makes great sport of Sancho's hunger and his eating habits (especially in Part II), but, given the circumstances in which he and his master travel, it is difficult to regard as a glutton someone who merely wants to eat regularly and enjoy a hot meal once in a while, and who is happy to sustain himself with a piece of bread, an onion, grapes, and cheese (see especially 20, *29, 31, 33, 37, 39, 40*).

Sancho is very talkative (34, *1-12*), but he is usually brief and direct, and very seldom do his speeches go beyond ten lines of text (see Appendix 34, "Lengths of Sancho's longer speeches")—in direct contrast to Don Quixote's long and winding interventions. Sancho's use of proverbs has come to be regarded as the quintessential characteristic of his personality. The widespread belief, however, that

he continually misuses them is quite mistaken. If one follows Sancho's train of thought, one soon sees that any one of the proverbs or
sayings of a particular series is perfectly appropriate to convey Sancho's reaction and answer to whatever has provoked it (as Don
Quixote tells him: "No más refranes, Sancho,...pues cualquiera de
los que has dicho basta para dar a entender tu pensamiento," II, 67,
551). For example, when Don Quixote tells Sancho that Queen
Madásima was never the mistress of the sage Elisabat, Sancho says:

> Allá se lo hayan; con su pan se lo coman; si fueron amanceba-
> dos, o no, a Dios habrán dado la cuenta; de mis viñas vengo, no
> sé nada; no soy amigo de saber vidas ajenas; que el que compra y
> miente, en su bolsa lo siente. Cuanto más, que desnudo nací,
> desnudo me hallo; ni pierdo ni gano; mas que lo fuesen, ¿qué me
> va a mí? Y muchos piensan que hay tocinos y no hay estacas.
> Mas ¿quién puede poner puertas al campo? Cuanto más, que de
> Dios dijeron (I, 25, 302).

Sancho cannot accept his master's assurances blindly, but remembering his fury when Cardenio stated that Queen Madásima and Elisabat were lovers, he simply answers in effect: "whatever they did is
their business, not mine. They'll get what they deserve," and in reply
to his master's "de aquí tomó el vulgo ignorante y mal intencionado
de decir y pensar que [la reina Madásima] era su manceba" (I, 25,
301), Sancho concludes by remarking that anything can be expected
from gossiping busybodies.

A more complex sequence of proverbs is Sancho's answer to the
licenciado when he tells master and squire that the wedding of Quiteria
to Camacho will be the death of Basilio:

> Dios lo hará mejor,...que Dios, que da lá llaga, da la medicina;
> nadie sabe lo que está por venir, de aquí a mañana muchas horas
> hay, y en una y aun en un momento, se cae la casa; yo he visto
> llover y hacer sol, todo a un mesmo punto; tal se acuesta sano la
> noche, que no se puede mover otro día. Y dígame, ¿por ventura
> habrá quien se alabe que tiene echado un clavo a la rodaja de la
> fortuna? No, por cierto, y entre el sí y el no de la mujer no me
> atrevería yo a poner una punta de alfiler, porque no cabría.
> Denme a mí que Quiteria quiera de buen corazón y de buena
> voluntad a Basilio; que yo le daré a él un saco de buena ventura;
> que el amor, según yo he oído decir, mira con unos antojos, que
> hacen parecer oro al cobre, a la pobreza riqueza, y a las lagañas
> perlas (II, 19, 181).

In other words, with this *sarta de necedades* Sancho is saying that the
future cannot be foretold, and he is warning the licenciado that Cama-

cho should not count his chickens before they are hatched. How pertinent and valid the *tonterías* just quoted are is well known. In Chapter 21 of Part II, Basilio pretends to kill himself and asks to be married to Quiteria before he dies; the company pleads on his behalf and his wish is granted; the local priest marries them; only then does Basilio stand up to reveal the trick (pp. 198-201). The direct and prophetic relationship between Sancho's proverbs and these later happenings is evident.

Dios lo hará mejor; que Dios, que da la llaga, da la medicina.	Basilio finds a way out of the problem. He does not die.
Nadie sabe lo que está por venir, de aquí a mañana muchas horas hay, y en una y aun en un momento, se cae la casa.	Camacho's wedding suddenly goes sour on him.
Yo he visto llover, y hacer sol, todo a un mesmo punto; tal se acuesta sano la noche, que no se puede mover otro día.	Basilio lies both mortally wounded and perfectly healthy simultaneously. Dying now—alive later.
¿Por ventura habrá quien se alabe que tiene echado un clavo a la rodaja de la fortuna? No, por cierto.	Camacho's triumph over Basilio does not last. His self-confidence proves unfounded.
Entre el *sí* y el *no* de la mujer no me atrevería yo a poner una punta de alfiler, porque no cabría.	Although Quiteria is in love with Basilio she accepts Camacho "el *sí*" only to back out later on "el *no*."
Denme a mí que Quiteria quiera de buen corazón y de buena voluntad a Basilio; que yo le daré a él un saco de buena ventura; que el amor, según yo he oído decir, mira con unos antojos, que hacen parecer oro al cobre, a la pobreza riqueza, y a las lagañas perlas.	Of course she does! Basilio and Quiteria become husband and wife. Quiteria prefers Basilio the Poor to Camacho the Rich.

The good sense ensconced in Sancho's string of proverbs would have become clear to Camacho when he realized that Quiteria had willingly accepted to marry Basilio and that both were in on the trick played on him. Don Quixote, however, pays no heed to the pertinence of Sancho's proverbs, and he reprimands him as usual:

¿Adónde vas a parar, Sancho, que seas maldito?...Que cuando comienzas a ensartar refranes y cuentos, no te puede esperar sino el mesmo Judas, que te lleve. Dime, animal, ¿qué sabes tú de clavos, ni de rodajas, ni de otra cosa ninguna?

Sancho's retort to this goes straight to the point, and also stands as an answer to the general misconception that holds that Sancho often does not know what he is talking about and misapplies his sayings.

¡Oh! Pues si no me entienden—respondió Sancho—, no es maravilla que mis sentencias sean tenidas por disparates. Pero no importa: yo me entiendo, y sé que no he dicho muchas necedades en lo que he dicho (II, 19, 181).

"If you do not understand me," Sancho tells his critics, "it would be safer not to judge me." In Chapter 43 of Part II we finally learn what lies behind Don Quixote's exaggerated annoyance at Sancho's ever-present habit:

¡Sesenta mil satanases te lleven a ti y a tus refranes! Una hora ha que los estás ensartando y dándome con cada uno tragos de tormento.... Dime, ¿dónde los hallas, ignorante, o cómo los aplicas, mentecato, que para decir yo uno y aplicarle bien, sudo y trabajo como si cavase?...Y con todo eso querría saber qué cuatro refranes te ocurrían ahora a la memoria que venían aquí a propósito, que yo ando recorriendo la mía, que la tengo buena, y ninguno se me ofrece (p. 364).

So, what annoys Don Quixote so greatly is not so much Sancho's frequent use of proverbs (30, *72, 73, 84*), or his misusing them (30, *14, 45, 90, 91, 126*), or even his setting them one after the other in endless chains (30, *60, 65, 90, 91, 125, 138*), as his own inability to imitate his squire's skill in finding and applying proverbs suited to every occasion.

One last example. When in Part II, Chapter 43, Don Quixote is advising Sancho how to behave in his governorship he tells him:

Sancho, no has de mezclar en tus pláticas la muchedumbre de refranes que sueles; que...muchas veces los traes tan por los cabellos, que más parecen disparates que sentencias.

Sancho replies:

Viénenseme tantos juntos a la boca cuando hablo, que riñen, por salir, unos con otros; pero la lengua va arrojando los primeros que encuentra, aunque no vengan a pelo. Mas yo tendré cuenta de aquí adelante de decir los que convengan a la gravedad de mi cargo; que en casa llena, presto se guisa la cena; y quien destaja no baraja; y a buen salvo está el que repica; y el dar y el tener, seso ha menester.

—¡Eso sí, Sancho!—dijo don Quijote—. ¡Encaja, ensarta, enhila refranes; que nadie te va a la mano! ¡Castígame mi madre, y yo trómpogelas! Estoyte diciendo que escuses [refranes], y en un instante has echado aquí una letanía dellos, que así cuadran con lo que vamos tratando como por los cerros de Úbeda (pp. 361-62).

This is the only instance I can find in which Sancho's proverbs are apparently not suited to the occasion. But in this passage Sancho is purposely misusing his proverbs to provoke and exasperate his master. He is fed up with having Don Quixote constantly correcting his speech and telling him that he misapplies his proverbs, especially since he had already made clear that when it came to using proverbs he knew very well what he was about. So, he retaliates, first craftily acknowledging and repeating what Don Quixote has just told him, and then emphasizing his cheekiness with four perfectly misapplied proverbs. The vexation of Don Quixote's angry reply is just what Sancho was aiming at. Blind to Sancho's irony, Don Quixote sees only that he is right in his evaluation of Sancho's annoying habit, without realizing that Sancho's wit and inventiveness have, once again, simultaneously boosted the high opinion he has of himself and rendered him harmless (as in the case of the "enchanted" *requesones*; 10, 8).

In such passages, Sancho's sense of humor, craftiness, cheekiness, and skill at getting his own way are at their best. One can find in the passages quoted above what, in my opinion, are the four most important characteristics given by Cervantes to his creation: 1) an awareness and acceptance of both his own weaknesses ("viénenseme tantos [refranes] juntos a la boca cuando hablo, que riñen, por salir, unos con otros," II, 43, 362) and his strengths ("no importa: yo me entiendo, y sé que no he dicho muchas necedades," II, 19, 181); 2) an innate ability to construct his dialogue from the same materials used by those who surround him (to Don Quixote's "mienten...los que tal pensaren y dijeren," Sancho answers: "ni yo lo digo ni lo pienso," I, 25, 302);[137] 3) a talent for winning his battles by humoring his adversaries ("la lengua va arrojando los primeros que encuentra,

[137] As usual, Sancho reverses in his answer the order of some of the elements used by his interlocutor ("pensaren y dijeren"—"digo...pienso"), which is another characteristic of his speech. See for another instance

aunque no vengan a pelo," II, 43, 362);[138] and 4) a keen sense of humor. When Sancho puts these four gifts to work simultaneously the results could not be more to his satisfaction, as the following example will show.

In Part I, Chapter 26, Sancho is on his way to deliver Don Quixote's letter to Dulcinea. He reaches the inn in which he and his master had recently spent an eventful night, but even though he is very hungry, he hesitates to enter, remembering the blanketing he had received there. The priest and the barber, who had left their village in search of Don Quixote, and who happen to be at the door of the inn when Sancho arrives, recognize him immediately, where-upon they approach him and inquire the whereabouts of Don Quixote. When Sancho, in an attempt to protect his master, gives them an evasive answer, they accuse him of having murdered and robbed the knight. Sancho then decides to tell them the truth:

> Y luego, de corrida y sin parar, les contó de la suerte que quedaba [su amo], las aventuras que le habían sucedido, y cómo llevaba la carta a la señora Dulcinea del Toboso, que era la hija de Lorenzo Corchuelo, de quien estaba enamorado hasta los hígados.
>
> Quedaron admirados los dos de lo que Sancho Panza les contaba; y aunque ya sabían la locura de don Quijote y el género della, siempre que la oían se admiraban de nuevo. Pidiéronle a Sancho Panza que les enseñase la carta que llevaba a la señora Dulcinea del Toboso. El dijo que iba escrita en un libro de memoria, y que era orden de su señor que la hiciese trasladar en papel en el primer lugar que llegase; a lo cual dijo el cura que se la mostrase; que él la trasladaría de muy buena letra. Metió la mano en el seno Sancho Panza, buscando el librillo, pero no le halló, ni le podía hallar si le buscara hasta agora, porque se había quedado don Quijote con él, y no se le había dado, ni a él se le acordó de pedírsele.
>
> Cuando Sancho vio que no hallaba el libro, fuésele parando mortal el rostro; y tornándose a tentar todo el cuerpo muy apriesa, tornó a echar de ver que no le hallaba, y, sin más ni más, se echó entrambos puños a las barbas, y se arrancó la mitad de ellas, y luego, apriesa y sin cesar, se dio media docena de puñadas en el rostro y en las narices, que se las bañó todas en sangre. Visto lo cual por el cura y el barbero, le dijeron que qué le había sucedido, que tan mal se paraba.

Sancho's imitation of Don Quixote's speech in the episode of the fulling hammers: "Sancho amigo, has de saber"—"Has de saber, ¡oh Sancho amigo!"; "la de oro, o la dorada"—"la dorada, o de oro"; "las grandes hazañas"—"las hazañas grandes" (I, 20, 238-39 and 248). For a detailed study of Sancho's language see my article "Sancho's Rustic Speech," forthcoming.

[138] Note the humorous twist Sancho gives to Don Quixote's "muchas veces los traes por los *cabellos*," which becomes "aunque no vengan a *pelo*" (my italics).

—¿Qué me ha de suceder —respondió Sancho—, sino el haber perdido de una mano a otra, en un estante, tres pollinos, que cada uno era como un castillo?

—¿Cómo es eso? —replicó el barbero.

He perdido el libro de memoria —respondió Sancho—, donde venía carta para Dulcinea, y una cédula firmada de su señor, por la cual mandaba que su sobrina me diese tres pollinos, de cuatro o cinco que estaban en casa.

Y con esto, les contó la pérdida del rucio. Consolóle el cura, y díjole que, en hallando a su señor, él le haría revalidar la manda y que tornase a hacer la libranza en papel, como era uso y costumbre, porque las que se hacían en libros de memoria jamás se acetaban ni cumplían.

Con esto se consoló Sancho, y dijo que, como aquello fuese ansí, que no le daba mucha pena la pérdida de la carta de Dulcinea, porque él la sabía casi de memoria, de la cual se podría trasladar donde y cuando quisiesen.

—Decildo, Sancho, pues —dijo el barbero—; que después la trasladaremos.

Paróse Sancho Panza a rascar la cabeza, para traer a la memoria la carta, y ya se ponía sobre un pie, y ya sobre otro; unas veces miraba al suelo, otras al cielo, y al cabo de haberse roído la mitad de la yema de un dedo, teniendo suspensos a los que esperaban que ya la dijese, dijo al cabo de grandísimo rato:

—Por Dios, señor licenciado, que los diablos lleven la cosa que de la carta se me acuerda; aunque en el principio decía; «Alta y sobajada señora».

—No diría —dijo el barbero— *sobajada*, sino sobrehumana o soberana señora.

—Así es —dijo Sancho—. Luego, si mal no me acuerdo, proseguía..., si mal no me acuerdo: «el llego y falto de sueño, y el ferido besa a vuestra merced las manos, ingrata y muy desconocida hermosa», y no sé qué decía de salud y de enfermedad que le enviaba, y por aquí iba escurriendo, hasta que acababa en «Vuestro hasta la muerte, el Caballero de la Triste Figura».

No poco gustaron los dos de ver la buena memoria de Sancho Panza, y alabáronsela mucho, y le pidieron que dijese la carta otras dos veces, para que ellos, ansimesmo, la tomasen de memoria para trasladalla a su tiempo. Tornóla a decir Sancho otras tres veces, y otras tantas volvió a decir otros tres mil disparates. Tras esto, contó asimesmo las cosas de su amo; pero no habló palabra acerca del manteamiento que le había sucedido en aquella venta en la cual rehusaba entrar. Dijo también como su señor, en trayendo que le trujese buen despacho de la señora Dulcinea del Toboso, se había de poner en camino a procurar cómo ser emperador, o, por lo menos, monarca; que así lo tenían concertado entre los dos, y era cosa muy fácil venir a serlo, según era el valor de su persona y la fuerza de su brazo; y que en siéndolo, le había de casar a él, porque ya sería viudo, que no podía ser menos, y le había de dar por mujer a una doncella de la emperatriz, heredera de un rico y grande estado de tierra firme, sin ínsulos ni ínsulas, que ya no las quería.

Decía esto Sancho con tanto reposo, limpiándose de cuando en cuando las narices, y con tan poco juicio, que los dos se admiraron de nuevo, considerando cuán vehemente había sido la locura de don Quijote, pues había llevado tras sí el juicio de aquel pobre hombre. No quisieron cansarse en sacarle del error en que estaba, pareciéndoles que, pues no le dañaba nada la conciencia, mejor era dejarle en él, y a ellos les sería de más gusto oír sus necedades. Y así, le dijeron que rogase a Dios por la salud de su señor; que cosa contingente y muy agible era venir, con el discurso del tiempo, a ser emperador, como él decía, o, por lo menos, arzobispo, o otra dignidad equivalente. A lo cual respondió Sancho.

—Señores, si la fortuna rodease las cosas de manera que a mi amo le viniese en voluntad de no ser emperador, sino de ser arzobispo, querría yo saber agora: ¿Qué suelen dar los arzobispos andantes a sus escuderos?

—Suélenles dar —respondió el cura—, algún beneficio, simple o curado, o alguna sacristanía, que les vale mucho de renta rentada, amén del pie de altar, que se suele estimar en otro tanto.

—Para eso será menester —replicó Sancho— que el escudero no sea casado, y que sepa ayudar a misa, por lo menos; y si esto es así, ¡desdichado de yo, que soy casado y no sé la primera letra del abecé! ¿Qué será de mí si a mi amo le da antojo de ser arzobispo, y no emperador, como es uso y costumbre de los caballeros andantes?

—No tengáis pena, Sancho amigo —dijo el barbero—; que aquí rogaremos a vuestro amo, y se lo aconsejaremos, y aun se lo pondremos en caso de conciencia, que sea emperador y no arzobispo, porque le será más fácil, a causa de que él es más valiente que estudiante.

—Así me ha parecido a mí —respondió Sancho—; aunque sé decir que para todo tiene habilidad. Lo que yo pienso hacer de mi parte es rogarle a Nuestro Señor que le eche a aquellas partes donde él más se sirva y adonde a mí más mercedes me haga (pp. 322-25).

Taken in isolation and at its face value, this passage confirms Close's thesis that Sancho is an uncouth peasant, a simpleton, and a buffoon. First, we note the sharp contrast between Sancho's telling the priest and the barber that he knows by heart Don Quixote's letter to Dulcinea and the string of nonsense that follows, and also the incongruency between Sancho's initial caution (which shows that he perceived Don Quixote's fooleries for what they were) and his throwing it to the winds when he proceeds to give his eager listeners, "de corrida y sin parar," an account not only of where his master is and what he is doing, but also, unnecessarily, of all their previous adventures and misadventures. Secondly, we are faced with a rustic boor who scratches his head, shifts his weight from one foot to the other, stares at the ground and then at the sky, sucks his finger, babbles, fumbles, and cleans his nose, presumably with either his fingers or the back of his hand. Thirdly, Sancho seems to consider Don Quixote's fooleries simultaneously both a laughing matter and perfectly normal behavior. And he jumps from reality (his self-inflicted punishment for having lost the knight's message to Dulcinea along with Don Quixote's note instructing his niece to give three donkeys to Sancho) to the imaginary (fancying himself a widower and the husband of a lady-in-waiting to an empress), apparently without realizing the absurdity of this juxtaposition. Finally, Sancho shows greed and delusions of grandeur in his eagerness to see his master out of the Sierra Morena and beginning to bestow favors and honors upon his servant. In short, the common sense Sancho had shown in the previous chapters is nowhere to be found in this passage. Before, he advises Don Quixote, pokes fun at him when he learns who Dulcinea really is, brings to his master's attention the foolhardiness of the *penitencia* he proposes to carry out, and refuses to stay and see him make a fool of himself; now Sancho is depicted as a babbling idiot, an uncouth peasant, and a greedy servant who sees his relationship with his master only in terms of his personal benefit and profit.

The various questions, however, raised by the apparently irreconcilable contradictions between this episode and what preceded it disappear when one studies this passage within the context of *Don Quixote* as a whole.

To begin with, it is worth noting that the Sancho of Chapter 26 of Part I, with his weak and failing memory, is the exact opposite of the Sancho who at other times and when necessary shows that he has an excellent memory (25, *1-4, 6, 8-10, 12, 13, 16*). As recently as Chapter 20, he is able to quote in full Don Quixote's speech in the episode of the fulling hammers (25, *3*). This fact is the more remarkable because Sancho was able to memorize Don Quixote's speech though he was in fear of the noise made by the fulling hammers and heard the speech only once. Now, in Chapter 26, he forgets the content of a letter he pointedly had his master read and re-read to him. It is also worth noting that the only happening missing from Sancho's detailed account to the priest and the barber is the blanketing he received at the inn. Furthermore, Sancho is seen striking a posture he knows will show him in the role of an idiot; he himself informs us indirectly, through one of his sayings, that to suck one's finger is a sign of stupidity: "¡Llegaos, que me mamo el dedo!" (I, 29, 366). In addition, comparison of this episode with two other apparently unrelated episodes in *Don Quixote* will uncover the basic elements that make up Sancho's complex personality and will clarify and indeed explain away the contradictions noted above.

In the three episodes of the fulling hammers (I, 20), the cross-examination of Sancho by the priest and the barber (I, 26), and the trip of master and squire on Clavileño (II, 41), Sancho finds himself in similar difficulties as a consequence of events beyond his control. In the episode of the fulling hammers, Sancho is terrified because of the horrifying noises, the darkness, and the possibility that his master might leave him alone in the middle of the woods. In the second case, the view of the inn where he drank the potion of Fierabrás, suffered repeated beatings, was tossed on the blanket, and lost his saddlebags, coupled with his now being accused of having murdered and robbed his master have a similar effect on the bewildered squire. And the same bewilderment and terror result from Sancho's supernatural trip on Clavileño. All three experiences are, from Sancho's point of view, real and immediate causes for fear; and, as one would expect from Cervantes's craftsmanship in creating a consistent character, Sancho's reactions to these unexpected events are identical. First, Sancho tries to drown his fears by talking: "no hay que llorar,...que yo entretendré a vuestra merced contando cuentos desde aquí al día" (p. 241); "de corrida y sin parar, [Sancho] les contó de la suerte que quedaba [su amo].... Le pidieron que dijese la carta otras dos veces .... Tornóla a decir Sancho otras tres veces...Tras esto, contó asimesmo las cosas de su amo" (pp. 322 and 324); "[a la pregunta de la duquesa] Sancho respondió..." (pp. 353-54). Then, finding that he has an avid audience who want to be entertained ("díjole don Quijote que contase algún cuento para entretenerle," p. 241; "si vos no nos decís dónde queda [Don Quijote], imaginaremos, como ya imaginamos, que vos le habéis muerto y robado," p. 322; "preguntó la duquesa a Sancho que cómo le había ido en aquel largo viaje," p. 353), Sancho obliges, telling his listeners what they want to hear, but in a manner that will serve his own immediate purposes and needs.[139]

During the adventure of the fulling mill Don Quixote wants to hear an entertaining story, and Sancho intends to keep him busy until morning arrives; hence, he tells his master the shaggy-dog story about a goatherd who has to take three hundred goats across a river,

---

[139] When Sancho finds himself alone with his fears he talks to himself. For instance, when Don Quixote sends Sancho to look for Dulcinea in El Toboso, Sancho is afraid that he might be proven a liar and punished by his master, and so "comenzó a hablar consigo mesmo y a decirse..." (II, 10, 105); when he finds himself on the floor sandwiched between two planks during the mock battle of Barataria, Sancho, "que lo escuchaba y sufría todo, decía entre sí..." (II, 53, 443); and on his trip from Barataria to the ducal palace he picks up his courage by talking to his ass and to himself: "¡Ay—dijo Sancho—...!" Sancho "decía entre sí" (II, 55, 455 and 457).

one at a time. As extra precautions to keep his master's mind away from his adventures, Sancho informs him that throughout the story he will have to keep an exact count of how many goats have crossed the river, and then he narrates the tale in such a way that he forces Don Quixote to interrupt it repeatedly. The story ends, as Sancho had all along planned, with the arrival of the dawn ("la mañana, que ya venía...," p. 245).

In the second episode, Sancho knows that the priest and the barber consider that his master is a deranged man, and rightly suspects that they must think him a fool for following Don Quixote. Thus he decides to keep them entertained, and, at the same time, he dampens his own worries by making them believe that they are right on both counts. He therefore describes his master's adventures in full and plays the role of the village idiot. Furthermore, to lengthen the farce, Sancho picks up and develops ideas used or suggested by his listeners:

> Y así, [el cura y el barbero] le dijeron...que cosa contingente y muy agible era venir [su amo]...a ser emperador, como él decía, o, por lo menos arzobispo....
> Señores, si...a mi amo le viniese en voluntad de no ser emperador, sino de ser arzobispo, querría yo saber agora: ¿Qué suelen dar los arzobispos andantes a sus escuderos? (I, 26, 325).[140]

And, like Don Quixote in the previous episode, the priest and the barber take the bait that Sancho has so ably thrown to them:

> No poco gustaron los dos de ver la buena memoria de Sancho,... y alabáronsela mucho, y le pidieron que dijese la carta otras dos veces.... Los dos se admiraron de nuevo, considerando cuán vehemente había sido la locura de don Quijote, pues había llevado tras sí el juicio de aquel pobre hombre. No quisieron cansarse en sacarle del error en que estaba, pareciéndoles que... mejor era dejarle en él, y a ellos les sería de más gusto oír sus necedades (I, 26, 324-25).

Not only have the priest and the barber forgotten all about their accusation against Sancho, they are so pleased with themselves that they do not bother to ask him his reasons for not wanting to enter the inn, and they allow him to remain outside. Thus, Sancho's fears

---

140 It is no coincidence that Sancho makes reference to his master's becoming a bishop only when the priest and the barber are present (I, 26, 325 [3], 329 [2], 361, 363 [2]), or when he has them in mind (II, 13, 128).

melt away. He is no longer a suspected felon, he does not have to enter the inn right away, and he manages to have a hot meal at the expense of his unsuspecting audience ("de allí a poco el barbero le sacó de comer," I, 27, 326).

The results are equally satisfactory when Sancho narrates his trip on Clavileño. The Duke and Duchess enjoy Sancho's oriental fairy-tale immensely and accelerate his becoming governor of the *insula* Barataria, while Sancho forgets all about his previous misgivings.

> Con el felice y gracioso suceso de la aventura de la Dolorida quedaron tan contentos los duques, que determinaron pasar con las burlas adelante, viendo el acomodado sujeto que tenían para que se tuviesen por veras; y así... [al día siguiente] dijo el duque a Sancho que se adeliñase y compusiese para ir a ser goberna-dor, que ya sus insulanos lo estaban esperando como el agua de mayo (II, 42, 355).

Sancho, the consummate story-teller, has overcome all odds. His ability to entertain, his malleability that enables him to accept and adapt himself to the circumstances at hand, and his humor have triumphed, and he can finally sit on a high-backed chair as governor of Barataria.

Sancho's humor glitters throughout the various passages quoted above. It goes from the most subtle understatement to the most extravagant exclamation (10, *1-11*), but to catalogue here the gamut of forms it takes would be impossible. The use of proverbs, the adoption of the archaic language used by his master, the mixture of truth and fantasy, the exaggerations, and the wordplay are but a few of the many comical modes and devices interspersed in Sancho's dialogues. The following are examples of a few specific types of the squire's manifold humor. When Sancho finds himself dubious con-cerning the true nature of any object or action, he resorts to describ-ing it as a mixture of what it really is and what it is not. For instance, when the inkeeper's wife is taking care of Don Quixote's bruises from the beating suffered at the hands of the Yanguesian carriers, Sancho lies, telling her that Don Quixote fell from a rock. When he asks to be cured also, the innkeeper's wife says, "desa manera,... también debisteis vos de caer," to which Sancho replies, "no caí,... sino que del sobresalto que tomé de ver caer a mi amo, de tal manera me duele a mí el cuerpo, que me parece que *me han dado mil palos*—— (I, 16, 199; italics in this and the following quotations are mine). After Don Quixote gains possession of the helmet of Mambrino, the barber having fled leaving behind his basin and donkey, Sancho says to his master, "qué haremos deste caballo *rucio* rodado, que parece *asno pardo*," and "[este] almete...no semeja sino una *bacía de barbero* pintiparada" (I, 21, 255 and 256). During Don Quixote's battle with the wineskins Sancho tells the astonished guests, "yo vi...la cabeza [del gigante] cortada y caída a un lado, que es tamaña como un gran *cuero de vino*" (I, 35, 438). But the best examples of this subtle but very effective type of humor are Sancho's calling the barber's basin, "baciyelmo" (I, 44, 540), and his referring to the flippant Dorotea as "tocada honrada" (I, 46, 551).

Sancho's exaggerations go from complex and extravagant outbursts to simple and innocent remarks. Examples of the simpler types will be found in Appendix 15. For Sancho's extravagant outbursts see his reactions 1) when Don Quixote defeats the Bizcayan squire (I, 10, 147), 2) when Don Quixote has apparently been killed by one of the men carrying the statue of the Virgin Mary (I, 52, 601), 3) when the Caballero del Verde Gabán finishes describing himself and his life (II, 16, 153-54), 4) when Quiteria appears in her wedding dress (II, 21, 197), and 5) when knight and squire return to their village after their second sally (II, 72, 580).

The precise nature and purpose of Sancho's deliberate wordplay have been largely obscured by the unfortunate tendency of critics to group wordplay together with barbarisms, solecisms, and colloquialisms under misleading labels such as *prevaricaciones* or *desatinos idiomáticos*. Wordplay is, like punning, conscious and deliberate substitution or combination of words, whereas barbarisms, solecisms, and colloquialisms are generally unintentional. I shall deal with these elements of Sancho's language elsewhere (see above, footnote 137), merely noting here the humorous purpose and the comical effect of Sancho's wordplay, which are too obvious to need any further explanation or clarification.

In addition to his keen sense of humor and characteristic use of language, there are a few other major traits that contribute to making Sancho unique. He is stubborn (3, *23*), and he has a strong attachment to material things, acquisitiveness, some might call it (16, *1-11, 17, 20-23*), though at times he shows himself generous (16, *19*), honest (16, *12-16, 18*), and compassionate towards his fellow men (33, *1-5, 7, 8, 10, 12*) and even towards animals (33, *6*). Sancho's devotion to, and love for his master, are proverbial (27, *3-9, 11, 14, 17, 21, 23, 27*). There are contradictions, of course, such as his sometimes unkind words about Don Quixote (27, *10, 12, 13, 19, 20, 26*) and his occasional though infrequent threats to abandon his service (29, *2, 3, 9, 10*), and other passages show Sancho as a

highwayman, a thief, and a disrespectful believer (12, *1, 2, 4, 5;* 18, *7*),
a bully (12, *6*), and a bigoted racist (12, *8, 9, 11*); but such fluctuations
and extemporaneous remarks are only to be expected in a true-to-life
literary character (see also 12, *7, 10*). Moreover, this less flattering
evidence is greatly reduced in importance when it is set within the
overall context of Cervantes's novel as a whole, and when account is
taken of other episodes—Sancho's meeting with Ricote, for instance
—and the historical period in which Cervantes placed the action of
the story. To call Sancho greedy, avaricious, or a thief without taking
into consideration his compassion towards the needy and the dispossessed and the other passages that undermine this oversimplified
view of him, is unjust and betrays some critical bias. And the same is
true of labeling him a lazy slug without recognizing that all his
laziness amounts to is a strong dislike for walking great distances and
a gift for falling asleep, and sleeping soundly, under the most trying
of circumstances (6, *1-24*).

Another weakness of Sancho is his lying (26, *1-8, 10-16*). Like
talking, lying is an escape valve for Sancho's fears, except that in this
case he has no control over the repercussions of his fabrications as he
does with his tales. Sancho is not an inveterate liar (26, *9*), but his lies
keep echoing back to him. They are like little demons that wait for
him at every turn and force him to continue his fabricating in order
to avoid being caught lying.[141]

Sancho weeps, too, on several occasions. In most instances his
crying reflects his love for his master and his donkey, but in the
episodes of the the fulling hammers, the "enchanted bark," and
Clavileño he weeps out of fear (31, *1-2, 11, 13*). Although tears were
not then seen necessarily as a sign of weakness or cowardice, it is
none the less necessary to clear Sancho of the charge of being a
coward. In instances of accusations such as this the Appendixes
attached to this study prove most helpful because one can study most
of the appropriate passages together and draw conclusions directly
from Cervantes's text. For example, out of the seventy-two quotations listed in Appendix 9, only seventeen show Sancho as a character
who, if necessary, would fight against all odds to defend his master,
himself, or his *ínsula* (9, *2-4, 20, 25, 26, 29, 40-42, 54, 57, 58, 64, 70-
72*). With fifty-four quotations showing him being called a coward or
acting apparently pusillanimously, the logical conclusion would seem
to be that he is indeed a faint-hearted individual. With the Appendix
at hand, however, it is soon evident that in seven passages he is being

141 See Flores, 1970.

accused ironically or unjustly of being a coward (9, 1, 9, 12, 27, 36, 59, 63), and that in numerous other instances his fears are well justified by what might seem to him supernatural dangers (9, 5, 10, 11-21, 29, 31, 32, 35, 39, 44, 47, 65, 66, 68, 69). In fact, in some of these passages the visions and terrifying noises that master and squire must face send shivers through the spine not only of Sancho, but even of the reckless Don Quixote, and make his hair stand on end (9, 10, 11, 44, 69). In other passages Sancho is just pretending that he is afraid because either it is expected of him (9, 9, 46, 48) or he is humoring his master to boost his self-esteem and make him think himself superior to his squire (9, 24). At other times, Sancho is showing his awe at his master's uncontrolled anger (9, 28, 37), or he contradicts himself by doing the very thing he had just said he would not do (9, 4, 56-58). Thus, what at first had seemed a foregone conclusion changes its tone as the hard evidence slowly begins to dwindle away, and at the end the true Sancho appears, a Sancho who is not a coward, as he himself had stated at a very early stage (9, 2), but a cautious character with good sense, who does not like to take unnecessary risks but is ready and willing to fight when circumstances warrant it. Sancho reacts and responds to sudden, disquieting, and unexpected happenings just as most of us would were we to find ourselves facing the same perils.

In addition to helping us clarify our perception of the most important traits of Sancho, the Appendixes serve another very important function, giving us an unobstructed, overall view of Cervantes's characterization of Sancho. The Appendixes are:

1. Occupation and activities (I, 4, 94; II, 53, 444)
2. Means and possessions (I, 4, 94; II, 72, 580)
3. Home and family (I, 4, 94; II, 73, 583)
4. Stupidity, simplicity, and rusticity (I, 7, 125; II, 73, 582)
5. Love for his ass (I, 7, 126; II, 70, 565)
6. Laziness (I, 7, 126; II, 71, 573)
7. Soft spot for wine (I, 7, 127; II, 59, 489)
8. Ambitions and aspirations (I, 7, 127; II, 65, 537)
9. Cowardice (I, 8, 129; II, 69, 561)
10. Artfulness and humor (I, 8, 131; II, 71, 575)
11. Don Quixote and Sancho as opposites (I, 8, 132; II, 70, 565)
12. Sancho a thief, a heartless highwayman, a bigoted racist, a bully (I, 8, 134; II, 8, 94)
13. Physique and appearance (I, 9, 144; II, 49, 404)
14. Education (I, 10, 148; II, 51, 427)
15. Exaggerations (I, 10, 149; II, 72, 577)
16. Desire for wealth (I, 10, 149; II, 74, 591)

17. Sancho praised or his advice accepted (I, 10, 150; II, 74, 590)
18. Catholicism (I, 10, 151; II, 73, 582)
19. Complaints (I, 10, 153; II, 71, 570)
20. Love of food (I, 10-11, 153; II, 67, 551)
21. Gullibility (I, 13, 177; II, 67, 547)
22. Quixotification (I, 15, 191; II, 74, 590)
23. Wordplay (I, 15, 192; II, 68, 556)
24. Sexual temperance (I, 15, 194; II, 70, 569)
25. Memory (I, 15, 195; II, 51, 427)
26. Lies (I, 16, 198; II, 72, 580)
27. Opinion of, and attitude towards, Don Quixote (I, 16, 199; II, 74, 586)
28. From *loco* to *gracioso* (I, 17, 209; II, 72, 577)
29. Homesickness and eagerness to continue their adventures (I, 18, 216; II, 74, 590)
30. Sayings and proverbs (I, 18, 217; II, 73, 583)
31. Sancho weeps (I, 20, 239; II, 74, 591)
32. References to salary (I, 20, 251; II, 42, 357)
33. Compassion (I, 22, 270; II, 73, 581)
34. Loquacity (I, 25, 300; II, 31, 280)

The order in which the Appendixes are listed obeys the sequence in which the various topics first appear in the book, thus: the first reference dealing with Sancho appears in Chapter 4 of Part I, "[Don Quixote] determinó volver a su casa...haciendo cuenta de recebir [como escudero] a un labrador vecino suyo" (p. 94): *labrador* gives us "Occupation and activities" as the topics of Appendix 1; the second reference immediately follows the sentence just quoted, "que era pobre" (p. 94): *pobre* gives us "Means and possessions" as the topics of Appendix 2, etcetera. The references in parentheses in the index to the Appendixes are generally to the first and last quotations in the book relating to each aspect; Appendixes 10 and 26, however, list only representative quotations, and 28 and 34, quote the views of other characters about Sancho.

As the chapters of *Don Quixote* now stand the various traits of Sancho listed in the Appendixes (excluding Appendix 28, which deals with a change that Sancho apparently undergoes through the novel) are introduced for the first time as follows:[142]

Chapter 4 (3 traits), 7(7), 8(3), 9(1), 10(6), 11(1), **12(0)**, 13(1), **14(0)**, 15(4), 16(2), **17(0)**, 18(2), **19(0)**, 20(2), **21(0)**, 22(1)[143]

---

[142] Sancho's sense of humor (Appendix 10) and his talkativeness (Appendix 34) have been counted here under Chapter 7, because these traits are evident from the moment he first appears.

[143] Bold face shows those chapters where no new traits are introduced.

However, in my article "Cervantes at Work: The Writing of *Don Quixote*, Part I," I showed that the text of Part I went through several stages of revision and that the order in which the episodes now appear in the printed text is in certain cases not the order in which they were written.[144] If the conclusions reached in this article are correct, it should logically follow that the characterization of Sancho will show a smoother and more even progress when the chapters are restored to their original order. Following that order Sancho's successive new traits would therefore originally have been introduced as follows:[145]

[144] *Journal of Hispanic Philology*, 3 (1979), 135-60.

[145] The order of the Appendixes would then be readjusted:
1 to 9 remain unchanged.
10. [Counted in Chapter 7.]
11 and 12 remain unchanged.
14. Education (I, old Chapter 9; see "Cervantes at Work," Table, STATE 2a).
15. Exaggerations (I, old Chapter 9)
16. Desire for wealth (I, old Chapter 9)
17. Sancho praised or his advice accepted (I, old Chapter 9)
18. Catholicism (I, old Chapter 9)
19. Complaints (I, old Chapter 9)
22. Quixotification (I, old Chapter 9)
23. Wordplay (I, old Chapter 9)
24. Sexual temperance (I, old Chapter 9)
25. Memory (I, old Chapter 9)
26. Lies (I, old Chapter 10)
27. Opinion of, and attitude towards, Don Quixote (I, old Chapter 10).
28. [Deals with a progressive development not belonging to a particular chapter or chapters.]
29. Homesickness and eagerness to continue their adventures (I, old Chapter 12)
30. Sayings and proverbs (I, old Chapter 12)
21. Gullibility (I, old Chapter 13—the Appendix would begin with quotation 2 because quotation 1 belongs to a later interpolation; see "Cervantes at Work," Table, STATE 4).
31. Sancho weeps (I, old Chapter 14)
32. References to salary (I, old Chapter 14)
13. Physique and appearance (I, old Chapter 15—the Appendix would begin with quotation 2 because quotation 1 belongs to a later interpolation; see "Cervantes at Work," Table STATE 3).
33. Compassion (I, old Chapter 16)
20. Love of food (I, old Chapter 18—the Appendix would begin with quotation 3 because quotations 1 and 2 belong to a later interpolation; see "Cervantes at Work," Table, STATE 4).
34. [Counted in Chapter 7.]

Chapter 4 (3 traits), 7(7), 8(3), old 9(10), old 10(2), old **11(0)**, old 12(2), old 13(1), old 14(2), old 15(1), old 16(1), old 17(0), old **18(1)**

This sequence shows a smoother, faster, and more consistent characterization of Sancho, as would be expected from Cervantes's genius and craftsmanship (I am using both nouns advisedly). In the original order of the episodes Sancho was already fully characterized by Chapter 18 of Part I, and only old Chapters 11 and 17 did not include any new traits, whereas in the present order the characterization is not complete until Chapter 22, with five chapters not including any new traits (Chapters 12, 14, 17, 19, and 21).

Whether we accept the original or the present sequence one thing is certain: the Appendixes demonstrate beyond doubt that Dámaso Alonso's theory that Cervantes drew "el alma de Sancho sin prisa y sin preocuparse del orden mismo de las pinceladas" ("Sancho Quijote," p. 62) is, at best, a misconception. The Appendixes also show that Sancho is basically the same complex character from the beginning to the end of the novel. Except for Appendix 12 (with a last quotation from Chapter 8 of Part II), all the Appendixes supply consistent evidence about Sancho's character, job, family, and milieu from Chapter 4 of Part I to the last chapters of Part II. This fact demolishes the theory propounded by Casalduero, Savj-López, Romero Flores, Leif Sletsjöe, and Brantley that there are two different Sanchos in *Don Quixote*, and also the theory of the Romantics that Cervantes sacrificed the knight in Part II by altering Sancho's personality and giving him more exposure and more emphasis. Of course Sancho is more visible in Part II (so is Don Quixote), because he appears in twice as many pages as in Part I, and, naturally, the Appendixes reflect this imbalance (306 quotations from Part I against 632 from Part II).[146] But as to altering Sancho's personality, true, the Sancho of Appendix 12 (thief, highwayman, racist, bully) vanishes early in Part II, and Sancho uses far more sayings and proverbs in Part II than in Part I, but otherwise there is no noticeable change in Sancho, as de Chasca and Urbina have noted (see above, footnote 124 and pp. 89-90), or in the manner in which he reacts to outside circumstances.

It is true also that Sancho receives more praise in the sequel (fifty-four instances, Appendix 17) than in Part I (twenty-seven instances),

---

[146] The almost exact 1:2 ratio shown between the total number of quotations listed from Part I and Part II was not intentional. This striking coincidence is of no particular significance.

and that other characters and Cervantes see him changing from *loco* in Part I (28, *1-6*) to *gracioso* in Part II (28, *7, 9, 11-21*), but this change is so gradually and skilfully introduced (*loco*, 28, *1-6*; *gracioso*, 28, *7*; *loco*, 28, *8*; *gracioso*, 28, *9*; *loco*, 28, *10* gracioso, 28, *11-21*) that it alone cannot be responsible for the reader's changing view of the squire. Moreover, Sancho's stupidity, simplicity, and rusticity, whether real or imaginary, are still very much in evidence in Part II (Part I, 4, *1-21*; Part II, 4, *22-74*).

What, then, is the reason for critics' insisting that there is a sudden change in Sancho's personality between Parts I and II? There is more than one reason, of course. In the last chapters of Part I Don Quixote is depicted as a madman who needs to be caged, and most of his windmill-idealism of the early chapters has subsided; hence, Sancho's good sense and love for his master become more evident. Also, in Part II Cervantes's other characters begin to appreciate and praise, if not fully understand all the complexities of, Sancho's keen sense of humor. But perhaps a more important reason for this more favorable image of Sancho projected by the text is a drastic structural change that Cervantes decided upon between the writing of the Parts. In my article "The Rôle of Cide Hamete in *Don Quixote*," I suggested that Cide Hamete plays two totally different roles in Cervantes's novel.[147] The dispensable Cide Hamete of Part I becomes in Part II a dominant and fundamental element of the narrative, and as a consequence Cervantes becomes a less biased and more cautious narrator because he now has entrenched between himself and his characters the continuous presence of Cide Hamete and the "Moorish translator." This change in the technique of the narration in some degree conditions the perception readers have of Cervantes's characters.

In Part I, Cervantes makes twenty clear-cut unkind or ironical remarks concerning Sancho (3, *6*; 4, *1-3, 11-14, 19-21*; 6, *8*; 7, *2, 3*; 9, *12*; 16, *3*; 19, *2*; 20, *2, 3*; 28, *3*), exactly the same number of such remarks as he makes in Part II (4, *28, 32, 33, 47, 52, 57, 78*; 6, *15, 19*; 7, *9, 10*; 9, *36, 61, 67*; 16, *21*; 18, *17*; 20, *8, 17, 41*; 30, *52*), even though Sancho appears, as note before, in twice as many pages as in Part I.[148] This lessening of authorial intervention with critical or

147 *Bulletin of Hispanic Studies*, 59 (1982), 3-14.

148 Four additional negative remarks appear in Part II, but they are explicitly laid at the door of the translator (4, *26, 27, 61*) and Cide Hamete (21, *23*). Cervantes's criticism of Sancho may appear either as humorous exaggeration: "Sancho se arrancó la mitad [de las barbas]" (4, *11*), "[Sancho, la bota] puesta a la boca, estuvo mirando las estrellas un cuarto de hora" (7, *9*),

unflattering intent is particularly surprising if one compares the number of quotations listed for the different Parts in Appendixes 4 ("Stupidity, simplicity, and rusticity," 21/53), 17 ("Sancho praised or his advice accepted," 27/54), and 28 ("From *loco* to *gracioso*," 6/15). The 1:2 ratio shown in these three appendixes is, unlike that of the total number of quotations (see footnote 146), of great interest. Not only does it in general give evidence of Cervantes's virtuosity; it also underscores the unexpectedness of the equal number of authorial remarks in the Parts (20/20). One would have expected at least forty such remarks in Part II. Furthermore, four quotations from Part II show a critical balance which is totally absent in Part I:

> "[Sancho], aunque tonto, no andaba...muy fuera de camino" (4, *30*).

> "Maguer era tonto, bien se le alcanzaba [a Sancho] que las acciones de su amo...eran disparatadas" (4, *48*).

> "[Sancho] se las tenía tiesas a todos, maguera tonto, bronco y rollizo" (4, *62*).

> "Andaban mezcladas [las palabras de Sancho] y sus acciones, con asomos discretos y tontos" (4, *63*).

Hence, thanks to the dominant presence of Cide Hamete and the Translator in the text of Part II Cervantes became a more detached and more objective narrator than in Part I, and this structural change of emphasis is evident not only in the smaller number, comparatively speaking, of authorial remarks one finds in the sequel, but also in how the other characters see Sancho in Part II, as will be seen below.

These facts and Appendixes 4, 17, 21, and 28 can also be used to test, once again, Close's theory that Sancho is a simpleton and a buffoon. The fact that Sancho's words and actions are seen first as *locuras* and then as *gracias* seems to uphold Close's contention that "on occasions Sancho is manifestly wise, sporadically in *Don Quixote* Part I, increasingly in Part II.... Vestigially throughout the novel and pal-

---

"[el lacayo y Sancho] despabilaron y dieron fondo con todo el repuesto de las alforjas, con tan buenos alientos, que lamieron el pliego de las cartas sólo porque olía a queso" (20, *41*); ironic commentary: "destas lágrimas, y determinación tan honrada...saca el autor desta historia que [Sancho] debía ser bien nacido, y, por lo menos, cristiano viejo" (3, *6*), "[Sancho], sepultado en sueño y tendido sobre el albarda de su jumento, no se acordaba en aquel instante de la madre que lo había parido" (6, *8*); or sharp putdown: "[Sancho] tenía] muy poca sal en la mollera" (4, *1*), "quisiera Sancho que [la noche] fuera del todo escura, por hallar en su escuridad disculpa de su sandez" (4, *32*).

pably in the episodes in the Duke's palace, Sancho exhibits the jester's typical attributes of conduct" (p. 344). Appendix 17 and pages 125-28 of this study clearly demonstrate, however, that Close's statements are incorrect. Both Sancho's sense of humor and his good sense show palpably from the very beginning and remain unchanged, though obviously not constant, throughout the novel. Moreover, on the basis of what has already been said here about the picture Cervantes gives us of Sancho, perhaps a more appropriate description would be entertainer rather than buffoon or court-jester. Sancho never over-steps the fine border-line that separates what is harmlessly and amusingly funny from what is grossly abusive or at the expense or to the detriment of another person or animal, something which cannot be said of several other Cervantine characters. It must be kept in mind, too, that the quotations listed in Appendix 28 do not tell us what Sancho is, but how he is perceived by other characters. They change from regarding him as *loco* to regarding him as *gracioso*; Sancho himself does not change. If this is so, what *is* Sancho? *Loco* or *gracioso*, simpleminded and gullible (Appendixes 4 and 21) or commonsensical and trustworthy (Appendix 17)? Does Cervantes mean us to accept it as fact when he tells us that, "no se dejó de reír don Quijote de la simplicidad de su escudero" (4, 3), or that, "le admiraba [al canónigo] la necedad de Sancho" (4, 20)? Or is he putting his own words and bias in the minds of his characters? Or do Cervantes's words reflect the bias in the characters' minds? Perhaps the following passages will help to answer these apparently complex and unsolvable questions.

In Chapter 33 of Part II, the Duchess tells Sancho that Dulcinea is truly enchanted, to which fabrication Sancho cunningly answers:

> Bien puede ser todo eso, ... porque de mi ruin ingenio no se puede ni debe presumir que fabricase en un instante tan agudo embuste (p. 301).

Notice the adaptability and malleability of Sancho. He immediately realizes that he cannot insist that it is all his own invention without indirectly calling the Duchess a liar, and so he bends ("bien puede ser todo eso") and apparently accepts that he is an idiot ("mi ruin ingenio"), only to bounce up and, without the Duchess's noticing his irony, unashamedly praise his own imagination and inventiveness for having thought up in a split second "tan agudo embuste." Sancho is merely playing the Duchess's game, as he often plays Don Quixote's, but the Duchess in her ignorance is amazed at her having duped Sancho so easily:

> De lo que más la duquesa se admiraba era que la simplicidad de Sancho fuese tanta, que hubiese venido a creer ser verdad

infalible que Dulcinea del Toboso estuviese encantada, habiendo sido él mesmo el encantador (II, 34, 304).

The Duke tells Sansón Carrasco about Sancho's fabrication and how his wife's felicitous invention turned the tables on the squire: "De que no poco se rió y admiró el bachiller, considerando la ... agudeza y simplicidad de Sancho" (II, 70, 564). But, in fact, Sancho had not been fooled at all by what the Duchess told him.

> Renovóse la admiración ... en Sancho, en ver que, a despecho de la verdad, querían que estuviese encantada Dulcinea (II, 34, 310).

"Bien puede ser todo," and the ironical contrast "ruin ingenio" and "agudo embuste" are not the chance utterances of a simpleton who did not know what he was saying. Sancho was aware all along of where the truth lay and was perfectly conscious of his irony. The dupes are the Duchess, the Duke, Sansón, and all the others, not Sancho.

Sancho clearly is not feeble-minded, nor a court-jester. Clearly also we can trust Cervantes, but not the judgment of his characters; nor can we accept Sancho's own statements of self-abasement and ignorance at their face value (4, 31, 35, 41, 45, 53, 54, 64, 72, 74). Cervantes is not putting his own words in the minds of his characters; they are presented as indeed believing however mistakenly, that Sancho is *simple* and *necio*.[149] Even Cide Hamete shows himself at times misled by Sancho's supposed docility and rustic simplicity (cf. 21, 23 and 24). It can be noted also that Appendix 21 ("Gullibility") is more a demonstration of Sancho's non-gullibility (26 instances: 2, 4, 5, 8, 9, 11-17, 20-22, 24-33, 35) than of his imagined *simplicidad* (9 instances: 1, 3, 6, 7, 10, 18, 19, 23, 34), and the evidence in Sancho's favor is strengthened when the twenty-six instances of non-gullibility put us on our guard against taking the quotations of the other group at their face value (cf. 3 and 4; 6 and 11, 12, 14-17, and 22; 19 and 20). And it is worth pointing out that a great number of the quotations listed in Appendix 4 are remarks spoken by Don Quixote in anger, which, like those expressing his annoyance at Sancho's

---

[149] In my article "The Rôle of Cide Hamete in *Don Quixote*" I stated: "[Cervantes's unkind remarks] may seem harmless in isolation, but the accumulation of tens upon tens of them in Part I builds up a coat of prejudice," p. 4. When I wrote this article I was counting as Cervantes's also the remarks made by his characters. I was mistaken. As I have shown above, Cervantes's characters do not speak for their creator.

loquacity, are futil attempts to silence Sancho's good sense and the unwelcome truths he is stating (5, 7-10, 15-17, 38, 39, 43, 44, 49-51, 56, 58-60, 67, 68, 73).

All this textual evidence also suggests that Sancho's Quixotification might be merely another critical mirage. Simple common sense dictates that a middle-aged person (or a well drawn character) set in his ways, and with a strong and clearly defined personality does not, short of a miracle or a mental crisis, completely change his life-long views, his habits, his beliefs, and his very nature in a short period of time. Because neither Cervantes nor any of his other characters sees Don Quixote as a saint or even (with the sole exception of Doña Rodríguez) as a heroic figure, clinical, miraculous, and mythical causation should be discarded altogether. How, then, are we to explain Sancho's use of archaisms, his following Don Quixote into battle, and his apparent acceptance of the existence of his master's imaginary world (22, 1 and passim), his correcting Teresa's malapropisms (22, 8), his good sense, sound advice, and polite manners (17, 1-81; 22, 9-16)?

The very first dialogue between master and squire, and many other conversations, thoughts, and actions of Sancho in the early chapters seem to suggest that he is indeed a simpleton at the beginning of the story. The passages just considered above demonstrate, on the other hand, that he is no-one's fool at the end. So there might seem to be some grounds for the Quixotification theory. The first dialogue between master and squire goes as follows:

Dijo... Sancho Panza a su amo:
—Mire vuestra merced, señor caballero andante, que no se le olvide lo que de la ínsula me tiene prometido; que yo la sabré gobernar, por grande que sea.
A lo cual le respondió don Quijote:
—Has de saber, amigo Sancho Panza, que fue costumbre muy usada de los caballeros andantes antiguos hacer gobernadores a sus escuderos de las ínsulas o reinos que ganaban, y yo tengo determinado de que por mí no falte tan agradecida usanza; antes pienso aventajarme en ella: porque ellos algunas veces, y quizás las más, esperaban a que sus escuderos fuesen viejos, y ya después de hartos de servir y de llevar malos días y peores noches, les daban algún título de conde, o, por lo mucho, de marqués, de algún valle o provincia de poco más a menos; pero si tú vives y yo vivo, bien podría ser que antes de seis días ganase yo tal reino, que tuviese otros a él adherentes, que viniesen de molde para coronarte por rey de uno dellos. Y no lo tengas a mucho; que cosas y casos acontecen a los tales caballeros por modos tan nunca vistos ni pensados, que con facilidad te podría dar aún más de lo que te prometo.

—De esa manera —respondió Sancho Panza—, si yo fuese rey por
algún milagro de los que vuestra merced dice, por lo menos, Juana
Gutiérrez, mi oíslo, vendría a ser reina, y mis hijos infantes.
—Pues ¿quién lo duda? —respondió don Quijote.
—Yo lo dudo —replicó Sancho Panza—; porque tengo para mí que,
aunque lloviese Dios reinos sobre la tierra, ninguno asentaría bien sobre
la cabeza de Mari Gutiérrez. Sepa, señor, que no vale dos maravedís para
reina; condesa le caerá mejor, y aun Dios y ayuda.
—Encomiéndalo tú a Dios, Sancho —respondió don Quijote—, que Él
dará lo que más le convenga; pero no apoques tu ánimo tanto, que te
vengas a contentar con menos que con ser adelantado.
—No haré, señor mío —respondió Sancho—, y más teniendo tan
principal amo en vuestra merced, que me sabrá dar todo aquello que me
esté bien y yo pueda llevar (pp. 127-28).

If after reading this extract we immediately regard Sancho as a
simpleton who accepts and believes in the promises and fantasies of
child-like Don Quixote, then everything the squire says or does
afterwards would be fool's business. If, however, we give him the
benefit of the doubt and consider this passage in relation to other
passages our conclusions might be different. If we compare this
conversation with two others in Part II where Sancho asks his master
to explain to him the meaning of one of his sayings (II, 58) and talks
with him about playing shepherds instead of knight and squire (II,
67), the similarities between them will bring the apparent inanity of
Sancho's first speeches into sharper focus. Here is the first excerpt:

—Yo así lo creo —respondió Sancho—, y quería que vuestra
merced me dijese qué es la causa por que dicen los españoles
cuando quieren dar alguna batalla, invocando aquel San Diego
Matamoros: «¡Santiago, y cierra España!» ¿Está por ventura España
abierta, y de modo que es menester cerrarla, o qué ceremonia es
ésta?
—Simplicísimo eres, Sancho —respondió don Quijote—; y mira
que este gran caballero de la cruz bermeja háselo dado Dios a
España por patrón y amparo suyo, especialmente en los rigurosos
trances que con los moros los españoles han tenido, y así, le
invocan y llaman como a defensor suyo en todas las batallas que
acometen, y muchas veces le han visto visiblemente en ellas,
derribando, atropellando, destruyendo y matando los agarenos
escuadrones; y desta verdad te pudiera traer muchos ejemplos que
en las verdaderas historias españolas se cuentan.
Mudó Sancho plática, y dijo a su amo...." (pp. 474-75)

No one can doubt that Sancho is here jokingly feigning ignorance in his first question. We know he had previously used this saying appositely (II, 4, 70), and we recognize the deliberate silliness of his next question: "¿Está por ventura España abierta, y de modo que es menester cerrarla?" Don Quixote's answer is typical: "Simplicísimo eres Sancho"; and then he embarks on a lengthy explanation, until Sancho changes the subject.

This is basically the same as happens in Sancho's first dialogue with his master. It is important to note, moreover, that Cervantes does not make Sancho derive his conversations from what he, the author, states or from what the other characters think or say when Sancho is not present or behind his back, but from what they say directly to him; hence, we should not see Sancho's opening words in the book as resulting from, proving, or supporting Cervantes's preceding remark that "iba Sancho...con mucho deseo de verse ya gobernador de la ínsula" (I, 7, 127), but rather as a continuation of his unrecorded talks with Don Quixote:

> Tanto le dijo [don Quijote], tanto le persuadió y prometió... Decíale...[que] tal vez le podía suceder aventura que ganase, en quítame allá esas pajas, alguna ínsula y le dejase a él por gobernador della (I, 7, 125).

To ignore Cervantes's derogatory and ironic remarks ("de muy poca sal en la mollera," "el pobre villano," "iba...con mucho deseo de verse ya gobernador") altogether is impossible; but knowing Sancho's good common sense, and his sense of humor, can we accept his questions as merely those of an uneducated, stupid, and credulous peasant? Is it possible, on the other hand, to think Sancho so tactless and foolhardy that he would start his first recorded conversation with Don Quixote by telling him that he realizes that all his promises and chivalric fantasies are sheer nonsense? Of course not. What, then, is he doing? We find a partial answer to this question in the second conversation from Part II mentioned earlier. Finding themselves in a place they have been before, Don Quixote says to Sancho:

> —Este es el prado donde topamos a las bizarras pastoras y gallardos pastores que en él querían renovar e imitar a la pastoral Arcadia, pensamiento tan nuevo como discreto, a cuya imitación, si es que a ti te parece bien, querría, ¡oh Sancho!, que nos convirtiésemos en pastores, siquiera el tiempo que tengo de estar recogido. Yo compraré algunas ovejas, y todas las demás cosas que al pastoral ejercicio son necesarias, y llamándome yo *el pastor Quijotiz*, y tú *el pastor Pancino*, nos andaremos por los montes, por las selvas y por los prados, cantando aquí, endechando allí,

bebiendo de los líquidos cristales de la fuentes, o ya de los limpios arroyuelos, o de los caudalosos ríos. Daránnos con abundantísima mano de su dulcísimo fruto las encinas, asiento los troncos de los durísimos alcornoques, sombra los sauces, olor las rosas, alfombras de mil colores matizadas los estendidos prados, aliento el aire claro y puro, luz la luna y las estrellas, a pesar de la escuridad de la noche; gusto el canto, alegría el lloro, Apolo versos, el amor conceptos, con que podremos hacernos eternos y famosos, no sólo en los presentes, sino en los venideros siglos.

—Pardiez -dijo Sancho—, que me ha cuadrado, y aun esquinado, tal género de vida; y más, que no la ha de haber aún bien visto el bachiller Sansón Carrasco y maese Nicolás el barbero, cuando la han de querer seguir, y hacerse pastores con nosotros; y aun quiera Dios no le venga en voluntad al cura de entrar también en el aprisco, según es de alegre y amigo de holgarse.

—Tú has dicho muy bien —dijo don Quijote—; y podrá llamarse el bachiller Sansón Carrasco, si entra en el pastoral gremio, como entrará sin duda, *el pastor Sansonino*, o ya *el pastor Carrascón*; el barbero Nicolás se podrá llamar *Miculoso*, como ya el antiguo Boscán se llamó *Nemoroso*; al cura no sé qué nombre le pongamos, si no es algún derivativo de su nombre, llamándole *el pastor Curiambro*. Las pastoras de quien hemos de ser amantes, como entre peras podremos escoger sus nombres; y pues el de mi señora cuadra así al de pastora como al de princesa, no hay para qué cansarme en buscar otro que mejor le venga; tú, Sancho, pondrás a la tuya el que quisieres.

—No pienso —respondió Sancho— ponerle otro alguno sino el de *Teresona*, que le vendrá bien con su gordura y con el propio que tiene, pues se llama Teresa; y más, que celebrándola yo en mis versos vengo a descubrir mis castos deseos, pues no ando a buscar pan de trastrigo por las casas ajenas. El cura no será bien que tenga pastora, por dar buen ejemplo; y si quisiere el bachiller tenerla, su alma en su palma.

—¡Válame Dios —dijo don Quijote—, y qué vida nos hemos de dar, Sancho amigo! Qué de churumbelas han de llegar a nuestros oídos, qué de gaitas zamoranas, qué tamborines, y qué de sonajas, y qué de rabeles! Pues ¡qué si destas diferencias de músicas resuena la de los albogues! Allí se verá casi todos los instrumentos pastorales.... Y hanos de ayudar mucho al parecer en perfeción este ejercicio el ser yo algún tanto poeta, como tú sabes, y el serlo también en estremo el bachiller Sansón Carrasco. Del cura no digo nada; pero yo apostaré que debe de tener sus puntas y collares de poeta; y que las tenga también maese Nicolás, no dudo en ello, porque todos, o los más, son guitarristas y copleros. Yo me quejaré de ausencia; tú te alabarás de firme enamorado; el pastor Carrascón, de desdeñado; y el cura Curiambro, de lo que él más puede servirse, y así, andará la cosa que no haya más que desear.

A lo que respondió Sancho:

—Yo soy, señor, tan desgraciado, que temo no ha de llegar el día en que en tal ejercicio me vea. ¡Oh, qué polidas cuchares tengo de hacer cuando pastor me vea! ¡Qué de migas, qué de natas, qué de guirnaldas y qué de zarandajas pastoriles, que, puesto que no me granjeen fama de discreto, no dejarán de granjearme la de ingenioso! Sanchica mi hija nos llevará la comida al hato. Pero, ¡guarda! que es de buen parecer, y hay pastores más maliciosos que simples, y no querría que fuese por lana y volviese trasquilada (pp. 548-50).

All three excerpts clearly show how Sancho builds his conversation from what has previously been given to him (*caballero, ínsula,* etc.; San Diego Matamoros; *pastores*), and also how he stores in his memory apparently unimportant bits of information for future use. When Sancho pointedly says "aquel San Diego Matamoros," he is referring back not to Don Quixote's preceding speech, but to the previous episode when his master used that name for the Saint (II, 58, 472), a fact emphasized by Sancho's use of the pronoun "aquel," which is not needed for the question he is asking.

Looking back now to the opening dialogue, we can safely assume that Sancho knows that Don Quixote's chivalric world (like the pastoral world) is imaginary, a game devised by the knight, and that he, Sancho, now a part of it, is trying to learn the rules by which he will have to play. He is acting in his first dialogue with Don Quixote as he is to act from then on throughout the novel. He is cunningly winding up his master with the knight's own key (*caballero andante, ínsula, rey, reina, infantes, reinos, condesa*), mainly to keep the conversation going, but also to get out of him the rules of the game they are playing. In Part I Sancho is somewhat confused when other characters (the priest, the barber, Dorotea, the company in the inn) join the game. At first he plays along with them gingerly because he realizes that they are bringing their own rules with them, but by Chapter 67 of Part II he is a proficient and confident player. He therefore at that time not only jumps eagerly at the invitation to play shepherds, but also hopes to have as fellow-players the priest, the barber, and Sansón.

By this stage of the novel the reader knows well the kind of person Sancho is, his sense of humor, and his malleability, and no longer takes his exclamations and illusory pastoral plans (Teresa becomes *la pastora Teresona*; "Sanchica nos llevará la comida al hato") as the inane talk of a simpleton; and yet, the elements in this excerpt are essentially the same as those of Sancho's first dialogue with Don Quixote ("Juana Gutiérrez...vendría a ser reina, y mis hijos infantes") Furthermore, in the closing pages of the novel Sancho once again attempts to wind up his master with Don Quixote's own key: "No se muera,...no sea perezoso, sino levántese desa cama, y vámonos al campo vestidos de pastores,...quizá tras de alguna mata hallaremos a la señora Dulcinea desencantada" (II, 74, 589-90). But on this occasion, and for the first and only time, Sancho's efforts fail. His master dies. He leaves Sancho with unforgettable memories and many tales to tell, but otherwise very much as Cervantes had first introduced him to the reader some one hundred and twenty-two chapters earlier. It should now be clear that from the very beginning Sancho does not take his master's promises simplemindedly ("si yo fuese rey por algún *milagro* de los que vuestra merced dice," my italics). And he unequivocally tells Don Quixote in Part II: "Si sucediese, lo cual no lo creo ni , lo espero, que vuesa merced me diese la ínsula que me tiene prometida..." (7, 88). It is worth noting also that, although Sancho does not receive much praise in his first three chapters, his advice and good sense are consistently accepted and acknowledged from Chapter 10 of Part I to Chapter 74 of Part II (Appendix 17).

When Sancho first appears in Chapter 7 of Part I, he is ready and willing to range mountains and woods in squire-dress, govern *ínsulas*, pass laws, and lead men; similarly at the conclusion of the novel he wants to herd goats, recite poetry, and "range hills and dales in shepherd-dress" (Entwistle, p. 133). In fact, of all the fantasies of his master and all the adventures they face, the only made-up things in which Sancho apparently really believes àre the *ínsula* Barataria and his governorship.

And thus the donnish, mythical, and spiritual columns that have been built to support the architrave of the Quixotification theory turn out to be made of sand. Sancho is already whole from the start. All he learns with his master are the complex rules of the imaginary games they play together.

In view of these conclusions, we should see Sancho's ambitions and references to salary as part of the game. It should be emphasized that Don Quixote is the first to mention *ínsulas* and *condados* (Appendix 8; see especially *10* and *30*), and that the first reference to salary comes from the lips of the knight himself, not from Sancho! There is, therefore, no firm basis, *pace* Aubrun, for considering that master and servant see their relationship with different eyes—Don Quixote as a feudal contract between lord and vassal, and Sancho as a civil contract between master and servant—even in Part II (Appendix 32; see especially *3*).

A more difficult task, superficially at least, is to show that master and squire are not a pair of opposites as proposed by Romantic critics. Don Quixote is a passably well-off, educated *hidalgo*: Sancho is a poor, uneducated peasant. He is stout and short: his master is tall and thin. The squire is down-to-earth, modest, cautious, and funny: the knight, solemn, foolhardy, arrogant, and less practical. The Don lectures: Sancho Panza entertains. The Governor of Barataria redresses wrongdoings: Don Quixote of La Mancha maims. One spins his talk from what he has read and dreamt: the other from what he hears and from the life he lives. The contrasts are all too evident. And this polarity, deliberately stressed by Cervantes (Appendix 11, *1-3, 5-7, 11, 12, 15, 16, 18, 20*) and by the knight himself vaingloriously (*11, 4, 9, 14, 17, 19*), lies at the very core of the novel, giving tension and dynamism to the story; but, characteristically, Sancho is the one who reacts against these oversimplifications. "No hay tanta diferencia de mí a mi amo, que a él le laven con agua de ángeles y a mí con lejía de diablos" (II, 32, 294), he would say at the Ducal palace. In the end, however, what rules out the theory that Don Quixote and Sancho are simple opposites is not any high degree of similarity between them or any process of Quixotification or Sanchification that brings them together, but rather the sheer complexity of their characters and their overlapping.

Now that the massive amount of textual evidence has been examined and the various items have been seen both in the specific context of the passage where they appear and in the overall context of the novel, the consistency of Cervantes's characterization of Sancho and his delicate labor of creation shine out over the maligning the squire has been subjected to by the other characters in the novel and by numerous writers and critics. True, there are some blatant textual contradictions: Teresa is thin (*3, 22*) and fat (*3, 25*): Sancho states that he can sign his name (*14, 8, 11*) and later that he cannot (*14, 13*); Cervantes writes that Panza is probably a nickname (*13, 1*), only to be contradicted by Sancho (*3, 10, 18, 19, 23*); but these contradictions are only minor authorial slips. There are some apparent inconsistencies, too, in the character of the squire, though one of the inconsistent traits is always clearly dominant. Sancho is presented now as a thief and highwayman, then as honest and compassionate. He is disrespectful and deferential, greedy and generous. His great love for his ass is at times non existent, as when Sancho uses him as a shield to avoid being stoned or hurt (*5, 5, 16*; see also *25*). He complains repeatedly (and no one can deny that he always has good reasons to do so, see Appendix 19); none the less, he is eager to continue with his master despite the voice of common sense that gnaws at his mind (Appendix 29). We can no longer argue that Sancho must be stupid simply because he left his family and village to follow Don Quixote. It has been shown here that the text does not support this view. I cannot elaborate on Sancho's true motives for following his neighbor, except to suggest that it is the love and respect that he shows towards the knight which impel him to accept Don Quixote's offer and remain with him throughout most of the story. Boredom and a yearning for adventure have also been suggested as the main reasons. for Sancho's escapades, and this theory seems to me plausible; but the text does not have anything to support or deny this hypothesis, and I have only the text as my guide. Moreover, to consider that only an idiot would follow a madman is tantamount to ignoring human nature. It would not be too hard to find numerous examples of otherwise intelligent men and women who in real life, and in all good faith or for the sake of the adventure, have followed, and follow, clowns, visionaries, liars, hypocrites, criminals, false prophets, and madmen. Love, curiosity, respect, friendship, admiration, the seeking of higher truths, and veneration, all play important roles in this apparent contradiction between being and doing. The apparent inconsistencies in Sancho's personality arise when he finds himself under different circumstances, and they are the natural result of human weaknesses. Such are to be expected in a well-drawn, true-to-life character, and, in my opinion, they make Sancho even more endearing. He might not be a perfectly consistent human being; no human being ever is and Sancho was never intended to be such, but he is perfect as a work of art. As in Genesis the first man emanated instantly whole from the mind of his Creator, so I consider did the Sancho of Chapter 7 of Part I.

PLATE 10 Sancho Panza
by Dubout (Paris: Les Presses de l'Union Typographique, 1938)
Courtesy of the British Library, Cerv.700, vol. 3, p. 21

PLATE 11 Sancho and the Baratarian doctor
(Moscow: n.p., 1953-1954)
        Courtesy of the British Library, Cerv.736, vol. 2, p. 264

❧ In Closing ❧

THE MOST DIFFICULT TASK I had during the writing of this book was to keep Sancho as separate as possible from Cervantes and Don Quixote in order to avoid seeing him as merely the satellite of more massive bodies, reflecting rather than emitting light, though, of course, it would have been altogether impossible to ignore or dismiss the forces that bind together creator and creation, master and squire.

Then there were the enticing songs of sirens luring me towards treacherous reefs. Here is Thomas Mann in his "Voyage with Don Quixote":

> [Avellaneda] drove Cervantes to compose a second part (p. 435), . . . though, as Goethe remarks, the theme was really exhausted in the first part (p. 435). . . . The second part has no longer the happy freshness and carelessness of the first (p. 436). . . . [First Cervantes conceived his work] modestly, as a pretty crude and downright satire, without a notion of the extent to which his hero was destined to grow, . . . [a process which] causes a considerable identification of the author with his hero, an inclination to assimilate his intellectual attainments to the author's own, to make him the mouthpiece of Cervantes's convictions (p. 444).

What nonsense! How textually baseless many such critical remarks are, and how maddening to let them pass unchallenged. But I closed my eyes and covered my ears, and eventually, the alluring songs were heard no more.

We have seen that, suggestive, imaginative, and original as some of the critical interpretations considered in this study might be, they are clearly not defensible from the text. By attributing to Cervantes goals and intentions which go beyond what can be ascertained from the text itself, these interpretations have given us distorted views of Cervantes's work. Most critics have examined isolated strains of Sancho under the lenses of their personal microscopes and have catalogued him according to their individual likes and dislikes, with little concern for other textual evidence which might contradict their theories.

The overall picture of Sancho criticism is one of disarray, irrelevance, and repetition. We, the critics, seem to move awkwardly under the majesty of the high trees of the literary forest and frequently lose ourselves amongst the underbrush. When faced with the inventiveness and creativity of Cervantes, we become so nearsighted, so enwrapped in our own pet theories, that we rush our hobbyhorses into print oblivious of anything else. We make idols and gods of clay in our own image and likeness.

For Avellaneda, Gayton, and D'Urfey, Sancho is nought but a babbling sot, a liar, and a glutton; for Molière, Ayres, and Close he is a buffoon and a court-jester; for Pitaval and Frederick II he is a sage governor and a just law-maker; for the Romantics and their followers he is always the less commendable element of any pair of opposites; for Unamuno he is the proselyte and acolyte of a man in a cathartic mission; for Menéndez Pidal and Joly he is a traditional character exuding plain folk wisdom; for Castro he represents History; for Shevill, Hatzfeld, Oelschläger, Sainz, and Tharpe he is a none-too-brilliant undergraduate under his master's exemplary tutoring; for Brenan he is the feminine half of a connubial partnership; for Herder, Lunacharski, Tubino, and Aubrun he is the symbol of class struggle; for Urbina he is a parody of the squires of the romances of chivalry; for Maldonado de Guevara and Willis he is an unrepentant, uneducated peasant; for Romero Flores and Moore he is the down-to-earth, unidealistic half of his creator; for Dámaso Alonso and Sletsjöe he is an unaccomplished and unconvincing character.

One has to look at Partridge, Jerry Tugwell, Sam Weller, and Sam Gamgee, and at their relationship with their masters to be able to grasp and understand Sancho's true character and his true relationship with Don Quixote. The elements that draw and tie both characters together are the friendship and mutual dependence and encouragement that might arise between two individuals of different social, economic, and intellectual levels. They are a master and servant who find themselves travelling alone on unfamiliar roads, fighting off dangers together, enjoying the sunny days, creating novel adventures, and encountering unexpected situations; but who, once back in their home town, automatically reassume the character of their original condition, none the less having done and experienced in a short span of time what in all probability neither of them would have experienced or done in all their lives had they never left their village and broken the constraints of the unwritten but rigid rules of social intercourse. Sancho might not be the donzel prescribed by courtly romances of chivalry, nor the worker of miracles recommended by Arabian fairytales, but he is the ideal companion to take on a long and uncomfortable journey. He is the perfect antidote, both loving and mischievous, to the cheerless Don Quixote.

Moreover, it should now be clear that Sancho is basically the same complex character from beginning to end; that what changes is in fact the other characters' opinion of him; that what to the reader might seem farcical, feebleminded, and even crass in the early chapters acquires a totally different color once the reader is better acquainted with Sancho's character, with his good sense, humor, cunning, and adaptability ("[yo] uso de los tiempos como los hallo," he says in Chapter 62 of Part II, p. 509); and that Cervantes himself is less critical and less sparing in his praise of Sancho in Part II than in Part I, thanks to the interposition of Cide Hamete Benengeli and the Moorish translator between him and his characters. And thus many theories about Sancho prove to be critical sand castles that wash away under the relentless tide of textual evidence.

But perhaps more important for understanding the fundamental relationship between the author and his characters in *Don Quixote* is the fact that Cervantes seems not to have forced his own bias into what he has his characters say or think. When Cervantes comments directly about Sancho he usually means what he writes, but he allows his characters to agree or disagree with him and change their opinion as the story unfolds, constantly increasing the number of the manifold points of view manifested in his novel.

What new challenges await Sancho in the path that lies ahead? Only time will tell.

R. M. FLORES

October 10, 1981

PLATE 12 Sancho in the battle of Barataria
(Moscow: n.p., 1953-1954)
        Courtesy of the British Library, Cerv.736, vol. 2, p. 302

BIBLIOGRAPHIES

BIBLIOGRAPHY I. General Bibliography.

Includes all works mentioned in this study with cross-references, when pertinent, to BIBLIOGRAPHIES II and III.

BIBLIOGRAPHY II. Sancho Criticism.

Lists critical monographs dealing chiefly with Sancho.

BIBLIOGRAPHY III. Works of Fiction.

Lists in chronological order those works which I have consulted (all pertinent bibliographical data given) and those mentioned from other critical sources (only author, title, and year are given).

NOTE: Entries published in or after 1900 do not give the names of printers or publishers, except when the absence of these data could lead to confusion.

BIBLIOGRAPHY I

General Bibliography

Abaurre y Mesa, José. See Bibliography III, 1901.

Allen, John Jay. See Bibliography II.

Almeida, Filinto de. See Bibliography III, 1905.

Alonso, Amado. See Bibliography II.

Alonso, Dámaso. See Bibliography II.

Ames, Van Meter *Aesthetics of the Novel*. Chicago, 1928.

Anonymous. See Bibliography III, 1614, 1616, 1617 Cervantes, 1650, 1658, 1680, 1700, 17th Century, 1714, 1722, 1772, 1774, 1800, 18th Century, 1900.

Araujo, Joaquim de. See Bibliography III, 1905.

Ares Montes, José. "Don Quijote en el teatro portugés del siglo XVIII," *Anales Cervantinos*, 3 (1953), 349-52.

Armas y Cárdenas, José de. *El "Quijote" y su época*. Madrid, 1915. Reprinted in *Cervantes y el "Quijote"*. Havana, 1945.

Arouet, François Marie. See Voltaire.

Aubrun, Charles Vincent. See Bibliography II.

Aude, Jean. See Bibliography III, 1807.

Aveleyra Arroyo de Anda, Teresa. See Bibliography II.

Avellaneda. See Bibliography III, 1614, Fernández de Avellaneda, Alonso.

Ayres, James. See Bibliography III, 1742.

Bardon, Maurice. *"Don Quichotte" en France au XVII*^e *et au XVIII*^e *siècle 1605-1815.* 2 vols. Paris, 1931.

————. *"Don Quichotte* en France: L'Interprétation romantique," *Les Lettres Romanes*, 3 (1949), 263-82.

Bastel von der Sohl, Pahsch. See Bibliography III, 1648, Cervantes.

Baudoin, Nicolas. Translator. See Bibliography III, 1608, Cervantes.

Beaumont, Francis. See Bibliography III, 1620, Fletcher, John.

Belloni, Antonio. *Il Seicento.* 1929.

Benardete, Maír José. Editor of *Cervantes Across the Centuries.* New York, 1947.

Bergel, Lienhard. "Cervantes in Germany," in *Cervantes Across the Centuries.* Edited by Angel Flores and Maír José Benardete. New York, 1947, pp. 305-42.

Bertrand, Jean Jacques Achille. "Génesis de la concepción romántica de Don Quijote en Francia," *Anales Cervantinos*, 3 (1953), 1-41.

————. "Génesis de la concepción romántica de Don Quijote en Francia: Segunda parte," *Anales Cervantinos*, 4 (1954), 41-76.

Bertuch, Friedrich Justin. Translator. See Bibliography III, 1775, Cervantes.

Bleznick, Donald William. See Bibliography II.

Blumenfeld, Walter. See Bibliography II.

Boissel. See Bibliography III, 1789.

Boyer, Jean Baptiste de. See Bibliography III, 1736.

Brackenridge, Hugh Henry. See Bibliography III, 1792.

Brantley, Franklin Oakes. See Bibliography II.

Brasol, Boris Leo. Translator. Dostoievski, Fedor Mikhailovich.

Brazier, Nicolas. See Bibliography III, 1807.

Brenan, Edward Fitz-Gerald. *The Literature of the Spanish People: From Roman Times to the Present Day.* 2nd ed. Cambridge, 1965. First published 1951.

Brett-Smith, Herbert Francis Brett. Editor. See Bibliography III, 1627, Drayton, Michael.

Brooke, Henry. See Bibliography III, 1766.

Burke, Ulick Ralph. See Bibliography II.

Butler, Samuel. See Bibliography III, 17th Century.

Caballero Calderón, Eduardo. Editor. See Bibliography II, Suárez, Marco Fidel.

Calandrelli, M. See Bibliography III, 1904.

Calderón de la Barca, Pedro. See Bibliography III, 1633.

Camp, Jean. See Bibliography III, 1933.

Carreras y Artau, Tomás. *La filosofía del derecho en el "Quijote".* Madrid, 1903.

Casalduero, Joaquín. "The Composition of *Don Quixote,*" in *Cervantes Across the Centuries.* Edited by Angel Flores and Maír José Benardete. New York, 1947, pp. 56-93.

Castro, Américo. "Incarnation in *Don Quixote,*" in *Cervantes Across the Centuries.* Edited by Angel Flores and Maír José Benardete. New York, 1947, pp. 136-78.

Cavestany y González Nandín, Juan Antonio. See Bibliography II.

Cervantes Saavedra, Miguel de. See Bibliography III, 1605, 1608, 1612, 1613, 1614, 1615, 1617, 1618, 1620, 1648, 1700, 1775, 1799, 1863, 1866, 1929, 1978.

Champein, Stanislas. See Bibliography III, 1789.

Close, Anthony J. *The Romantic Approach to "Don Quixote": A Critical History of the Romantic Tradition in "Quixote" Criticism.* Cambridge, 1978. See also Bibliography II.

Colerdige, Samuel Taylor. "Lecture viii: Don Quixote: Cervantes." In *Coleridge's Miscellaneous Criticism,* edited by Thomas Middleton Raysor. London, 1936. Read in 1818.

Collier, Jeremy. *Short View of the Immorality, and Profaneness of the English Stage.* 2nd ed. London: S. Keble, 1698.

Cramail, Adrien de Montluc, Count of. See Bibliography III, 1633.

Cuvelier de Trie, Jean Guillaume Antoine. See Bibliography III, 1799, 1816.

Daireaux, Max. *Cervantès.* Paris, 1948.

D'Avenant, William. See Bibliography III, 1630.

Day, Cyrus Lawrence. Editor. See Bibliography III, 1933, D'Urfey, Thomas.

De Andrea, Peter Frank. See Bibliography II.

De Chasca, Edmund Villela. See Bibliography II.

De Cordova, Rafael J. "The *Don Quixote* of Cervantes," *The Knickerbocker,* 38 (1851), 190.

De Lollis, Cesare, *Cervantes reazionario e altri scritti d'ispanistica.* Edited by Silvio Pellegrini. Florence, 1947.

Derjavin, Constantin Nicolaievich. "La crítica cervantina en Rusia," *Boletín de la Real Academia de la Historia,* 94 (1929), 215-38.

Despois, Eugène André. Editor. See Bibliography III, 1670, Molière.

Deutsch, Helene. See Bibliography II.

Dickens, Charles. *The Heart of Charles Dickens: As Revealed in His Letters to Angela Burdett-Coutts.* Edited by Edgar Johnson. New York, 1952. See also Bibliography III, 1836, Dickens, Charles.

Doré, Paul Gustave. Illustrator. See Bibliography I, Bertrand, Jean Jacques Achille, 1953, and Romera-Navarro, Miguel. See Bibliography III, 1863, Cervantes.

Dostoievski, Fedor Mikhailovich. *The Diary of a Writer.* Translated by Boris Leo Brasol. New York, 1954.

Drake, Dana Blackmar. *"Don Quijote" (1894-1970): A Selective Annotated Bibliography.* Chapel Hill, North Carolina, 1974.

————. *"Don Quijote" (1894-1970): A Selective and Annotated Bibliography, Volume Two, with an Index to Volumes One and Two.* Miami, Florida, 1978.

Drayton, Michael. See Bibliography III, 1627.

Dudden, Frederick Homes. *Henry Fielding: His Life, Works, and Times.* 2 vols. Oxford, 1952.

Dufresny, Charles Rivière. See Bibliography III, 1694.

Durán, Manuel. "El *Quijote* a través del prisma de Mikhail Bakhtine: carnaval, disfraces, escatología y locura," in *Cervantes and the Renaissance.* Edited by Michael D. McGaha. Easton, Pennsylvania, 1980, pp. 71-86.

D'Urfey, Thomas. See Bibliography III, 1694, 1696, 17th Century.

Dyce, Alexander. Editor. See Bibliography III, c. 1620, Fletcher, John.

Efron, Arthur. "Satire Denied: A Critical History of English and American *Don Quixote* Criticism." Unpublished dissertation, University of Washington, 1964.

Engelbert, Jo Anne. See Bibliography II.

Entwistle, William James. *Cervantes 1547-1616.* Oxford, 1940.

Erasmus, Desiderius. *Institutio principis christiani.*

Favart, Charles Simon. See Bibliography III, 1743.

Féletz, Charles Marie Dorimond, Abbot of. *Mélanges de philosophie, d'histoire et de littérature.* 1828-1830.

Fernández, Marcos. See Bibliography III, 1655.

Fernández de Avellaneda, Alonso. See Bibliography III, 1614.

Fernández Suárez, Alvaro. *Los mitos del "Quijote".* Madrid, 1953.

Fielding Henry. "Proceedings at the Court of Censorial Enquiry," in *The Covent-Garden Journal,* edited by Gerard Edward Jensen. 2 vols. Oxford, 1915. Vol. I. First published 1752. See also Bibliography III, 1734, 1742, 1749.

Figueiredo, Fidelino de Sousa. "O thema do *Quixote* na litteratura portuguesa do seculo XVIII," *Revista de Filología Española,* 7 (1920), 47-56.

————. "O thema do *Quixote* na litteratura portuguesa do seculo XIX," *Revista de Filología Española,* 8 (1921), 161-69.

Fitzgerald, Percy Hetherington. Editor. Lamb, Charles.

Fitzmaurice-Kelly, James. "Cervantes in England," *Proceedings of the British Academy 1905-1906*, 2 (1906), 11-29.

Flaccomio, Rosaria. *La fortuna del "Don Quijote" in Italia nei secoli XVII e XVIII e il "Don Chisciotti" di G. Meli.* Palermo, 1928.

Fletcher, John. See Bibliography III, c. 1620.

Flores, Angel. Editor of *Cervantes Across the Centuries.* New York, 1947.

Flores, Robert M. "Cervantes at Work: The Writing of *Don Quixote*, Part I," *Journal of Hispanic Philology*, 3 (1979), 135-60.

————. "The Loss and Recovery of Sancho's Ass in *Don Quixote*, Part I," *Modern Language Review*, 75 (1980), 301-10.

————. "The Rôle of Cide Hamete in *Don Quixote*," *Bulletin of Hispanic Studies*, 59 (1982), 3-14. See also Bibliography II.

Florian, Jean Pierre Claris de. Translator. See Bibliography III, 1799, Cervantes.

Foucault, Michel Paul. *Les Mots et les choses: Une archéologie des sciences humaines.* Mayenne, 1966.

Fourcroy, Bonaventure. See Bibliography III, 1659.

Fowles, John. See Bibliography III, 1969.

Frank, Waldo David. "The Career of the Hero," in *Cervantes Across the Centuries.* Edited by Angel Flores and Maír José Benardete. New York, 1947, pp. 183-94.

Friche, Vladimir Maksimovich. "Shekspir i Servantes," *Sovremenny Mir*, 4 (1916), 110-23.

Gale, George Stafford. "Don Nixon's Sancho Panza?" *Spectator*, 243 (1979), 17-18.

Gale, Steven H. "The Relationship between Beaumont's *The Knight of the Burning Pestle* and Cervantes' *Don Quixote*," *Anales Cervantinos*, 11 (1972), 87-96.

————. "Cervantes' Influence on Dickens, with Comparative Emphasis on *Don Quijote* and *Pickwick Papers*," *Anales Cervantinos*, 12 (1973), 135-56.

Gaultier. See Bibliography III, 1713.

Gayot de Pitaval, François. *Causes célèbres.* 1749.

Gayton, Edmund. See Bibliography III, 1654.

Gebhart, Emile. *De Panurge à Sancho Pança: Mélanges de littérature européenne.* Paris, 1911.

Geoffroy, Julien Louis. *Cours de littérature dramatique.* 1819-1820.

Gigli, Girolamo. See Bibliography III, 1698.

Girard, René Noel. *Mensonge romantique et vérité romanesque.* Paris, 1961.

Goldmann. See Bibliography III, 1807.

González, Manuel Pedro. "La más afortunada imitación del *Quijote*," *Hispania*, 9 (1926), 275-83.

Graves, Richard. See Bibliography III, 1773.

Guérin de Bouscal, Guyon. See Bibliography III, 1641.

Hatzfeld, Helmut. *El "Quijote" como obra de arte del lenguaje*. Translated by M. C. de I. Madrid, 1949. First German edition 1927.

Hendrix, William Samuel. See Bibliography II.

Henley, William Ernest. Editor. See Bibliography III, 1760, Smollett, Tobias.

Herrero-García, Miguel. *Estimaciones literarias del siglo XVII*. Madrid, 1930.

Hilborn, Harry Warren. See Bibliography II.

Houdar de la Motte, Antoine. *Réflexions sur la Critique*. 1715.

I., M. C. de. Translator. Hatzfeld, Helmut.

Jensen, Gerard Edward. Editor. Fielding, Henry.

Johnson, Edgar. Editor. Dickens, Charles.

Joly, Monique. See Bibliography II.

Karelin, V. Translator. See Bibliography III, 1866, Cervantes.

Kazantzakis, Nikos. *Spain*. New York, 1963. First Greek edition 1957. See also Bibliography III.

Klinger, Friedrich Maximilian von. "Reflections on World and Literature." 1803.

Knowles, Jr., Edwin Blackwell. "The Vogue of *Don Quixote* in England from 1605 to 1660." Unpublished dissertation, New York University, 1938.

————. "Don Quixote in England before 1660," in "Dissertations: Literature and Art," at the University of Oregon Library, 800/D632/v. 1.

————. "*Don Quixote* through English Eyes," *Hispania*, 23 (1940), 103-15.

————. "Cervantes and English Literature," in *Cervantes Across the Centuries*. Edited by Angel Flores and Maír José Benardete. New York, 1947, pp. 267-93.

Kracauer, Siegfried. *History: The Last Things before the Last*. Oxford, 1969.

Krzhevski, B. A. "*Don Kikhot* na fone ispanskoi literatury XVI-XVII st." In the Russian Academy edition of *Don Quixote*, pp. xxxix-lxxix. See Bibliography III, 1929, Cervantes.

Lagniet, Jacques. Engraver. See Bibliography III, 17th Century.

LaGrone, Gregory Gough. *The Imitations of "Don Quixote" in the Spanish Drama*. Philadelphia, 1937.

Lamb, Charles. "Barrenness of the Imaginative Faculty in the Production of Modern Art." In *The Life, Letters and Writings of Charles Lamb*. Edited by Percy Hetherington Fitzgerald. 6 vols. London: E. Moxon and Co., 1876. Vol. IV.

Larra y Wetoret, Luis Mariano de. See Bibliography III, 1864.

Larraz López, José. See Bibliography III, 1961.

Larsen, Joan. "S. T. Coleridge: His Theory of Knowledge," *Transactions of the Wisconsin Academy of Sciences, Arts and Letters*, 48 (1959), 221-32.

Leary, Lewis Gaston. Editor. See Bibliography III, 1792, Brackenridge, Hugh Henry.

Lennox, Charlotte. See Bibliography III, 1752.

Lewis, Dominic Bevan Wyndham. *The Shadow of Cervantes*. New York, 1962.

López Fanego, Otilia. See Bibliography II.

López del Arco, A. Editor. See Bibliography II.

Lorenzi, Giovanni Battista. See Bibliography III, 1773.

Lowe-Porter, Helen Tracy. Translator. Mann, Thomas.

Lukács, Georg Szegedi. *Teoría de la novela*. Translated from the French by Juan José Sebreli. Barcelona, 1971. First German edition 1920.

Lunacharski, Anatoli Vasilevich. *Istoria zapadno-yevropeiskoi literatury*. Moscow, 1924.

Machen, Arthur. *Hieroglyphics: A Note upon Ecstacy in Literature*. New York, 1923.

Madariaga y Rojo, Salvador de. *Guía del lector del "Quijote": ensayo psicológico sobre el "Quijote"*. Bilbao, 1926.

Máinez, Ramón León. *Cervantes y su época*. Jerez de la Frontera, 1901.

Maldonado de Guevara y Andrés, Francisco. "Apuntes para la fijación de las estructuras esenciales en el *Quijote*," *Anales Cervantinos*, 1 (1951), 159-231.

Mancing, Howard Terrance. See Bibliography II.

Mann, Thomas. "Voyage with *Don Quixote*." In *Essays of Three Decades*. Translated by Helen Tracy Lowe-Porter. New York, 1948. This essay was written in 1934.

Maqueda, José. See Bibliography III, 1812.

Márquez, Juan. *Gobernador cristiano*. 1615.

Márquez Villanueva, Francisco. See Bibliography II.

Martial. *Epigrams*. 1st Century A.D.

McGaha, Michael D. Editor. Durán, Manuel.

Mele, Eugenio. "Per la fortuna del Cervantes in Italia nel Seicento," *Studi di Filologia Moderna*, 2 (1909), 229-55.

Meli, Giovanni. See Bibliography III, 1787.

Melz, Christian Fritz. "An Evaluation of the Earliest German Translation of *Don Quixote: Juncker Harnisch aus Fleckenland*," *University of California Publications in Modern Philology*, 27, No. 5 (1945), 301-42.

Menéndez Pidal, Ramón. *De Cervantes y Lope de Vega*. Buenos Aires, 1940.

Meregalli, Franco. "Cervantes nella critica romantica tedesca," *Annali di Ca'Foscari*, 11 (1972), 381-95.

—————. "La critica cervantina dell'ottocento in Francia e in Spagna," *Anales Cervantinos*, 15 (1976), 121-48.

Merejkovski, Dmitiri Sergeievich. "Don Kikhot i Sancho," *Severny Viestnik* (1881).

Mesnard, Paul, Editor. See Bibliography III, 1670, Molière.

Miró Quesada Sosa, Aurelio. *Cervantes, Tirso y el Perú*. Lima, 1947.

Molas y Casas, Juan. See Bibliography III, 1881.

Molho, Maurice. See Bibliography II.

Molière [pseud. of Jean Baptiste Poquelin]. See Bibliography III, 1660, 1661, 1666, 1670.

Molina, Tirso de [pseud. of Gabriel Téllez]. See Bibliography III, 1611, 1612, 1622, 1638.

Montalvo, Juan. See Bibliography III, 1895.

Moore, John Aiken. See Bibliography II.

Morel-Fatio, Alfred Paul Victor. "Social and Historical Background," in *Cervantes Across the Centuries*. Edited by Angel Flores and Maír José Benardete. New York, 1947, pp. 101-27.

Morera y Galicia, Magín. See Bibliography III, 1905.

Morón-Arroyo, Ciriaco. "Cooperative Mimesis: Don Quixote and Sancho Panza," *Diacritics*, 8 (1978), 75-86. (This review-article of César Bandera's *Mimesis conflictiva: ficción literaria y violencia en Cervantes y Calderón* has little to do with Sancho.)

Morosini, Marco. See Bibliography III, 1680.

Motteux, Peter Anthony. Translator. See Bibliography III, 1700, Cervantes.

Murillo, Luis Andrés. *The Golden Dial: Temporal Configuration in "Don Quijote"*. Oxford, 1975. See also Bibliography III, 1978, Cervantes.

Niehus, Edward L. "Quixote Figures in the Novels of Smollet," *Durham University Journal*, 40 (1979), 233-43.

Novitsky, Pavel I. "Thematic Design," in *Cervantes Across the Centuries*. Edited by Angel Flores and Maír José Benardete. New York, 1947, pp. 239-45.

Oelschläger, Victor Rudolph Bernhardt. See Bibliography II.

Ortega y Gasset, José. *Meditaciones del "Quijote"*. 1914.

Ostrovski, Aleksandr Nicolaievich. See Bibliography III, 1870.

Oudin, César. Translator. See Bibliography III, 1614, Cervantes.

Pabón, Núñez, Lucio. See Bibliography II.

Papini, Giovanni. "Don Chisciotte dell'inganno," *La Voce*, 8 (1916), 193-205.

————. "Cervantes" in *Stroncature*. 5th edition. Florence, 1920, pp. 347-57. First published 1916.

Pellegrini, Silvio. Editor. De Lollis, Cesare.

Pelorson, J. M. See Bibliography II.

Pérez Capo, Felipe. *El "Quijote" en el teatro: Repertorio cronológico de 290 producciones escénicas relacionadas con la inmortal obra de Cervantes*. Barcelona, 1947.

Perier. See Bibliography III, 1905.

Petrov, Dmitri Konstanovich (Review of vol. II of L. Yu. Shepelevich's *'Don Kikhot" Servantesa, Zhizn Servantesa i yego proizvedenia*, in *Zhurnal Ministerstva Narodago Prosveschenia* (1904), pp. 163-79).

Philidor, François. See Bibliography III, 1762.

Pilon, Frederick. See Bibliography III, 1785.

Pitollet, Camille. See Bibliography II.

Poinsinet, Antoine Alexandre Henri. See Bibliography III, 1762.

Pope, Alexander, See Bibliography III, 1711, 1728, 1731.

Poquelin, Jean Baptiste. See Bibliography III, 1670, Molière.

Quevedo y Villegas, Francisco de. See Bibliography III, 1616.

Quilter, Daniel Edward. "The Image of the *Quijote* in the Seventeenth Century." Unpublished dissertation, University of Illinois, 1962.

Raysor, Thomas Middleton. Editor. Coleridge, Samuel Taylor.

Redondo, Augustin. See Bibliography II.

Riley, Edward Calverley. *Cervantes's Theory of the Novel*. Oxford, 1964. First published 1962.

Rodríguez Marín, Francisco. *El "Quijote" y don Quijote en América*. Madrid, 1911.

Rondani, A. See Bibliography II.

Romera-Navarro, Miguel. *Interpretación pictórica del "Quijote" por Doré*. Madrid, 1946.

Romero Flores, Hipólito R. See Bibliography II.

Rosset, François de. Translator. See Bibliography III, 1618, Cervantes.

Rossi, Giuseppe Carlo. "Una 'fantasia' italiana su *Don Chisciotte*," *Hispano-Italic Studies*, 2 (1979), 87-92.

—————. "Interpretaciones cervantinas en la literatura italiana del siglo XVIII," *Actas del II Simposio sobre el P. Feijóo, 1976*. Forthcoming.

Rousseau, Jean-Jacques. See Bibliography III, 1761.

Rubio García, Luis. See Bibliography II.

Ruskin, John. *Modern Painters*. 5 vols. 1843-1860. Vol. I (1843).

Saint-Amant, Marc-Antoine. See Bibliography III, 17th Century.

Saint-Just, Louis Antoine Léon de. See Bibliography III, c. 1790.

Sainz, Fernando. See Bibliography II.

Sánchez y Escribano, Federico. See Bibliography II.

Santos, Joseph. See Bibliography III, 1776.

Savj-López, Paolo. *Cervantes*. Naples, 1913.

Scarron, Paul. See Bibliography III, 1645, 1646.

Schevill, Rudolph. *Master Spirits of Literature: Cervantes*. London, 1919.

Schürr, Friedrich. "Cervantes y el romanticismo," *Anales Cervantinos,* 1 (1951), 41-70.

Sckommodau, Hans. See Bibliography II.

Sebreli, Juan José. Translator. Lukács, Georg Szegedi.

Sedgwick, Jr., Henry Dwight. "Don Quixote," *Atlantic Monthly,* 77 (1896), 256-64.

Shelton, Thomas. Translator. See Bibliography III, 1612, 1620, Cervantes.

Shepelevich, Lev Ylianovich. *"Don Kikhot" Servantesa, Zhizn Servantesa i yego proizvedenia.* 2 vols. 1901-1903.

———. "Trekhsotletie *Don Kikhota* Servantesa," *Vestnik Yevropy,* 223 (1905), 328-40.

Shirley, James. See Bibliography III, 1633.

Silva, Antonio José da. See Bibliography III, 1733.

Skinner, J. L. "Changing Interpretations of *Don Quixote* from *Hudibras* to *Pickwick.*" Unpublished dissertation, Cambridge, 1973.

Sletsjöe, Leif. See Bibliography II.

Smollet, Tobias George. See Bibliography III, 1760.

Socorro, Manuel. See Bibliography II.

Sorel, Charles. See Bibliography III, 1627.

Sterne, Laurence. See Bibliography III, 1760.

Suárez, Marco Fidel. See Bibliography II.

Téllez, Gabriel. See Bibliography III, 1611, 1612, 1622, 1638, Molina, Tirso de.

Tharpe, Dorothy. See Bibliography II.

Tolkien, John Ronald Reuel. See Bibliography III, 1954.

Tubino, Francisco María. "¿Necesita el *Quijote* comentarios?" In *Cervantes y el "Quijote": estudios críticos.* Madrid, 1872, pp. 197-218.

Turgenev, Ivan Sergeievich. "Hamlet i Don Kikhot." 1860.

Turkevich, Ludmilla Buketoff. *Cervantes in Russia.* Princeton, 1950.

Unamuno y Jugo, Miguel de. *Vida de Don Quijote y Sancho según Miguel de Cervantes Saavedra, explicada y comentada por Miguel de Unamuno.* 6th Austral edition. Buenos Aires, 1945. First published 1905.

Urbina, Eduardo. See Bibliography II.

Valdivielso, Josef de. See Bibliography III, 1622.

Vega Carpio, Lope Félix de. See Bibliography III, 1611, 1618, 1635.

Vélez de Guevara, Juan. See Bibliography III, 1675.

Viardot, Louis. Translator. See Bibliography III, 1863, Cervantes.

Voltaire [pseud. of François Marie Arouet]. *Dictionnaire philosophique.* 1764.

Wagner, Horst Ernst. "Zur Frage der Erzähleinschübe im *Don Quijote* und in den *Pickwick Papers*," *Arcadia,* 9 (1974), 1-22.

Waller, Alfred Rayney. Editor. See Bibliography III, 17th Century, Butler, Samuel.

Warburton, William. Editor. See Bibliography III, 1731, Pope, Alexander.

Wellek, René. *Immanuel Kant in England 1793-1838.* Princeton, 1931.

Welsh, Alexander. "Waverly, Pickwick, and Don Quixote," *Nineteenth-century Fiction,* 22 (1967-68), 19-30.

Willis, Raymond Smith. See Bibliography II.

Wilson, Edward Meryon. "Edmund Gayton on Don Quixote, Andrés, and Juan Haldudo," *Comparative Literature,* 2 (1950), 64-72.

Zaldumbide, Gonzalo. See Bibliography III, 1895, Montalvo, Juan.

Zeno, Apostolo. See Bibliography III, 1727.

BIBLIOGRAPHY II

Sancho Criticism

Allen, John Jay. "The Governorship of Sancho and Don Quijote's Chivalric Career," *Revista Hispánica Moderna,* 38 (1974-1975), 141-52.

Alonso, Amado. "Las prevaricaciones idiomáticas de Sancho," *Nueva Revista de Filología Hispánica,* 2 (1948), 1-20. Reprinted in *Don Quijote, Forschung und Kritik.* Darmstadt, 1968, pp. 37-80.

Alonso, Dámaso. "Sancho-Quijote, Sancho-Sancho," *Homenaje a Cervantes,* 2 vols. (Valencia, 1950), II, pp. 5-63. Reprinted in *Del Siglo de Oro a este siglo de siglas.* Madrid, 1962, pp. 9-19.

Aubrun, Charles Vincent. "Sancho Panza, paysan pour de rire, paysan pour de vrai," *Revista Canadiense de Estudios Hispánicos,* 1 (1976), 16-29.

Aveleyra Arroyo de Anda, Teresa. "Un hombre llamado Sancho Panza," *Nueva Revista de Filología Hispánica,* 22 (1973), 1-16.

Bleznick, Donald William. "Don Quijote's Advice to Governor Sancho Panza," *Hispania,* 40 (1957), 62-65.

Blumenfeld, Walter. "Don Quijote y Sancho Panza como tipos psicológicos," *Revista de las Indias,* 2nd Series, No. 38 (1942), pp. 338-68.

Brantley, Franklin O. "Sancho's Ascent into the Spheres," *Hispania,* 53 (1970), 37-45.

Burke, Ulick Ralph. *Sancho Panza's Proverbs, and Others which Occur in "Don Quixote": With a Literal English Translation, Notes, and an Introduction.* London: Whittingham and Co., 1892.

Cavestany y González Nandín, Juan Antonio. "Sobre una frase oscura de Sancho Panza," *Anales Cervantinos,* 11 (1972), 163-69. [Meaning of *adminícula.*]

Close, Anthony J. "Sancho Panza: Wise Fool," *Modern Language Review,* 68 (1973), 344-57.

Coy, José Luis. "'Incitado y movido del ejemplo de su amo': deseo y mimetismo en el *Quijote*," *The American Hispanist*, 3 (1977), 6-10. [This article only repeats commonplaces.]

De Andrea, Peter Frank. "El 'gobierno de la ínsula Barataria', *Speculum Principis* cervantino," *Filosofía y Letras*, 13, No. 26 (1947), 241-57.

De Chasca, Edmund Villela. "Sancho-Sanchuelo, Sancho-Sancho, Sancho-Sanchísimo," *Estudios literarios de hispanistas norteamericanos dedicados a Helmut Hatzfeld con motivo de su 80 aniversario* (Barcelona, 1974), pp. 73-86.

Deutsch, Helene. "Don Quijote und Donquijotismo," *Almanach der Psychoanalyse*, 10 (1935), 151-60.

Engelbert, Jo Anne. "A Sancho for Saint Francis," *Hispania*, 46 (1963), 287-89.

Flores, R. M. "Sancho's Fabrications: A Mirror of the Development of His Imagination," *Hispanic Review*, 38 (1970), 174-82.

—————. "Playing Chess in *Don Quixote*," *Romance Notes*, 22 (1981), 202-07.

Hendrix, William Samuel. "Sancho Panza and the Comic Types of the Sixteenth Century," *Homenaje a Menéndez Pidal: Miscelánea de estudios lingüísticos e históricos*, 3 vols. (Madrid, 1925), II, pp. 485-94.

Hilborn, Harry Warren. "Lo subconsciente en la psicología de Sancho Panza," *Studia Iberica, Festschrift für Hans Flasche* (Bern-Munich, 1973), pp. 267-80.

Joly, Monique. "Ainsi parlait Sancho Pança," *Les Langues Néo-latines*, 69 (1975), 3-37.

—————. "Tres autores en busca de un personaje: Cervantes, Avellaneda y Lesage frente a Sancho Panza," *Actas del Quinto Congreso Internacional de Hispanistas*, 2 vols. (Bordeaux, 1977), II, pp. 489-99.

López del Arco, A., editor. *Refranes de Sancho Panza. Aventuras y desventuras, malicias y agudezas del escudero de don Quijote*. Madrid, 1905.

López Fanego, Otilia. "Un ejemplo de la erudición de Sancho," *Anales Cervantinos* 16 (1977), 243-46. [Classical sources of the expression «más los pies que las manos».]

Mancing, Howard Terrance. "La retórica de Sancho Panza," *Actas del Séptimo Congreso Internacional de Hispanistas*. Forthcoming. [I was not able to consult this monograph.]

Márquez Villanueva, Francisco. "Sobre la génesis literaria de Sancho Panza," *Anales Cervantinos*, 7 (1958), 123-55. Reprinted in *Fuentes literarias cervantinas*. Madrid, 1973, pp. 20-94.

Molho, Maurice. "Raíz folklórica de Sancho Panza," *Cervantes: Raíces folklóricas*. Madrid, 1976, pp. 215-336.

Moore, John Aiken. "The Idealism of Sancho Panza," *Hispania*, 41 (1958), 73-76.

Morón-Arroyo, Ciriaco. See Bibliography I.

Oelschläger, Victor Rudolph Bernhardt. "Sancho's Zest for the Quest," *Hispania*, 35 (1952), 18-24.

Pabón Núñez, Lucio. "Sancho, o la exaltación del pueblo español," *Cuadernos Hispanoamericanos*, 58 (1964), 541-80.

Pelorson, J. M. "Le Discours des armes et des 'lettres' et l'épisode de Barataria," *Les Langues Néo-latines*, 69 (1975), 40-58.

Pitollet, Camille. "Sur un jugement rendu par Sancho Panza dans son île," *Bulletin Hispanique*, 39 (1937), 105-19. [The two old men and the hollow cane filled with gold coins.]

Redondo, Augustin. "Tradición carnavalesca y creación literaria: Del personaje de Sancho Panza al episodio de la ínsula Barataria en el *Quijote*," *Bulletin Hispanique*, 80 (1978), 39-70.

Romero Flores, Hipólito R. *Biografía de Sancho Panza, filósofo de la sensatez*. Barcelona, 1952. Second edition, 1955.

Rondani, Alberto. *A proposito di Sancho Panza e Don Abbondio*. 1905. [I was not able to consult this monograph.]

Rubio García, Luis. "La ínsula Barataria," *Estudios literarios dedicados al profesor Mariano Baquero Goyanes*. Murcia, 1974, pp. 639-53. [The *ínsula* is an out-of-the-way, inland hamlet located near the ducal palace, and Barataria stands for *fraude, falsedad, engaño*.]

Sainz, Fernando. "Don Quijote educador de Sancho," *Hispania*, 34 (1951), 363-65.

Sánchez Escribano, Federico. "Sancho Panza y su cultura popular: Un aspecto de sociología cervantina," *Asomante*, 3 (1948), 33-40.

Sckommodau, Hans. "Insula: Zu einem Abenteuer Sancho Panzas," *Die Neueren Sprachen*, 2nd Series, 13 (1964), 512-25.

————. "Die *Insula Barataria*, die *Insula Firme* und das Schloss Chambord," *Beiträge zur Romanischen Philologie*. Berlin, 1967, pp. 92-104.

Sletsjöe, Leif. *Sancho Panza, hombre de bien*. Madrid, 1961.

Socorro, Manuel. *La ínsula de Sancho en el reino de Don Quijote*. Las Palmas, 1947 [cover, 1948].

Suárez, Marco Fidel. "Sancho Panza," *Cervantes en Colombia*. Edited by Eduardo Caballero Calderón. Madrid, 1948, pp. 219-40.

Tharpe, Dorothy. "The 'Education' of Sancho as Seen in His Personal References," *Modern Language Journal*, 45 (1961), 244-48.

Urbina, Eduardo. "Sancho Panza 'escudero sin par': Parodia y creación en *Don Quijote* (1605, 1615)." Unpublished dissertation, University of California at Berkeley. 1979.

————. "Sancho Panza y Gandalín, escuderos," *Cervantes and the Renaissance*. Easton, Pennsylvania, 1980, pp. 113-24.

————. "El enano artúrico en la génesis literaria de Sancho Panza," *Actas del Séptimo Congreso Internacional de Hispanistas*. Forthcoming.

Willis, Raymond Smith. "Sancho Panza: Prototype for the Modern Novel," *Hispanic Review*, 37 (1969), 207-27.

BIBLIOGRAPHY III

Works of Fiction (listed in chronological order)

1605. Cervantes Saavedra, Miguel de. *El ingenioso hidalgo don Quixote de la Mancha. Con Privilegio, en Madrid.* Madrid: Juan de la Cuesta, 1605.

———. *El ingenioso hidalgo don Quixote de la Mancha. Con priuilegio de Castilla, Aragon, y Portugal.* Madrid: Juan de la Cuesta, 1605.

1608. Cervantes. *Le Curieux impertinent.* Translated by Nicolas Baudouin. Paris: Jean Richer, 1608.

1611. Molina, Tirso de. *El cobarde más valiente.* 1611.

———. *La mujer que manda en casa.* 1611.

Vega Carpio, Lope Félix de. *Barlán y Josafá.* 1611.

1612. Cervantes. *The History of the Valorous and Wittie Knight-Errant, Don-Quixote of the Mancha.* Translated by Thomas Shelton. London: E. Blounte, 1612.

Molina, Tirso de. *No le arriendo la ganancia.* 1612.

1613. Cervantes. *Rinconete y Cortadillo.* 1613. [*Novelas ejemplares*]

1614. Anonymous. *Le Ballet de Don Quichot.* 1614?

Cervantes. *L'Ingénieux Don Quixote de la Manche.* Translated by César Oudin. Paris: J. Foüet, 1614.

Fernández de Avellaneda, Alonso [pseud.]. *El Quijote: Segundo tomo del ingenioso hidalgo don Quijote de la Mancha, que contiene su tercera salida y es la quinta parte de sus aventuras.* Second Aguilar edition. Madrid, 1947. [First edition. Tarragona: Felipe Roberto, 1614]

1615. Cervantes. *Segunda parte del ingenioso cavallero don Quixote de la Mancha.* Madrid: Juan de la Cuesta, 1615.

———. *Entremés del rufián viudo.* 1615. [Comedias y entremeses]

———. *Entremés de la elección de los alcaldes de Daganzo.* 1615. [*Comedias y entremeses*]

1616. Anonymous. *L'Entrée en France de Don Quichot de la Manche.* Between 1616 and 1625.

Quevedo y Villegas, Francisco de. *Testamento de don Quijote.* 1616.

1617. Cervantes. *Isaac Winkelfelder und Jobst von der Schneid.* Anonymous Germanized version of *Rinconete y Cortadillo.* 1617.

———. *Unzeitiger Fürwitz.* Anonymous German translation of *El curioso impertinente.* 1617.

1618. Cervantes. *Seconde Partie de l'Histoire de l'Ingénieux, et Redoutable Chevalier Dom-Quichot de la Manche.* Translated by François de Rosset. Paris: V. J. du Clou et D. Moreau, 1618.

Vega Carpio, Lope Félix de. *La mejor enamorada, la Magdalena.* 1618.

——————. *El Antecristo.* 1618.

1620. Cervantes. *The History of Don-Quichote. The First Parte. (The Second Part of the History of the Valorous and Witty Knight-Errant, Don Quixote of the Mancha).* 2 vols. London: E. Blounte, 1620.

Fletcher, John. *The Double Marriage.* In *The Works of Beaumont and Fletcher,* edited by Alexander Dyce. 11 vols. London: Edward Moxon, 1843-1846. Vol. VI (1844). First staged c. 1620.

1622. Molina, Tirso de. *Antona García.* 1622.

Valdivielso, Josef de. *El hijo pródigo.* 1622.

1627. Drayton, Michael. *Nimphidia, The Court of Fayrie.* Edited by Herbert Francis Brett Brett-Smith. Oxford, 1921. First published 1627.

Sorel, Charles. *Le Berger extravagant.* 1627.

1630. D'Avenant, William. *The Cruell Brother.* London: A. Mathews, 1630.

1633. Calderón de la Barca, Pedro. *La devoción de la cruz.* 1633.

Cramail, Adrien de Montluc, Count of. *La Comédie de proverbes.* 1633.

Shirley, James. *The Triumph of Peace.* London: John Norton, 1633.

1635. Vega Carpio, Lope Félix de. *Audiencias del rey don Pedro.* 1635.

——————. *Auto del Nacimiento de Nuestro Salvador.* 1635.

1638. Molina, Tirso de. *El laberinto de Creta.* 1638.

1641. Guérin de Bouscal, Guyon. *Le Gouvernement de Sancho Pansa.* 1641.

1645. Scarron, Paul. *Jodelet ou le Maître valet.* 1645.

1646. Scarron, Paul. *Les Trois Dorotées ou le Jodelet souffleté.* 1646.

1648. Cervantes. *Don Kichote de la Mantzscha, Das ist: Juncker Harnisch auss Fleckenland.* Frankfurt: Thomas Matthias Götz 1648. *Erster Theil der abenthewerlichen Geschichte des scharpffsinnigen Lehns- und Ritter-sassen Juncker Harnisches auss Fleckenland.* Hofgeismar: Salomon Schadewitz, 1648. Translated by Pahsch Bastel von der Sohle [pseud. of Joaquim Caesar from Halle].

1650. Anonymous. *El visir de la Perdularia.* 1650.

1654. Gayton, Edmund. *Pleasant Notes upon Don Quixot.* London: n.p., 1654.

1655. Fernández, Marcos. *Olla podrida a la española.* 1655.

1658. Anonymous. *The History of Don Quixote.* London? 1658?

1659. Fourcroy, Bonaventure. *Sancho Pança.* 1659.

1660. Molière. *Sganarelle ou le Cocu imaginaire.* 1660.

1661. Molière. *Les Fâcheux.* 1661.

1666. Molière. *Le Misanthrope.* 1666.

1675. Vélez de Guevara, Juan. *Mancebón de los palacios.* 1675.

1670. Molière. *Le Bourgeois gentilhomme.* In *OEuvres de Molière,* edited by Eugène André Despois and Paul Mesnard. 13 vols. Paris: Librairie Hachette, 1873-1900. Vol. VIII (1883). First staged 1670.

1680. Anonymous. *El rey de los tiburones.* 1680.

Morosini, Marco. *Don Chisciotte della Mancia.* 1680.

1687. Cleveland, John. *The Works of Mr. John Cleveland.* 1687.

1694. Dufresny, Charles. *Sancho Pança.* 1694.

D'Urfey, Thomas. *The Comical History of Don Quixote.* London: Samuel Briscoe, 1694.

—————. *The Comical History of Don Quixote. Part the Second.* London: Samuel Briscoe, 1694.

1696. D'Urfey, Thomas. *The Comical History of Don Quixote. The Third Part. With the Marriage of Mary the Buxome.* London: Samuel Briscoe, 1696.

1698. Gigli, Girolamo. *Il "Don Chisciotte", ovvero Un pazzo guarisce l'altro.* 1698.

17th Century
Anonymous. Discursos de la viuda de veinte y cuatro maridos. [17th Century]

Anonymous. "Fábula de Jesucristo y la Magdalena." [17th Century]

Butler, Samuel. "Wit and Folly," in *Samuel Butler: Characters and Passages from Note-Books.* Edited by Alfred Rayney Waller. Cambridge, 1908. [17th Century]

D'Urfey, Thomas. *The Songs of Thomas D'Urfey.* Edited by Cyrus Lawrence Day. Cambridge, Massachusetts, 1933. [17th Century]

Lagniet, Jacques. *Les Advantures du fameaux Chevalier Dom Quixot de la Manche et de Sancho Pansa, son escuyer.* [Engravings] [17th Century]

Saint-Amant, Marc-Antoine. "La Chambre du débauché." [17th Century]

1700. Anonymous. *Mascarade de don Quichotte.* 1700.

Cervantes. English translation of *Don Quixote.* Translated by Peter Anthony Motteux. 1700-1712.

1711. Pope, Alexander. *An Essay On Criticism.* 1711. Published anonymously.

1713. Gaultier. *Basile et Quitterie.* 1713?

1714. Anonymous. *Les Regrets de Sancho-Pança sur la mort de son asne: ou Dialogue de Sancho et de Don Quichotte sur le même sujet, et autres Nouvelles en vers.* 1714.

1722. Anonymous. *Suite nouvelle et veritable de l'histoire et des avantures de l'incomparable Don Quichotte de la Manche. Traduite d'un Manuscrit Espagnol de Cide-Hamet Benengely son veritable historien.* 6 vols. Paris, 1722-1726.

1727. Zeno, Apostolo. *Don Chisciotte in corte della duchessa.* 1727?

1728. Pope, Alexander. *Dunciad.* 1728.

1731. Pope, Alexander. "Moral Essays, Epistle IV," in *The Works of Alexander Pope Esq.,* edited by William Warburton. 9 vols. London: Printed for J. and P. Knapton, 1751. Vol. III. First published 1731.

1733. Silva, Antonio José da. *Vida do grande D. Quixote de la Mancha e do gordo Sancho Pança.* 1733.

1734. Fielding, Henry. *Don Quixote in England. A Comedy. As it is Acted at the New Theatre in the Hay-Market.* London: Printing-Office in Wild-Court, 1734.

1736. Boyer, Jean Baptiste de. *Lettres juives.* 1736.

1742. Ayres, James. *Sancho at Court: or, The Mock Governor.* 1742.

Fielding, Henry. *Joseph Andrews.* 1742.

1743. Favart, Charles. *Don Quichotte chez la Duchesse.* 1743.

1749. Fielding, Henry. *Tom Jones.* 1749.

1752. Lennox, Charlotte. *The Female Quixote, or The Adventures of Arabella.* 1752.

1760. Smollett, Tobias. *The Adventures of Sir Launcelot Greaves.* In *The Works of Tobias Smollett,* edited by William Ernest Henley. 12 vols. Westminster, 1899-1901. Vol. X (1900). First published 1760-1762.

Sterne, Laurence. *Tristram Shandy.* 1760-1767.

1761. Rousseau, Jean-Jacques. *La Nouvelle Héloïse.* 1761.

1762. Philidor, François, and Antoine Poinsinet. *Sancho Pança dans son Isle.* 1762.

1766. Brooke, Henry. *The Fool of Quality; or, The History of Henry Earl of Moreland.* 5 vols. London: W. Johnston, 1766-1770.

1772. Anonymous. *Squire Badger.* 1772.

1773. Graves, Richard. *The Spiritual Quixote: or, The Summer's Ramble of Mr. Geoffry Wildgoose.* 3 vols. London: Printed for J. Dodsley, 1773.

Lorenzi, Giovanni Battista. *L'idolo cinese.* 1773.

1774. Anonymous. *O grande governador da Ilha dos Lagartos.* 1774.

1775. Cervantes. German translation of *Don Quixote.* Translated by Friedrich Justin Bertuch. 1775-1777.

1776. Santos, Joseph. *Las caperuzas de Sancho.* 1776.

1785. Pilon, Frederick. *Barataria: or, Sancho Turn'd Governor.* Dublin: Printed for Wilkinson et alii, 1785.

1787. Meli, Giovanni. *Don Chisciotti e Sanciu Panza.* 1787.

1789. Boissel and Stanislas Champein. *Le Nouveau Don Quichotte.* 1789.

1790. Saint-Just, Louis Antoine Léon de. *Organt.* c. 1790.

1792. Brackenridge, Hugh Henry. *Modern Chivalry: containing the Adventures of Captain John Farrago and Teague O'Regan, His Servant.* Edited by Lewis Gaston Leary. New Haven, Connecticut, 1965. First published 1792-1805.

1799. Cervantes. *Don Quichotte de la Manche.* Translated by Jean Pierre Claris de Florian. Paris: P. Didot l'Aîné, 1799.

Cuvelier de Trie, Jean Guillaume Antoine. *L'Empire de la folie: ou la Mort et l'apothéose de Don Quichotte.* 1799.

18th Century

Anonymous. *Insula Barataria: o Todo el reino es una quinta.* n. d. [18th Century].

—————. *Sancho Panza*. [18th Century].

1800. Anonymous. *Sancho Panza en su ínsula*. c. 1800.

1807. Brazier, Nicolas. *Rodomont: ou le Petit Dom Quichotte*. 1807.

Goldmann and Jean Aude. *Bédeno: ou le Sancho de Bisnagar*. 1807.

1812. Maqueda, José. *Sancho Panza en su gobierno*. 1812.

1816. Cuvelier de Trie, Jean Guillaume Antoine. *Sancho dans l'Isle de Barataria*. 1816.

1836. Dickens, Charles. *The Posthumous Papers of The Pickwick Club*. Oxford, 1964. First published in installments 1836; first edition 1837.

1840. *Master Humphrey's Clock*, in *"The Mystery of Edwin Drood" and "Master Humphrey's Clock"*, Charles Dickens Centennial Edition, Edito-Service S.A., Geneva, n.d. First published in installments 1840.

1863. Cervantes. French translation of *Don Quixote*. Translated by Louis Viardot. 1863. Illustrated by Paul Gustave Doré.

1864. Larra y Wetoret, Luis Mariano de. *La ínsula Barataria*. 1864.

1866. Cervantes. Russian translation of *Don Quixote*. Translated by V. Karelin. 1866.

1870. Ostrovski, Aleksandr Nicolaievich. *The Forest*. 1870.

1881. Molas y Casas, Juan. *Sancho Panza*. 1881.

1895. Montalvo, Juan. *Capítulos que se le olvidaron a Cervantes: Ensayo de imitación de un libro inimitable*. Edited by Gonzalo Zaldumbide. Mexico City, 1972. First published 1895.

1900. Anonymous. *El gran Sancho Panza*. c. 1900.

1901. Abaurre y Mesa, José. *Historia de varios sucesos ocurridos en la aldea después de la muerte del ingenioso hidalgo don Quijote de la Mancha*. Madrid, 1901.

1904. Calandrelli, M. *Sancho en la ínsula Barataria*. 1904.

1905. Almeida, Filinto de. Two sonnets in *Discursos pronunciados na sessão commemorativa do tricentenario da publicação do D. Quixote*. 1905.

Araujo, Joaquim de. "Visões do Quixote" [a short poem] in *Discursos pronunciados na sessão commemorativa do tricentenario da publicação do D. Quixote*. 1905.

Morera y Galicia, Magín. *Un desgobernado gobernador*. 1905.

Perier. *La ínsula Barataria*. 1905.

1929. Cervantes. *Khitroumny idalgo Don Kikhot Lamanchski*. 2 vols. 1929.

1933. Camp, Jean. *Sancho*. Paris, 1933.

1953. Kazantzakis, Nikos. *Saint Francis*. Translated by P. A. Bien. New York, 1962. First Greek edition 1953.

1954. Tolkien, John Ronald Reuel. *The Lord of the Rings*. 3 vols. 2nd Houghton Mifflin Company edition. Boston, 1967. First published 1954-1955.

19611.. Larraz López, José. *¡Don Quijancho, maestro! (Biografía fabulosa)*. Ma

1969. Fowles, John. *The French Lieutenant's Woman*. Boston, 1969.

1978. Cervantes. *Don Quijote de la Mancha*. Edited by Luis Andrés Murillo. 3 vols. Madrid: Clásicos Castalia, 1978.

1980. Chapman, Robin. *The Duchess's Diary*. London, 1980.

Appendixes

1. Occupation and Activities
2. Means and Possessions
3. Home and Family
4. Stupidity, Simplicity, and Rusticity
5. Love for His Ass
6. Laziness
7. Soft Spot for Wine
8. Ambitions and Aspirations
9. Cowardice
10. Artfulness and Humor
11. Don Quixote and Sancho as Opposites
12. Sancho a Thief, a Heartless Highwayman, a Bigoted Racist, a Bully
13. Physique and Appearance
14. Education
15. Exaggerations
16. Desire for Wealth
17. Sancho Praised or His Advice Accepted
18. Catholicism
19. Complaints
20. Love of Food
21. Gullibility
22. Quixotification
23. Wordplay
24. Sexual Temperance
25. Memory
26. Lies
27. Opinion of, and Attitude towards, Don Quixote
28. From *loco* to *gracioso*
29. Homesickness and Eagerness to Continue Their Adventures
30. Sayings and Proverbs
31. Sancho Weeps
32. References to Salary
33. Compassion
34. Loquacity

APPENDIX 1

OCCUPATION AND ACTIVITIES

1. "[Don Quijote] determinó volver a su casa...haciendo cuenta de recebir [como escudero] a un labrador vecino suyo" (I, 4, 94).
2. "Solicitó don Quijote a un labrador vecino suyo" (I, 7, 125).
3. "Sancho Panza, que así se llamaba el labrador...asentó por escudero de su vecino" (I, 7, 125-26).
4. "La ciencia que aprendí cuando era pastor" (I, 20, 239).
5. "Un tiempo fui muñidor de una cofradía" (I, 21, 264).
6. "Id, [Sancho],...a labrar vuestros pegujares" (II, 2, 53).
7. "Cuando yo servía...[al labrador] Tomé Carrasco,...dos ducados ganaba cada mes, amén de la comida" (II, 28, 258).
8. "[Yo] había ido por aquel tiempo a segar a Tembleque" (II, 31, 280).
9. "Labrador soy" (II, 32, 296).
10. "Podría ser que...supiese más [del oficio de gobernador] que de la labor del campo, en que me he criado" (II, 33, 300).
11. "[Si te hinchas] como la rana que quiso igualarse con el buey,...vendrá a ser feos pies de la rueda de tu locura la consideración de haber guardado puercos en tu tierra.

    —Así es verdad—respondió Sancho—, pero fue cuando muchacho; pero después, algo hombrecillo, gansos fueron los que guardé, que no puercos" (II, 42, 358).
12. "No te desprecies de decir que vienes de labradores" (II, 42, 358).
13. "Fui prioste en mi lugar" (II, 43, 363).
14. *"Sacado de gobernar un hato de cabras, no pueden imaginar para qué gobierno pueda ser bueno* [Sancho]" (II, 52, 437).
15. *"¿Quién podía pensar que un pastor de cabras había de venir a ser gobernador de ínsulas?"* (II, 52, 438).
16. "Mejor se me entiende a mí de arar y cavar, podar y ensarmentar las viñas" (II, 53, 444).

APPENDIX 2

MEANS AND POSSESSIONS

1. "[Don Quijote hizo] cuenta de recebir [como escudero] a un labrador vecino suyo, que era pobre y con hijos" (I, 4, 94).
2. "Si es que [el] título [de hombre de bien] se puede dar al que es pobre" (I, 7, 125).
3. "[Sancho dijo que]...pensaba llevar un asno que tenía" (I, 7, 126).

4. "Las alforjas que hoy me faltan, con todas mis alhajas, ¿son de otro que del [hijo de mi padre]?" (I, 18, 225).
5. "Aunque pobre,...no debo nada a nadie" (I, 47, 563).
6. "[No] tengo tantos bienes que pueda ser envidiado" (II, 8, 94).
7. "A mí no me falta [una caña de pescar]—respondió Sancho—: verdad es que no tengo rocín; pero tengo un asno" (II, 13, 129).
8. "Abre los ojos, deseada patria, y mira que vuelve a ti Sancho Panza...no muy rico" (II, 72, 580).

Appendix 3

Home and Family

1. "[Don Quijote hizo] cuenta de recebir [como escudero] a un labrador vecino suyo, que era pobre y con hijos" (I, 4, 94).
2. "[Sancho] dejó su mujer y hijos...[y] sin despedirse [de ellos], ni don Quijote de su ama y sobrina, una noche se salieron del lugar" (I, 7, 126).
3. "Aunque lloviese Dios reinos sobre la tierra, ninguno asentaría bien sobre la cabeza de Mari Gutiérrez. Sepa, señor, que no vale dos maravedís para reina; condesa le caerá mejor, y aun Dios y ayuda" (I, 7, 128).
4. "Sabiendo [Sancho] quién era [don Quijote] y habiéndole conocido desde su nacimiento" (I, 13, 177).
5. "Nunca tal nombre ni tal princesa había llegado jamás a su noticia, aunque [Sancho] vivía tan cerca del Toboso" (I, 13, 177).
6. "Destas lágrimas y determinación tan honrada...saca el autor desta historia que debía de ser bien nacido, y, por lo menos, cristiano viejo" (I, 20, 247).
7. "Me entristece el haberme de apartar de ti y de mis hijos,...pues [la alegría] que tengo va mezclada con la tristeza del dejarte" (II, 5, 73).
8. "Sanchico tiene ya quince años cabales, y es razón que vaya a la escuela, si es que su tío el abad le ha de dejar hecho de la Iglesia. Mirad también que Mari Sancha, vuestra hija, no se morirá si la casamos; que me va dando barruntos que desea tanto tener marido como vos deseáis veros con gobierno" (II, 5, 74).
9. "Séase [Mari Sancha] *señoría*, y venga lo que viniere" (II, 5, 75).
10. "Ya sabe todo el mundo...quién fueron los Panzas, de quien yo deciendo (II, 7, 90).
11. "Dos [hijos] tengo yo...que se pueden presentar al Papa en persona" (II, 13, 129).
12. "[Mari Sancha tiene] quince años, dos más a menos,...pero es tan grande como una lanza, y tan fresca como una mañana de abril, y tiene una fuerza de un ganapán" (II, 13, 129).
13. "Tuve en mi linaje por parte de mi padre los dos más excelentes mojones que en luengos años conoció la Mancha" (II, 13, 133).

14. "Dos linajes solos hay en el mundo, como decía una agüela mía, que son el tener y el no tener; aunque ella al del tener se atenía" (II, 20, 193-94).
15. "Quisiera haber oído lo que vuesa merced aquí ha dicho antes que me casara; que quizá dijera yo agora: «El buey suelto bien se lame».
   —¿Tan mala es tu Teresa, Sancho?—dijo don Quijote.
   —No es muy mala,...pero no es muy buena; a lo menos, no tan buena como yo quisiera.
   —Mal haces, Sancho,...en decir mal de tu mujer, que, en efecto, es madre de tus hijos.
   —No nos debemos nada,...que también ella dice mal de mí cuando se le antoja, especialmente cuando está celosa; que entonces súfrala el mesmo Satanás" (II, 22, 204-05).
16. "Es [Teresa] una bienaventurada, y a no ser celosa, no la trocara yo por la giganta Andandona" (II, 25, 236).
17. "No...dejaba de ser hijo de mis padres, que eran honradísimos" (II, 27, 255).
18. "Por el siglo de todos mis pasados los Panzas" (II, 40, 339).
19. "Yo no tengo *don*, ni en todo mi linaje le ha habido: Sancho Panza me llaman a secas, y Sancho se llamó mi padre, y Sancho mi agüelo, y todos fueron Panzas, sin añadiduras de *dones* ni *donas*" (II, 45, 376).
20. "A Sancho le vinieron deseos y barruntos de casar al [hijo de Diego de la Llana] con Sanchica su hija, y determinó de ponerlo en plática a su tiempo (II, 49, 415).
21. "[Sanchica] mostraba ser de edad de catorce años, poco más a menos" (II, 50, 416).
22. "Teresa Panza...no era muy vieja, aunque mostraba pasar de los cuarenta, pero fuerte, tiesa, nervuda y avellanada" (II, 50, 417).
23. "Yo soy del linaje de los Panzas, que todos son testarudos" (II, 53, 445).
24. "¿Por ventura, cabeza,...volveré a ver a mi mujer y a mis hijos?" (II, 62, 516).
25. "[El nombre de Teresona] le vendrá bien con su gordura y con el propio que tiene" (II, 67, 549).
26. "[Sanchica] es de buen parecer" (II, 67, 550).
27. "Quiero [a Teresa] más que a las pestañas de mis ojos" (II, 70, 569).
28. "El amor de mis hijos y de mi mujer me hace que me muestre interesado" (II, 71, 571).
29. "Abrazó Sanchica a su padre, y preguntóle si traía algo,...y asiéndole de un lado del cinto, y su mujer de la mano, tirando su hija al rucio, se fueron a su casa" (II, 73, 583).

APPENDIX 4

STUPIDITY, SIMPLICITY, AND RUSTICITY

1. "[Sancho era] hombre de bien,...pero de muy poca sal en la mollera" (I, 7, 125).
2. "El pobre villano se determinó de salirse con él" (I, 7, 125).

3. "No se dejó de reír don Quijote de la simplicidad de su escudero" (I, 8, 131).
4. "Mucho mejor me sabe lo que como en mi rincón sin melindres ni respetos, aunque sea pan y cebolla, que los gallipavos de otras mesas donde me sea forzoso mascar despacio, beber poco, limpiarme a menudo, no estornudar ni toser si me viene gana, ni hacer otras cosas que la soledad y libertad traen consigo" (I, 11, 154).
5. "No esperaba yo otra cosa de tu buen discurso; mas no me maravillo, pues quizá estos golpes...te deben de tener turbado el entendimiento" (I, 20, 244).
6. "Le vino en voluntad y deseo de hacer lo que otro no pudiera hacer por él;...y echó al aire entrambas posaderas....Tornó otra vez a probar ventura, y sucedióle tan bien, que, sin más ruido ni alboroto...se halló libre de la carga que tanta pesadumbre le había dado" (I, 20, 245).
7. "Ten más cuenta con tu persona y con lo que debes a la mía" (I, 20, 246).
8. "Como villano ruin que sois, criado y nacido entre ellos" (I, 20, 249).
9. "Tienes el más corto entendimiento que tiene ni tuvo escudero" (I, 25, 306).
10. "Aunque de ingenio boto, muchas veces despuntas de agudo; mas, para que veas cuán necio eres tú..." (I, 25, 313).
11. "[Sancho] se echó entrambos puños a las barbas, y se arrancó la mitad de ellas, y...se dio media docena de puñadas en el rostro y en las narices, que se las bañó todas en sangre" (I, 26, 323).
12. "[Tornó a decir la carta] Sancho otras tres veces, y otras tantas volvió a decir otros tres mil disparates.... Decía esto...con tanto reposo, limpiándose de cuando en cuando las narices, y con tan poco juicio, que los dos se admiraron de nuevo" (I, 26, 324).
13. "[Al cura y al barbero] les sería de más gusto oír sus necedades" (I, 26, 325).
14. "Quedó...el cura admirado de su simplicidad" (I, 29, 363).
15. ¡Oh, qué necio y qué simple que eres!" (I, 31, 388).
16. "Ahora te digo, Sanchuelo, que eres el mayor bellacuelo,...ladrón vagamundo" (I, 37, 460).
17. "Eres un mentecato" (I, 37, 460).
18. "No os despechéis...de las sandeces que vuestro buen escudero ha dicho" (I, 46, 553).
19. "No quiso responder el barbero a Sancho, porque no descubriese con sus simplicidades lo que él y el cura tanto procuraban encubrir" (I, 47, 563).
20. "Le admiraba [al conónigo] la necedad de Sancho" (I, 50, 588).
21. "Habiendo recebido grande gusto de las simplicidades de Sancho" (I, 52, 602).
22. "Don Quijote, temeroso que Sancho se descosiese y desbuchase algún montón de maliciosas necedades,...le llamó" (II, 2, 53-54).
23. "Me maravillo...de la simplicidad del escudero" (II, 2, 54).
24. "Las locuras del señor sin las necedades del criado no valían un ardite" (II, 2, 54).
25. "El vulgo tiene a vuestra merced por grandísimo loco, y a mí por no menos mentecato" (II, 2, 56).

26. "El traductor desta historia...dice que [tiene este quinto capítulo] por apócrifo, porque en él habla Sancho Panza con otro estilo del que se podía prometer de su corto ingenio, y dice cosas tan sutiles, que no tiene por posible que él las supiese" (II, 5, 73).

27. "Estas razones que aquí va diciendo Sancho son las segundas por quien dice el tradutor que tiene por apócrifo este capítulo, que exceden a la capacidad de Sancho" (II, 5, 78).

28. "En tanto que Sancho Panza y su mujer Teresa Cascajo pasaron la impertinente referida plática..." (II, 6, 79).

29. "[Sansón confirmó a Sancho] por uno de los más solenes mentecatos de nuestros siglos" (II, 7, 91).

30. "[Sancho], aunque tonto, no andaba...muy fuera de camino" (II, 8, 92).

31. "Es verdad que soy algo malicioso, y que tengo mis ciertos asomos de bellaco; pero todo lo cubre y tapa la gran capa de la simpleza mía, siempre natural y nunca artificiosa" (II, 8, 94).

32. "Quisiera Sancho que [la noche] fuera del todo escura, por hallar en su escuridad disculpa de su sandez" (II, 9, 99).

33. "Todas o las más veces que Sancho quería hablar de oposición y a lo cortesano, acababa su razón con despeñarse del monte de su simplicidad al profundo [abismo] de su ignorancia" (II, 12, 122).

34. "Nunca he visto yo escudero—replicó el del Bosque—que se atreva a hablar donde habla su señor" (II, 12, 127).

35. "Aunque parezco hombre, soy una bestia para ser de la Iglesia" (II, 12, 128).

36. "Pareciéndole buena y santa [la vida de don Diego de Miranda] y que quien la hacía debía de hacer milagros, se arrojó [Sancho] del rucio, y con gran priesa le fue a asir del estribo derecho, y con devoto corazón y casi lágrimas le besó los pies una y muchas veces" (II, 16, 153).

37. "Vos, sí, [Sancho], que debéis de ser bueno, como vuestra simplicidad lo muestra" (II, 16, 154).

38. "Dime, animal, ¿qué sabes tú de clavos, ni de rodajas, ni de otra cosa ninguna? (II, 19, 181).

39. "Tus rústicos términos" (II, 20, 195).

40. "Rióse don Quijote de las rústicas alabanzas de Sancho" (II, 21, 196).

41. "Para preguntar necedades y responder disparates no he menester yo andar buscando ayuda de vecinos" (II, 22, 207).

42. "Espantóse el primo así del atrevimiento de Sancho Panza como de la paciencia de su amo...[que] palabras y razones le dijo Sancho, que merecían molerle a palos; porque realmente le pareció que había andado atrevidillo con su señor" (II, 24, 224).

43. "A trueco de que a vos no os duela nada, tendré yo por gusto el enfado que me dan vuestras impertinencias" (II, 28, 258).

44. "A trueco de verme sin tan mal escudero, holgáreme de quedarme pobre y sin blanca.... Éntrate, éntrate, malandrín, follón y vestiglo, que todo lo pareces.... En fin, como tú has dicho otras veces, no es la miel..., etcétera. Asno eres, y asno has de ser, y en asno has de parar cuando se te acabe el curso de la vida; que para mí tengo que antes llegará ella a su

último término que tú caigas y des en la cuenta de que eres bestia" (II, 28, 260).

45. "Yo confieso que para ser del todo asno no me falta más de la cola.... Vuestra merced...advierta que sé poco" (II, 28, 260-61).

46. "Rióse don Quijote de la interpretación que Sancho había dado al nombre y al cómputo y cuenta del cosmógrafo Ptolomeo" (II, 29, 264).

47. "Volvieron a sus bestias, y a ser bestias, don Quijote y Sancho" (II, 29, 267).

48. "Maguer era tonto, bien se le alcanzaba [a Sancho] que las acciones de su amo...eran disparates" (II, 30, 268).

49. "Mi escudero, que Dios maldiga, mejor desata la lengua para decir malicias que ata y cincha una silla" (II, 30, 271).

50. "Dime, truhán moderno y majadero antiguo: ¿parécete bien deshonrar y afrentar a una dueña tan venerada?... Por quien Dios es, Sancho, que te reportes, y que no descubras la hilaza de manera que caigan en la cuenta de que eres de villana y grosera tela tejido" (II, 31, 277).

51. "Bien será—dijo don Quijote—que vuestras grandezas manden echar de aquí a este tonto, que dirá mil patochadas" (II, 31, 279).

52. "Por mudar de plática y hacer que Sancho no prosiguiese con otros disparates, preguntó la duquesa a don Quijote que qué nuevas tenía de la señora Dulcinea" (II, 31, 281).

53. "Si yo fuera discreto, días ha que había de haber dejado a mi amo" (II, 33, 298).

54. "De mi ruin ingenio no se puede ni debe presumir que fabricase en un instante tan agudo embuste" (II, 33, 301).

55. "De lo que más la duquesa se admiraba era que la simplicidad de Sancho fuese tanta, que hubiese venido a creer ser verdad infalible que Dulcinea del Toboso estuviese encantada, habiendo sido él mesmo el encantador" (II, 34, 304).

56. "Dejen a este tonto, señores míos" (II, 34, 308).

57. "A estas razones respondió con estas disparatadas Sancho" (II, 35, 318).

58. "Aunque tonto, [Sancho], eres hombre verídico" (II, 41, 347).

59. "Tú, que para mí, sin duda alguna, eres un porro..." (II, 42, 357).

60. "[No eres] otra cosa que un costal lleno de refranes y de malicias" (II, 43, 365).

61. "[El traductor] pensó, como él dice, que... la gala y artificio que [las novelas intercaladas en la primera parte] en sí contienen, el cual se mostrara bien al descubierto cuando por sí solas, sin arrimarse...a las sandeces de Sancho, salieran a luz" (II, 44, 366).

62. "[Sancho] se las tenía tiesas a todos, maguera tonto, bronco y rollizo" (II, 49, 404).

63. "Andaban mezcladas sus palabras y sus acciones, con asomos discretos y tontos" (II, 51, 425).

64. "Yo soy un hombre que tengo más de mostrenco que de agudo" (II, 51, 426).

65. *"En este pueblo todos tienen a mi marido por un porro, y que sacado de gobernar un hato de cabras, no pueden imaginar para qué gobierno pueda ser bueno"* (II, 52, 437).

66. "Quería que vuestra merced me dijese qué es la causa por que dicen los españoles... «¡Santiago, y cierra España!» ¿Está por ventura España abierta, y de modo que es menester cerrarla, o qué ceremonia es ésta? —Simplísimo eres, Sancho" (II, 58, 474).
67. "¿Es posible, ¡oh Sancho!, que haya en todo el orbe alguna persona que diga que no eres tonto, aforrado de lo mismo, con no sé qué ribetes de malicioso y de bellaco?" (II, 58, 480).
68. "Bestia—dijo don Quijote—, ¿qué quieres que te respondan" (II, 62, 516).
69. "Dio cuenta... como la duquesa su mujer había dado a entender a Sancho que... verdaderamente estaba encantada Dulcinea; de que no poco se rió y admiró el bachiller, considerando la... agudeza y simplicidad de Sancho" (II, 70, 564).
70. "No estaban los duques dos dedos de parecer tontos, pues tanto ahínco ponían en burlarse de dos tontos" (II, 70, 565).
71. "Dijo Sancho tantos donaires y tantas malicias, que dejaron de nuevo admirados a los duques, así con su simplicidad como con su agudeza" (II, 70, 568).
72. "Sin saber yo las más veces lo que me digo, hago reír a cuantos me escuchan" (II, 72, 577).
73. "Déjate desas sandeces—dijo don Quijote" (II, 72, 580).
74. "Según que yo imagino, aunque tonto" (II, 73, 582).

APPENDIX 5

LOVE FOR HIS ASS

1. "[Sancho dijo que] pensaba llevar un asno que tenía muy bueno" (I, 7, 126).
2. "[Sancho llevaba] del cabestro a su jumento, perpetuo compañero de sus prósperas y adversas fortunas" (I, 20, 247).
3. "Quisiera [llevarme este asno], o, por lo menos, trocalle con este mio, que no me parece tan bueno" (I, 21, 257).
4. "[Sancho] puso su jumento a las mil lindezas, dejándole mejorado en tercio y quinto" (I, 21, 257).
5. "Sancho se puso tras su asno, y con él se defendía de la nube y pedrisco que sobre entrambos llovía" (I, 22, 276).
6. "[El] llanto que anoche hice por el rucio" (I, 25, 316).
7. "Miré por el jumento, y no le vi; acudiéronme lágrimas a los ojos, y hice una lamentación, que si no la puso el autor de nuestra historia, puede hacer cuenta que no puso cosa buena" (II, 4, 67).
8. "Os conviene tener cuenta... con el rucio, de manera que esté para armas tomar: dobladle los piensos, [dijo Sancho a Teresa]" (II, 5, 74).
9. "Cada vez que [Sancho] veía levantar las vejigas en el aire y caer sobre las ancas de su rucio eran para él tártagos y sustos de muerte, y antes quisiera que aquellos golpes se los dieran a él en las niñas de los ojos que en el más mínimo pelo de la cola de su asno" (II, 11, 118).
10. "Tengo un asno que vale dos veces más que el caballo de mi amo" (II, 13, 129).

11. "Pero ninguna cosa le dio más pena que el oír roznar al rucio y el ver que Rocinante pugnaba por desatarse....
    —¡Oh carísimos amigos, quedaos en paz...!
    Y en esto, comenzó a llorar...amargamente" (II, 29, 263).
12. "Sancho, desamparando al rucio, se cosió con la duquesa;...[pero] remordiéndole la conciencia de que dejaba al jumento solo,...[pidió a una dueña que lo pusiera en la caballeriza, y dijo] que no le trocara [él] con el rocín del señor Lanzarote" (II, 31, 274 and 275).
13. "Es tan grande el cariño que tengo a mi jumento, que me pareció que no podía encomendarle a persona más caritativa" (II, 31, 276).
14. "Le suplicó [a la duquesa] le hiciese merced de que se tuviese buena cuenta con su rucio, porque era la lumbre de sus ojos" (II, 33, 303).
15. "No...quiso dejar [su rucio], aunque le daban un caballo" (II, 34, 305).
16. "Sancho se puso detrás de todos, sin apearse del rucio, a quien no osara desamparar, porque no le sucediese algún desmán,...[pero] en viendo al valiente [jabalí], desamparó al rucio y dio a correr cuanto pudo" (II, 34, 305).
17. "Dice Cide Hamete que pocas veces vio a Sancho Panza sin ver al rucio, ni al rucio sin ver a Sancho: tal era la amistad y buena fe que entre los dos se guardaban" (II, 34, 306).
18. *"El rucio está bueno,...y no le pienso dejar, aunque me llevaran a ser Gran Turco"* (II, 36, 322).
19. "Para andar reposado y llano, mi rucio,...[por] tierra, yo le cutiré con cuantos portantes hay en el mundo" (II, 40, 341).
20. "Volvía Sancho la cabeza de cuando en cuando a mirar a su asno, con cuya compañía iba tan contento, que no se trocara con el emperador de Alemaña" (II, 44, 368).
21. "Que se tenga cuenta con mi sustento y con el de mi rucio, que es lo que en este negocio importa" (II, 49, 406). .
22. "Llegándose al rucio, [Sancho] le abrazó y le dio un beso de paz en la frente, y no sin lágrimas en los ojos, le dijo:
    —Venid vos acá, compañero mío y amigo mío, y conllevador de mis trabajos y miserias: cuando yo me avenía con vos y no tenía otros pensamientos que los que me daban los cuidados de remendar vuestros aparejos y de sustentar vuestro corpezuelo, dichosas eran mis horas, mis días y mis años" (II, 53, 444).
23. "Nunca Sancho Panza se apartó de su asno, ni su asno de Sancho Panza....¡O compañero y amigo mío, qué mal pago te he dado de tus buenos servicios! Perdóname y pide a la fortuna, en el mejor modo que supieres, que nos saque deste miserable trabajo,...que yo prometo de ponerte una corona de laurel en la cabeza...y de darte los piensos doblados" (II, 55, 456).
24. "[Sancho] no quiso subir a ver al duque sin que primero no hubiese acomodado al rucio en la caballeriza" (II, 55, 460).
25. "Bien pudiera el Amor—dijo Sancho—[depositar el remedio de Altisidora en los martirios] de mi asno; que yo se lo agradeciera" (II, 70, 565).

Appendix 6

Laziness

1. "[Sancho] no estaba duecho a andar mucho a pie" (I, 7, 126).
2. "De un sueño [se llevó Sancho toda la noche], y no fueran parte para despertarle, si su amo no lo llamara, los rayos del sol, que le daban en el rostro, ni el canto de las aves" (I, 8, 132).
3. "[Sancho] estaba más para dormir que para oír canciones" (I, 11, 160).
4. "Duerme tú, [Sancho], que naciste para dormir" (I, 20, 241).
5. [Yo] soy mal caminante" (I, 25, 309).
6. "Podré...vivir descansado todos los días de mi vida" (I, 29, 366).
7. "Sólo Sancho Panza se desesperaba con la tardanza del recogimiento, y sólo él se acomodó mejor que todos, echándose sobre los aparejos de su jumento" (I, 42, 520).
8. [Sancho], sepultado en sueño y tendido sobre el albarda de su jumento, no se acordaba en aquel instante de la madre que lo había parido" (I, 43, 529).
9. "Hay hombres...que toman en arrendamiento los estados de los señores, y les dan un tanto cada año, y ellos se tienen cuidado del gobierno, y el señor se está a pierna tendida, gozando de la renta que le dan, sin curarse de otra cosa; y así haré yo,...que luego me desistiré de todo, y me gozaré mi renta como un duque, y allá se lo hayan" (I, 50, 587).
10. "Sancho se quedó dormido al pie de un alcornoque" (II, 12, 124).
11. "Llegándose a Sancho, que dormía, [don Quijote] le trabó del brazo, y con no pequeño trabajo le volvió a su acuerdo" (II, 12, 124).
12. "Llamó a su escudero Sancho, que aun todavía roncaba;...[el cual] ni despertara tan presto si don Quijote con el cuento de la lanza no le hiciere volver en sí. Despertó, en fin, soñoliento y perezoso" (II, 20, 185 and 186).
13. "Sancho respondió que...era verdad que tenía por costumbre dormir cuatro o cinco horas las siestas del verano" (II, 32, 296).
14. "Adelante, hermano, que es hora de dormir más que de negociar" (II, 47, 393).
15. "Sancho, que había merendado aquel día, se dejó entrar de rondón por las puertas del sueño" (II, 60, 491).
16. "No es cosa tan gustosa el caminar a pie, que me mueva e incite a hacer grandes jornadas" (II, 66, 542).
17. "Castíguese [vuestra merced] a sí mesmo, y no revienten sus iras...por la blandura de mis pies, queriendo que caminen más de lo justo" (II, 66, 543).
18. "[Sancho pasó la noche] durmiendo, y su amo velando" (II, 67, 551).
19. "Cumplió don Quijote con la naturaleza durmiendo el primer sueño, sin dar lugar al segundo; bien al revés de Sancho, que nunca tuvo segundo, porque le duraba el sueño desde la noche hasta la mañana, en que se mostraba su buena complexión y pocos cuidados" (II, 68, 552).
20. "En tanto que duermo, ni tengo temor, ni esperanza, ni trabajo, ni gloria; y bien haya el que inventó el sueño, capa que cubre todos los humanos

pensamientos, manjar que quita la hambre, agua que ahuyenta la sed, fuego que calienta el frío, frío que templa el ardor, y, finalmente, moneda general con que todas las cosas se compran, balanza y peso que iguala al pastor con el rey y al simple con el discreto" (II, 68, 553).

21. "Duerme tú, Sancho,...que naciste para dormir" (II, 68, 554).

22. "Vuesa merced coplee cuanto quisiere, que yo dormiré cuanto pudiere.

Y luego, tomando en el suelo cuanto quiso, se acurrucó y durmió a sueño suelto, sin que fianzas, ni deudas, ni dolor alguno se lo estorbase" (II, 68, 554).

23. "Durmió Sancho aquella noche...en el mesmo aposento de don Quijote, cosa que él quisiera escusarla,...porque bien sabía que su amo no le había de dejar dormir" (II, 70, 562).

24. "[A Sancho] durmiendo a sueño suelto, y [a don Quijote] velando a pensamientos desatados, les tomó el día y la gana de levantarse" (II, 70, 565).

25. "[Sancho] se durmió hasta que le despertó el sol" (II, 71, 573).

Appendix 7

Soft Spot for Wine

1. "Iba Sancho.Panza sobre su jumento como un patriarca, con sus alforjas y su bota" (I, 7, 127).

2. "De cuando en cuando empinaba [Sancho] la bota, con tanto gusto que le pudiera envidiar el más regalado bodegonero de Málaga .... Iba [Sancho] menudeando tragos" (I, 8, 132).

3. "[Sancho] tenía el estómago lleno, y no de agua de chicoria.... Al levantarse dió un tiento a la bota, y hallóla algo más flaca que la noche antes; y afligiósele el corazón, por parecerle que no llevaban camino de remediar tan presto su falta" (I, 8, 132).

4. "[Sancho] visitaba muy a menudo el...zaque" (I, 11, 158).

5. "Ya te entiendo, Sancho—le respondió don Quijote—; que bien se me trasluce que las visitas del zaque piden más recompensa de sueño que de música" (I, 11, 161).

6. "Como al primer trago vio que era agua, no quiso pasar adelante, y rogó a Maritornes que se le trujese de vino" (I, 18, 215).

7. "Sucedióles otra desgracia, que Sancho la tuvo por la peor de todas, y fue que no tenían vino" (I, 19, 236).

8. "¿No lo dije yo?—dijo oyendo esto Sancho—. Sí que no estaba yo borracho" (I, 35, 440).

9. "[Sancho, la bota] puesta a la boca, estuvo mirando las estrellas un cuarto de hora" (II, 13, 132).

10. "Tanto...bebieron los dos buenos escuderos, que tuvo necesidad el sueño de...templarles la sed, que quitársela fuera imposible ; y así, asidos entrambos de la ya casi vacía bota, con los bocados a medio mascar en la boca, se quedaron dormidos" (II, 13, 134).

11. "Dijo el primo a don Quijote que llegasen a [la ermita] a beber un trago. Apenas oyó esto Sancho Panza, cuando encaminó el rucio a la ermita,...

pero la mala suerte de Sancho parece que ordenó que el ermitaño no estuviese en casa" (II, 24, 226).

12. "En mi vida he bebido de malicia; con sed bien podría ser, porque no tengo nada de hipócrita; bebo cuando tengo gana, y cuando no la tengo [y me lo dan], por no parecer o melindroso o malcriado; que a un brindis de un amigo, ¿qué corazón ha de haber tan de mármol, que no haga la razón?" (II, 33, 302-03).

13. *Pensé venir a este gobierno a...beber frío, y...he venido a hacer penitencia, como si fuera ermitaño"* (II, 51, 430-31).

14. "El enemigo que yo hubiere vencido quiero que me le claven en la frente. Yo no quiero repartir despojos de enemigos, sino pedir y suplicar a algún amigo, si es que le tengo, que me dé un trago de vino" (II, 53, 443).

15. "[Sancho] pidió a Ricote la bota, y tomó su puntaría como los demás, y no con menos gusto que ellos.... Finalmente, el acabársele el vino fue principio de un sueño que dio a todos, quedándose dormidos sobre las mismas mesas y manteles; solos Ricote y Sancho quedaron alerta, porque habían comido más y bebido menos" (II, 54, 449-50).

16. "Acabó de cenar Sancho, y dejando [borracho] al ventero, se pasó a la estancia de su amo" (II, 59, 488).

17. "Que me maten, señores, si el autor deste libro que vuesas mercedes tienen quiere que no comamos buenas migas juntos; yo querría que ya que me llama comilón,...no me llamase también borracho,...[que el Sancho y el don Quijote de Cide Hamete], que somos nosotros: mi amo, valiente, discreto y enamorado; y yo, simple gracioso, y no...borracho" (II, 59, 488-89).

APPENDIX 8

AMBITIONS AND ASPIRATIONS

"[Don Quijote solicitó a Sancho, y] tanto le dijo, tanto le persuadió y prometió, que el pobre villano se determinó de salirse con él y servirle de escudero. Decíale, entre otras cosas,...[que] tal vez le podía suceder aventura que ganase...alguna ínsula y le dejase a él por gobernador della" (I, 7, 125).

1. "Iba Sancho...con mucho deseo de verse ya gobernador de la ínsula que su amo le había prometido,...[y dijo] a su amo:
— ...no se le olvide lo que de la ínsula me tiene prometido; que yo la sabré gobernar, por grande que sea" (I, 7, 127).

"Bien podría ser que antes de seis días ganase yo tal reino, que tuviese otros a él adherentes, que viniesen de molde para coronarte por rey de uno dellos" (I, 7, 127).

2. "Vuestra merced...me sabrá dar todo aquello que me esté bien y yo pueda llevar" (I, 7, 128).

3. "[Sancho] rogaba...que [en la batalla su amo] ganase alguna ínsula de donde le hiciese gobernador" (I, 10, 146-47).

4. "Sea... [servido] de darme el gobierno de la ínsula...que, por grande que

sea, yo me siento con fuerzas de saberla gobernar tal y tan bien como otro que haya gobernado ínsulas en el mundo" (I, 10, 147).

"No solamente os pueda hacer gobernador, sino más adelante" (I, 10, 147).

5. "Yo renuncio... el gobierno de la prometida ínsula, y no quiero otra cosa... [que] la receta de ese estremado licor" (I, 10, 149).

6. "[Quiero] que se llegue ya el tiempo de ganar esta ínsula... y muérame yo luego" (I, 10, 151).

"Que cuando faltare ínsula, [Sancho], ahí está el reino de Dinamarca o el de Soliadisa, que te vendrá como anillo al dedo," (I, 10, 151-52).

7. "[Sancho] propuso en su corazón... volverse a su tierra, aunque perdiese... las esperanzas del gobierno de la prometida ínsula" (I, 18, 225).

8. "Me ha rasgado mis esperanzas... de alcanzar aquella negra y malhadada ínsula" (I, 20, 239).

9. "Que si se usa en la caballería escribir hazañas de escuderos, que no pienso que se han de quedar las mías entre renglones" (I, 21, 258).

10. "[A Sancho] querría darle un condado que le tengo muchos días ha prometido; sino que temo que no ha de tener habilidad para gobernar su estado.

Casi estas últimas palabras oyó Sancho a su amo, a quien dijo:
—Trabaje vuestra merced... en darme ese condado tan prometido de vuestra merced, como de mí esperado; que yo le prometo que no me falte a mí habilidad para gobernarle" (I, 50, 586-87).

"Sólo sé que tan presto tuviese yo el condado como sabría regirle; que tanta alma tengo yo como otro" (I, 50, 587).

"Vos, [Teresa], me veréis presto conde, o gobernador de una ínsula, y no de las de por ahí, sino la mejor que pueda hallarse" (I, 52, 603).

11. "[Gobernadores] he visto por ahí... que, a mi parecer, no llegan a la suela de mi zapato" (II, 3, 63).

12. "Quizá mejor me sabrá el pan desgobernado que siendo gobernador; y ¿sé yo por ventura si en esos gobiernos me tiene aparejada el diablo alguna zancadilla donde tropiece y caiga y me haga las muelas? Sancho nací, y Sancho pienso morir; pero si, con todo esto... me deparase el cielo alguna ínsula,... no soy tan necio, que la desechase" (II, 4, 71).

13. "No echara mi señor el reino que me diera en saco roto; que yo he tomado el pulso a mí mismo, y me hallo con salud para regir reinos y gobernar ínsulas" (II, 4, 71).

14. "Si no pensase antes de mucho tiempo verme gobernador de una ínsula, aquí me caería muerto" (II, 5, 74).

15. "Si sucediese, lo cual ni lo creo ni lo espero, que vuesa merced me diese la ínsula que me tiene prometida,..." (II, 7, 88).

16. "[Del duque] tan gran bien espero como es verme gobernador" (II, 41, 346).

17. "Después que bajé del cielo, y después que desde su alta cumbre miré la tierra y la vi tan pequeña, se templó en parte en mí la gana que tenía tan grande de ser gobernador; porque ¿qué grandeza es mandar en un grano de mostaza, o qué dignidad o imperio el gobernar a media docena de

hombres tamaños como avellanas que, a mi parecer, no había más en toda la tierra? Si vuestra señoría fuese servido de darme una tantica parte del cielo, aunque no fuese más de media legua, la tomaría de mejor gana que la mayor ínsula del mundo" (II, 42, 355).

18. "Venga esa ínsula; que yo pugnaré por ser tal gobernador que a pesar de bellacos me vaya al cielo; y esto no es por codicia que yo tenga de salir de mis casillas ni de levantarme a mayores, sino por el deseo que tengo de probar a qué sabe el ser gobernador" (II, 42, 356).

19. "Yo no tengo *don*, ni en todo mi linaje le ha habido: Sancho Panza me llaman a secas, y Sancho se llamó mi padre, y Sancho mi agüelo, y todos fueron Panzas, sin añadidura de *dones* ni *donas*" (II, 45, 376).

20. "Si me dura el gobierno (que no durará, según se me trasluce)..." (II, 47, 391).

21. "Poniéndose de rodillas [el labrador], le pidió la mano para besársela. Negósela Sancho, y mandó que se levantase y dijese lo que quisiese" (II, 47, 392).

22. "Yo no nací para ser gobernador, ni para defender ínsulas ni ciudades de los enemigos que quisieren acometerlas. Mejor se me entiende a mí de arar y cavar, podar y ensarmentar las viñas, que de dar leyes ni de defender provincias ni reinos" (II, 53, 444).

23. "Por Dios que así me quede en éste, ni admita otro gobierno, aunque me le diesen entre dos platos, como volar al cielo sin alas" (II, 53, 445).

24. "He ganado... el haber conocido que no soy bueno para gobernar, si no es un hato de ganado" (II, 54, 453).

25. "Yo, señores, porque lo quiso así vuestra grandeza, sin ningún merecimiento mío, fui a gobernar vuestra ínsula Barataria" (II, 55, 460).

26. "Aquí está vuestro gobernador Sancho Panza, que ha granjeado en solos diez días que ha tenido el gobierno a conocer que no se le ha de dar nada por ser gobernador, no que de una ínsula, sino de todo el mundo" (II, 55, 461).

27. "Diez días... goberné [la ínsula] a pedir de boca; en ellos perdí el sosiego, y aprendí a despreciar todos los gobiernos del mundo; salí huyendo della" (II, 62, 510).

28. "¿Por ventura, cabeza, tendré otro gobierno? ¿Saldré de la estrecheza de escudero?" (II, 62, 516).

29. "Sancho, aunque aborrecía el ser gobernador, como queda dicho, todavía deseaba volver a mandar y a ser obedecido" (II, 63, 521).

30. "Yo, que dejé con el gobierno los deseos de ser más gobernador, no dejé la gana de ser conde" (II, 65, 537).

APPENDIX 9

COWARDICE

1. "Ellos son gigantes; y si tienes miedo, quítate de ahí" (I, 8, 129).

2. "Yo de mío me soy pacífico y enemigo de meterme en ruidos ni pendencias. Bien es verdad que en lo que tocare a defender mi persona no tendré mucha cuenta con [las leyes de caballería que dicen que no puedo pelear

hasta que sea armado caballero, que las leyes] divinas y humanas permiten que cada uno se defienda de quien quisiere agraviarle" (I, 8, 133).

3. "En esto de ayudarme contra caballero, [Sancho], has de tener a raya tus naturales ímpetus" (I, 8, 133).

4. "¿Qué diablos de venganza hemos de tomar—respondió Sancho—, si éstos son más de veinte, y nosotros no más de dos, y aun quizá nosotros sino uno y medio? [Pero don Quijote] arremetió a los gallegos, y lo mesmo hizo Sancho...incitado y movido del ejemplo de su amo" (I, 15, 191).

5. "[Sancho] con voz enferma y lastimada, dijo.... [A lo que] respondió don Quijote con el mesmo tono afeminado y doliente..." (I, 15, 192).

6. "Yo soy hombre pacífico, manso, sosegado, y sé disimular cualquiera injuria, porque tengo mujer y hijos que sustentar y criar.... En ninguna manera pondré mano a la espada...[y] perdono cuantos agravios me han hecho y han de hacer" (I, 15, 193).

7. "Tenía [a Rocinante] por persona...tan pacífica como yo" (I, 15, 194).

8. "Hace muy bien Pentapolín, y que le tengo de ayudar en cuanto pudiere" (I, 18, 219).

9. "El miedo que tienes—dijo don Quijote—te hace...que ni veas ni oyas a derechas" (I, 18, 223).

10. "[Sancho] comenzó a temblar como un azogado; y los cabellos...se le erizaron a don Quijote" (I, 19, 229).

11. "[Sancho] comenzó a dar diente con diente,...y creció más el batir y dentellar.... Esta estraña visión, a tales horas y en tal despoblado, bien bastaba para poner miedo en el corazón de Sancho, y aun en el de su amo" (I, 19, 230).

12. "[Sancho] naturalmente era medroso y de poco ánimo" (I, 20, 237).

13. "Pues no hay quien nos vea, menos habrá quien nos note de cobardes" (I, 20, 239).

14. "Yo, de miedo, dé mi ánima a quien quisiere llevarla" (I, 20, 239).

15. "Tiene [mi] miedo muchos ojos" (I, 20, 240).

16. "Tal era el miedo que tenía a los golpes, que todavía...sonaban" (I, 20, 241).

17. "Sancho dijo que sí hiciera, si le dejara el temor de lo que oía" (I, 20, 241).

18. "Era tanto el miedo que había entrado en su corazón..." (I, 20, 245).

19. "Sí tengo [mucho miedo]" (I, 20, 246).

20. "[Sancho] determinó de no [dejar a su amo] hasta el último tránsito y fin de aquel negocio" (I, 20, 247).

21. "[Sancho iba] por ver si vería ya lo que tan suspenso y medroso le tenía" (I, 20, 248).

22. "Yo me tengo en cuidado el apartarme" (I, 21, 253).

23. "Naturalmente eres cobarde, Sancho,...[así que voy a] apartarme de la furia que tanto temes" (I, 23, 277).

24. "En apartándome de vuestra merced, luego es conmigo el miedo, que me asalta con mil géneros de sobresaltos y visiones" (I, 23, 285).

25. "[Sancho], que de tal modo vio parar a su señor, arremetió al loco con el puño cerrado" (I, 24, 298).

26. "Sancho, que se vio acometer tan de improviso y oyó los vituperios que le decían, con la una mano asió de la albarda, y con la otra dio un mojicón al

barbero, que le bañó los dientes en sangre" (I, 44, 538).
27. "Si tú [tienes miedo], haces como quien eres" (I, 46, 551).
28. "A cuyas palabras y furibundos ademanes [de don Quijote] quedó Sancho
    tan encogido y medroso, que se holgara que en aquel instante se abriera
    debajo de sus pies la tierra y le tragara" (I, 46, 552).
29. "[El cabrero] saltó sobre don Quijote, y asiéndole del cuello con entrambas
    manos, no dudara de ahogalle, si Sancho Panza no llegara en aquel punto,
    y le asiera por [las] espaldas y diera con él encima de la mesa" (I, 52, 597).
30. "Pensar que tengo de poner mano a la espada...es pensar en lo escu-
    sado,...[porque] no pienso granjear fama de valiente" (II, 4, 70).
31. [Los] ladridos de perros...turbaban el corazón de Sancho" (II, 9, 99).
32. [El carro de Las cortes de la muerte], visto de improviso,...puso miedo en
    el corazón de Sancho" (II, 11, 116).
33. [Sancho refuses to fight with the squire of the Caballero del Bosque, and is
    afraid of the squire's nose (II, 14, 138-42).]
34. "[Sancho no] dejaba de aporrear al rucio para que se alejase del carro [de los
    leones]" (II, 17, 163).
35. "Tiraban [del castillo de madera] cuatro salvajes, todos vestidos de yedra y
    de cáñamo teñido de verde, tan al natural, que por poco espantaron a
    Sancho" (II, 20, 190-91).
36. "Sancho, a quien jamás pluguieron ni solazaron semejantes [batallas], se
    acogió a las tinajas" (II, 21, 201).
37. "Sancho Panza tuvo pavor grandísimo, porque...jamás había visto a su
    señor con tan desatinada cólera" (II, 26, 245).
38. "Fuese llegando a [los hombres armados] don Quijote, no con poca
    pesadumbre de Sancho, que nunca fue amigo de hallarse en semejantes
    jornadas" (II, 27, 252).
39. "Cuando Sancho se vio obra de dos varas dentro del río, comenzó a tem-
    blar temiendo su perdición" (II, 29, 263).
40. "[Al] que se llegare a lavarme ni a tocarme a un pelo...de mi barba...le
    daré tal puñada, que le deje el puño engastado en los cascos" (II, 32, 294).
41. "Tomen mi consejo y déjenle; porque ni [mi escudero] ni yo sabemos de
    achaque de burlas" (II, 32, 295).
42. "¡No, sino lléguense a hacer burla de [mí]; que así lo sufriré como ahora es
    de noche!" (II, 32, 295).
43. "Sólo Sancho, en viendo al valiente [jabalí]...dio a correr cuanto pudo"
    (II, 34, 305).
44. "Pasmose el duque [del ruido], suspendióse la duquesa, admiróse don
    Quijote, tembló Sancho Panza, y, finalmente, aun hasta los mesmos
    sabidores de la causa se espantaron" (II, 34, 309).
45. "Si yo veo otro diablo y oigo otro cuerno como el pasado, así esperaré yo
    aquí como en Flandes—dijo Sancho" (II, 34, 310).
46. "[El corazón] de Sancho vino a tierra [con el ruido], y dio con él desmayado
    en las faldas de la duquesa" (II, 34, 311).
47. "[De la] figura de la muerte, descarnada y fea,...Sancho [recibió] miedo"
    (II, 35, 313).
48. "De Sancho no hay que decir sino que el miedo le llevó a su acostumbrado
    refugio, que era el lado o faldas de la duquesa" (II, 36, 323).

49. "[En Clavileño]—dijo Sancho—yo no subo, porque ni tengo ánimo ni soy caballero" (II, 41, 344).

50. "[En Clavileño no subiré] yo—dijo Sancho—, ni de malo ni de buen talante,... bien puede buscar mi señor otro escudero que le acompañe,... que yo no soy brujo para gustar de andar por los aires" (II, 41, 345).

51. "Desde la memorable aventura de los batanes...nunca he visto a Sancho con tanto temor como ahora, y si yo fuera tan agorero como otros, su pusilanimidad me hiciera algunas cosquillas en el ánimo" (II, 41, 346).

52. "¿No estás, desalmada y cobarde criatura, en el mismo lugar que ocupó la linda Magalona?...Cúbrete, cubrete, animal descorazonado, y no te salga a la boca el temor que tienes" (II, 41, 349).

53. "Y en verdad que no sé de qué te turbas ni te espantas.... Destierra, [Sancho], el miedo" (II, 41, 350).

54. "Yo me avendré con cuantas espías y matadores y encantadores vinieren sobre mí y sobre mi ínsula" (II, 47, 391).

55. "[Sancho quedó] confuso y lleno de temor y espanto" (II, 53, 441).

56. "¿Qué me tengo de armar—respondió Sancho—, ni que sé yo de armas ni de socorros?" (II, 53, 441).

57. "Ármenme norabuena—replicó Sancho" (II, 53, 441).

58. "¿Cómo tengo de caminar...que no puedo jugar las choquezuelas de las rodillas, porque me lo impiden estas tablas que tan cosidas tengo con mis carnes? Lo que han de hacer es llevarme en brazos y ponerme, atravesado o en pie, en algún postigo, que yo le guardaré, o con esta lanza o con mi cuerpo" (II, 53, 442).

59. "Ande, señor gobernador—dijo otro [de los burladores]—, que más el miedo que las tablas le impiden el paso" (II, 53, 442).

60. "Sentóse sobre su lecho y desmayóse del temor, del sobresalto y del trabajo" (II, 53, 443).

61. "[Sancho] comenzó a caminar por aquella gruta adelante, por ver si hallaba alguna salida por otra parte. A veces iba a escuras, y a veces sin luz; pero ninguna vez sin miedo" (II, 55, 457).

62. "Ya no lo puedo llevar el estar aquí sepultado en vida, y me estoy muriendo de miedo" (II, 55, 459).

63. "[El] mayordomo...les encareció el asalto de la ínsula, y el miedo de Sancho" (II, 56, 461-62).

64. "Vuesa merced se esté quedo; si no, por Dios verdadero que nos han de oír los sordos.... [Pero don Quijote] procuraba y pugnaba por desenlazarle, viendo lo cual Sancho Panza, se puso en pie, y arremetiendo a su amo, se abrazó con él a brazo partido, y echándole una zancadilla, dio con él en el suelo boca arriba; púsole la rodilla derecha sobre el pecho, y con las manos le tenía las manos, de modo que ni le dejaba rodear ni alentar" (II, 60, 492).

65. "Alzando las manos [Sancho] topó con dos pies de persona, con zapatos y calzas. Tembló de miedo; acudió a otro árbol, y sucedióle lo mesmo. Dio veces llamando a don Quijote, que le favoreciese" (II, 60, 493).

66. "Pensó Sancho que el cielo se desencajaba de sus quicios y venía a dar sobre su cabeza; y agobiándola, lleno de miedo, la puso entre las piernas" (II, 63, 523).

67. "Sancho se agazapó debajo del rucio, poniéndose a los lados el lío de las armas y la albarda de su jumento,...temblando de miedo,...[que] ya se sabe su valentía" (II, 68, 553).
68. "Azoróse el [corazón] de Sancho, porque la gente que se les llegaba traía lanzas y adargas y venía muy a punto de guerra" (II, 68, 555).
69. "Creció en [don Quijote y Sancho] el miedo" (II, 68, 556).
70. "¡Voto a tal, así me deje yo sellar el rostro ni manosearme la cara como volverme moro!" (II, 69, 560).
71. "Bien podré yo dejarme manosear de todo el mundo; pero consentir que me toquen dueñas, ¡eso no!...Que me toquen dueñas no lo consentiré, si me llevase el diablo" (II, 69, 560).
72. "Todas las dueñas le sellaron, y otra mucha gente de casa le pellizcaron; pero lo que él no pudo sufrir fue el punzamiento de los alfileres; y así, se levantó de la silla, al parecer, mohíno, y asiendo de una hacha encendida que junto a él estaba, dio tras las dueñas, y tras todos sus verdugos, diciendo:
    —¡Afuera, ministros infernales; que no soy yo de bronce, para no sentir tan extraordinarios martirios!" (II, 69, 561).

Appendix 10

Artfulness and Humor

1. "Sabe Dios si yo me holgara que vuestra merced se quejara cuando alguna cosa le doliera. De mí sé decir que me he de quejar del más pequeño dolor que tenga, si ya no se entiende también con los escuderos de los caballeros andantes eso del no quejarse" (I, 8, 131).
2. "De aquí adelante yo proveeré las alforjas de todo género de fruta seca para vuestra merced, que es caballero, y para mí las proveeré, pues no lo soy, de otras cosas volátiles y de más sustancia" (I, 10, 152-53).
3. "Apenas puse mano a mi tizona..." (I, 15, 195).
4. "Pero,...dígame vuestra merced qué haremos deste caballo rucio rodado, que parece asno pardo" (I, 21, 256).
5. "Ni yo lo digo ni lo pienso—respondió Sancho—; allá se lo hayan; con su pan se lo coman; si fueron amancebados, o no, a Dios habrán dado la cuenta; de mis viñas vengo, no sé nada; no soy amigo de saber vidas ajenas; que el que compra y miente, en su bolsa lo siente. Cuanto más, que desnudo nací, desnudo me hallo: ni pierdo ni gano; mas que lo fuesen, ¿qué me va a mí? Y muchos piensan que hay tocinos y no hay estacas. Mas ¿quién puede poner puertas al campo? Cuanto más, que de Dios dijeron" (I, 25, 302).

6. "¿Qué me ha de suceder,...sino el haber perdido...tres pollinos, que cada uno era como un castillo?" (I, 26, 323).
7. "Los diablos lleven la cosa que de la carta se me acuerda; aunque en el principio decía: 'Alta y sobajada señora'" (I, 26, 324).
8. "Son requesones los que aquí me has puesto, traidor, bergante y mal mirado escudero.
   A lo que con gran flema y disimulación respondió Sancho:
   —Si son requesones, démelos vuesa merced; que yo me los comeré.... Pero cómalos el diablo que debió de ser el que ahí los puso.... A lo que Dios me da a entender también debo yo de tener encantadores que me persiguen" (II, 17, 159).
9. "A buena fe que [la novia] no viene vestida de labradora, sino de garrida palaciega. ¡Pardiez, que según diviso, que las patenas que había de traer son ricos corales, y la palmilla verde de Cuenca es terciopelo de treinta pelos! ¡Y montas que la guarnición es de tiras de lienzo, blanca! ¡Voto a mí que es de raso! Pues ¡tomadme las manos, adornadas con sortijas de azabache! No medre yo si no son anillos de oro, y muy de oro, y empedrados con pelras blancas como una cuajada, que cada una debe de valer un ojo de la cara. ¡Oh hideputa, y qué cabellos; que si no son postizos, no los he visto ni más luengos ni más rubios en toda mi vida! ¡No, sino ponedla tacha en el brío y en el talle, y no la comparéis a una palma que se mueve cargada de racimos de dátiles, que lo mesmo parecen los dijes que trae pendientes de los cabellos y de la garganta! Juro en mi ánima que ella es una chapada moza, y que puede pasar por los bancos de Flandes" (II, 21, 196).
10. "Sin duda—dijo Sancho—que este demonio debe de ser hombre de bien y buen cristiano; porque, a no serlo, no jurara *en Dios y en mi conciencia*. Ahora yo tengo para mí que aun en el mesmo infierno debe de haber buena gente" (II, 34, 309).
11. "Pardiez, señor—respondió Sancho—, que para [los latigazos] que yo pienso darme, eso se me da en casa que en el campo; pero con todo eso, querría que fuese entre árboles, que parece que me acompañan y me ayudan a llevar mi trabajo maravillosamente" (II, 71, 575).

APPENDIX 11

DON QUIXOTE AND SANCHO AS OPPOSITES

1. "Toda aquella noche no durmió don Quijote.... No la pasó ansí Sancho...[que] de un sueño se la llevó toda" (I, 8, 132).
2. "Cuanto fue de pesadumbre para Sancho no llegar a poblado, fue de contento para su amo dormir [la noche] al cielo descubierto" (I, 10, 153).
3. "Don Quijote le rogó [al pastor] que algo más cantase, no lo consintió Sancho" (I, 11, 160).

4. "A todos nos sabe bien [el sueño]—respondió Sancho.
   —No lo niego—replicó don Quijote—; pero acomódate tú,...que los
   de mi profesión mejor parecen velando que durmiendo" (I, 11, 161).
5. "[Sancho] durmió, no como enamorado desfavorecido, sino como hombre
   molido a coces" (I, 12, 167).
6. "Ya Sancho había dado al través con todo su esfuerzo. Lo contrario le
   avino a su amo" (I, 19, 230).
7. "[Sancho] que...era medroso y de poco ánimo [se asustó de los ruidos,
   los cuales] pusieran pavor a cualquier otro corazón que no fuera el de don
   Quijote,...[quien] acompañado de su intrépito corazón, saltó sobre Rocinante" (I, 20, 237-38).
8. "El [miedo] que yo tuve; que de vuestra merced ya yo sé que no le cono-
   ce, ni sabe qué es temor ni espanto" (I, 20, 249).
9. "Para que veas cuán necio eres tú y cuán discreto soy yo" (I, 25, 313).
10. "Que si tú [tienes miedo], haces como quien eres; y si yo no le tengo,
    hago como quien soy" (I, 46, 551).
11. "No por eso temió [don Quijote], como Sancho Panza, antes con gentil
    denuedo dijo al Caballero de los Espejos" (II, 14, 140).
12. "[Sancho no] dejaba de aporrear al rucio para que se alejase del carro [de
    los leones,...mientras que don Quijote] saltó del caballo, arrojó la lanza y
    embrazó el escudo, y desenvainando la espada, paso ante paso, con
    maravilloso denuedo y corazón valiente, se fue a poner delante del carro"
    (II, 17, 163).
13. "No hay tanta diferencia de mí a mi amo, que a él le laven con agua de
    ángeles y a mí con lejía de diablos" (II, 32, 294).
14. "Yo, Sancho, nací para vivir muriendo, y tú para morir comiendo" (II, 59,
    482).
15. "Sancho, que había merendado aquel día, se dejó entrar de rondón por las
    puertas del sueño; pero don Quijote, a quien desvelaban sus imagina-
    ciones mucho más que la hambre, no podía pegar sus ojos antes iba y
    venía con el pensamiento por mil géneros de lugares" (II, 60, 491).
16. "[Sancho pasó la noche] durmiendo, y su amo velando" (II, 67, 551).
17. "Yo, [Sancho], velo cuando tú duermes; yo lloro cuando cantas; yo me
    desmayo de ayuno cuando tú estás perezoso y desalentado de puro darto"
    desmayo de ayuno cuando tú estás perezoso y desalentado de puro
    harto" (II, 68, 552).
18. "Sintieron un sordo estruendo y un áspero ruido, que por todos aquellos
    valles se estendía. Levantóse en pie don Quijote y puso mano a la
    espada, y Sancho se agazapó debajo del rucio, poniéndose a los lados el lío
    de las armas y la albarda de su jumento, tan temblando de miedo como
    alborotado don Quijote. De punto en punto iba creciendo el ruido, y
    llegándose cerca a los dos temerosos; a lo menos, al uno, que al otro, ya
    se sabe su valentía" (II, 68, 553).
19. "Duerme tú, Sancho,...que naciste para dormir; que yo, que nací para
    velar..." (II, 68, 554).
20. "[Sancho y don Quijote], el uno durmiendo a sueño suelto, y el otro
    velando a pensamientos desatados, les tomó el día y la gana de levantarse;
    que las ociosas plumas...jamás dieron gusto a don Quijote" (II, 70, 565).

Appendix 12

Sancho a Thief, a Heartless Highwayman a Bigoted Racist, a Bully

1. [Sancho], que vio en el suelo al fraile...arremetió a él y le comenzó a quitar los hábitos...[diciendo] que aquello le tocaba a él ligitimamente, como despojos de la batalla que su señor...había ganado" (I, 8, 134).
2. "[Sancho] andaba ocupado desvalijando una acémila...y recogiendo todo lo que pudo y cupo en el talego" (I, 19, 233-34).
3. "Entristecióse mucho Sancho [de que Ginés no disparara la escopeta y dejara huir a los guardias] porque se le representó que los que iban huyendo habían de dar noticia del caso a la Santa Hermandad" (I, 22, 274-75).
4. "Desvalijando [Sancho] a la valija de su lencería, la puso en el costal de la despensa" (I, 23, 281).
5. "Pasaba Sancho la maleta, sin dejar rincón en toda ella,...porque no se quedase nada por diligencia ni mal recado; tal golosina habían despertado en él los hallados escudos, que pasaban de ciento" (I, 23, 284).
6. "Replicó Sancho Panza, y tornó a replicar el cabrero, y fue el fin de las réplicas asirse de las barbas y darse...puñadas" (I, 25, 299).
7. "Yo no soy hombre que robo ni mato a nadie" (I, 26, 322).
8. "Sólo le daba pesadumbre [a Sancho] el pensar que aquel reino era en tierra de negros y que la gente que por sus vasallos le diesen habían de ser todos negros,...[pero se dijo a sí mismo]: ¿Qué se me da a mí que mis vasallos sean negros? ¿Habrá más que cargar con ellos y traerlos a España, donde...[podré] vender treinta o diez mil vasallos en dácame esas pajas...?" (I, 29, 366).
9. "Mire vuestra merced que [escoja la parte de mi reino] hacia la marina, porque...pueda embarcar mis negros vasallos y hacer dellos lo que ya he dicho" (I, 31, 387).
10. "Yo no soy salteador de caminos; que en buena guerra ganó mi señor don Quijote estos despojos" (I, 44, 538).
11. "[Por] ser enemigo mortal, como lo soy, de los judíos, debían los historiadores tener misericordia de mí y tratarme bien en sus escritos" (II, 8, 94).

Appendix 13

Physique and Appearance

1. "Junto a [Rocinante] estaba Sancho, ...a los pies del cual estaba [un] rétulo que decía: *Sancho Zancas*, y debía de ser que tenía, a lo que mostraba la pintura, la barriga grande, el talle corto y las zancas largas, y por esto se le debió de poner nombre de Panza y de Zancas, que con estos dos sobrenombres le llama algunas veces la historia" (I, 9, 144).
2. "Tras esto, [Sancho] alzó la camisa lo mejor que pudo, y echó al aire entrambas posaderas, que no eran muy pequeñas" (I, 20, 245).

3. "Será menester que te rapes las barbas a menudo; que, según las tienes de espesas, aborrascadas y mal puestas,...a tiro de escopeta se echará de ver lo que eres" (I, 21, 264).
4. "[Yo] ya tengo edad para dar consejos" (I, 31, 387).
5. "Mientras más fuere entrando en edad Sancho, con la esperiencia que dan los años, estará más idóneo y más hábil para ser gobernador que no está agora" (II, 3, 62).
6. "Vuestra merced...se duela de mi mocedad" (II, 28, 260-61).
7. "Que si [me rapasen las barbas] a navaja, lo tendría a más beneficio" (II, 32, 288).
8. "Soy...moreno" (II, 41, 347).
9. "Una gran parte de mi barba se me ha chamuscado" (II, 41, 350).
10. "Esa gordura y esa personilla que tienes" (II, 43, 365).
11. "Las barbas, la gordura y pequeñez del nuevo gobernador [tenían] admirada a toda la gente" (II, 44, 376).
12. "[Sancho] se las tenía tiesas a todos, maguera tonto, bronco y rollizo" (II, 49, 404).

Appendix 14

Education

1. "Ni sé leer ni escrebir" (I, 10, 148).
2. "Yo no sé leer ni escrebir" (I, 10, 152).
3. "No sé la primera letra del abecé" (I, 26, 325).
4. "No sé leer" (I, 31, 388).
5. "No entiendo otra lengua que la mía" (II, 2, 55).
6. "Con la grama bien me avendría yo,...pero con la tica, ni me tiro ni me pago, porque no la entiendo" (II, 3, 63).
7. "No me he criado en la corte, ni he estudiado en Salamanca, para saber si añado o quito alguna letra a mis vocablos" (II, 19, 182).
8. "Yo no sé leer ni escribir, puesto que sé firmar" (II, 36, 321).
9. "Letras,...pocas tengo, porque aun no sé el abecé" (II, 42, 356).
10. "No sé leer ni escribir" (II, 43, 363).
11. "Bien se firmar mi nombre,...[que] aprendí a hacer unas letras como de marca de fardo, que decían que decía mi nombre" (II, 43, 363).
12. "Estaba [Sancho] mirando unas grandes y muchas letras que en la pared frontera de su silla estaban escritas; y como él no sabía leer, preguntó que qué eran aquellas pinturas" (II, 45, 376).
13. "Esto lo diera firmado de mi nombre, si supiera firmar" (II, 51, 427).

Appendix 15

Exaggerations

1. "En pago de mis muchos y buenos servicios" (I, 10, 149).
2. "Esta ínsula que tan cara me cuesta" (I, 10, 151)
3. "Me santiguaron los hombres con sus pinos" (I, 15, 195).

4. "No ha sino un mes que andamos buscando las aventuras" (I, 16, 200). [3rd day]
5. "Más de cuatrocientos moros me han aporreado a mí" (I, 17, 208).
6. "Muchas veces se me olvida cómo me llamo" (I, 25, 314).
7. "[He perdido] tres pollinos, que cada uno era como un castillo" (I, 26, 323).
8. "¡Por solos ocho meses de servicio [mi amo me tenía] dada la mejor ínsula que el mar ciñe y rodea!" (I, 52, 601). [three weeks]
9. "Obligado de mis muchos y buenos sercicios" (II, 4, 71).
10. "Ya sabe todo el mundo...quién fueron los Panzas" (II, 7, 90).
11. "Término lleva de quejarse un mes arreo" (II, 12, 125).
12. "El tal león...es mayor que una montaña" (II, 17, 162).
13. "Obra había cortada para tres días" (II, 20, 194).
14. "La palmilla verde de Cuenca es terciopelo de treinta pelos" (II, 21, 196).
15. "Debe de haber más de veinte años, tres días más o menos [que vuesa merced me prometió el gobierno de una ínsula]" (II, 28, 259).
16. "Ha muchos meses que ando en su compañía" (II, 32, 284).
17. "Sancho respondió...que le faltaban tres tocadores, que valían tres ciudades" (II, 60, 499-500).
18. "Mi señor don Quijote...sabe bien que con un puño de bellotas, o de nueces, nos solemos pasar entrambos ocho días" (II, 62, 509).
19. "Haga vuestra merced la experiencia, y ándese tras de mí, por lo menos un año" (II, 72, 577).

APPENDIX 16

DESIRE FOR WEALTH

1. "Valdrá la onza [del bálsamo] más de a dos reales, y no he menester yo más para pasar esta vida honrada y descansadamente" (I, 10, 149).
2. "Harto mejor sería no buscalle; porque si le hallamos y acaso fuese el dueño del dinero, claro está que lo tengo de restituir; y así, fuera mejor...que, por otra vía menos curiosa y diligente, pareciera su verdadero señor; y quizá fuera a tiempo que lo hubiera gastado [yo]" (I, 23, 285).
3. "[Sancho] les fue contando lo que les aconteció con el loco que hallaron en la sierra, encubriendo, empero, el hallazgo de la maleta y de cuanto en ella venía; que maguer que tonto, era un poco codicioso el mancebo" (I, 27, 328).
4. "[Sancho] díjose a sí mismo: ¿Qué se me da a mí que mis vasallos sean negros?...los podré vender,...de cuyo dinero podré comprar algún título" (I, 29, 366).
5. "Me alegra de pensar si podré hallar otros cien escudos" (II, 5, 73).
6. "El diablo me pone ante los ojos...un talego lleno de doblones, que me parece que a cada paso le toco con la mano, y me abrazo con él, y lo llevo a mi casa" (II, 13, 130).
7. "Dio Sancho [los cincuenta reales] de muy mala gana" (II, 29, 267).
8. "[A Sancho le] llegaba al alma llegar al caudal del dinero, pareciéndole que

todo lo que dél se quitaba era quitárselo a él de las niñas de sus ojos" (II, 30, 268).

9. "[Sancho] tomó el [vestido] que le dieron, con intención de venderle en la primera ocasión que pudiese" (II, 34, 305).

10. "*Voy* [al gobierno] *con grandísimo deseo de hacer dineros*" (II, 36, 322).

11. "[El buen gobernador] se muestra...muy codicioso" (II, 36, 322).

12. "Yo gobernaré esta ínsula sin perdonar derecho ni llevar cohecho" (II, 49, 405).

13. *"No te muestres, aunque por ventura lo seas—lo cual yo no creo—, codicioso"* (II, 51, 429).

14. "Sin blanca entré en este gobierno, y sin ella salgo, bien al revés de como suelen salir los gobernadores de otras ínsulas" (II, 53, 444-45).

15. "Saliendo yo desnudo, como salgo, no es menester otra señal para dar a entender que he gobernado como un ángel" (II, 53, 446).

16. "No soy nada codicioso; que, a serlo, un oficio dejé...donde pudiera hacer las paredes de mi casa de oro.... No fuera contigo, si como me prometes docientos escudos, me dieras aquí de contado cuatrocientos" (II, 54, 452).

17. "Estaba Sancho...contentísimo, porque el mayordomo del duque...le había dado un bolsico con docientos escudos de oro" (II, 57, 467).

18. "No es bien que se quede sin agradecimiento de nuestra parte docientos escudos de oro que en una bolsilla me dio el mayordomo del duque" (II, 58, 470-71).

19. "Pagó Sancho al ventero magníficamente" (II, 59, 490).

20. "No iba nada Sancho alegre, porque le entristecía ver que Altisidora no le había cumplido la palabra de darle las camisas,...[y] dijo a su amo:
    —Pues yo les voto a tal que si me traen a las manos otro algún enfermo, que antes que le cure, me han de untar las mías" (II, 71, 570).

21. "Azótate luego, [Sancho], y págate de contado....
    A cuyos ofrecimientos abrió Sancho los ojos y las orejas de un palmo....
    —Dígame vuestra merced: ¿cuánto me dará por cada azote que me diere?...[Y así] entraré en mi casa rico y contento, aunque bien azotado" (II, 71, 570,71).

22. "Dineros traigo, que es lo que importa" (II, 73, 583).

23. "Se regocijaba Sancho Panza; que esto del heredar algo borra o templa en el heredero la memoria de la pena que es razón que deje el muerto" (II, 74, 591).

Appendix 17

Sancho Praised or His Advice Accepted

1. "Has hablado y apuntado muy bien" (I, 10, 150).
2. "Así es—respondió don Quijote" (I, 17, 209).
3. "Sube...y guía, que yo te seguiré al paso que quisieres" (I, 18, 227).
4. "Tienes mucha razón" (I, 19, 228).
5. "Rióse don Quijote del donaire,...[pero] propuso de llamarse de aquel nombre" (I,19, 235).
6. "Pareciéndole que Sancho tenía razón, sin volverle a replicar le siguió" (I, 19, 236).
7. "Parecióle bien el consejo a don Quijote" (I, 20, 237).
8. "No dices mal, Sancho" (I, 21, 258).
9. "Digo que tienes razón" (I, 21, 264).
10. "Bien está eso" (I, 22, 275).
11. "Si yo hubiera creído lo que me dijiste, yo hubiera escusado esta pesadumbre.... Esta vez quiero tomar tu consejo" (I, 23, 277).
12. "Verdad dices" (I, 23, 282).
13. "Sea como tú quisieres, que no me parece mal tu designio" (I, 25, 309).
14. "[Al cura y al barbero] parecióles bien lo que Sancho Panza decía" (I, 27, 329).
15. "Dígote, Sancho,...que estás en lo cierto, y que habré de tomar tu consejo" (I, 31, 387).
16. "¡Qué de discreciones dices a las veces! No parece sino que has estudiado" (I, 31, 388).
17. "Sin que faltase el bueno de Sancho" (I, 36, 453).
18. "Estaba don Quijote delante, con mucho contento de ver cúan bien se defendía y ofendía su escudero, y túvole desde allí adelante por hombre de pro" (I, 44, 538-39).
19. "Sé yo bien de la bondad e inocencia [de Sancho], que no sabe levantar testimonios a nadie, [dijo Dorotea]" (I, 46, 553).
20. "Los muchos y buenos servicios [de Sancho]" (I, 46, 556).
21. "Verdad dices, Sancho" (I, 49, 575).
22. "Soy contento de hacer lo que dices, Sancho,...y cuando tú veas coyuntura de poner en obra mi libertad, yo te obedeceré en todo y por todo" (I, 49, 576).
23. "Vino más aliviado y con más deseos de poner en obra lo que su escudero ordenase" (I, 49, 577).
24. "Sancho Panza, mi escudero,...es el mejor hombre del mundo" (I, 50, 586).
25. "No son malas filosofías ésas, como tú dices, Sancho [—dijo el conónigo]" (I, 50, 587).
26. "[Sancho] es uno de los mejores escuderos que caballero andante ha tenido" (I, 50, 587).
27. "Tú estás en lo cierto, Sancho" (I, 50, 590).
28. "Decid, Sancho amigo; pasá adelante, que habláis hoy de perlas" (II, 7, 87).
29. "También confieso esa verdad.... Todo eso es así" (II, 9, 98).

30. "Has dicho, Sancho,... mil sentencias encerradas en el círculo de breves palabras: el consejo que ahora me has dado le apetezco y recibo de bonísima gana" (II, 9, 103).
31. "Sancho bueno, Sancho discreto, Sancho cristiano y Sancho sincero" (II, 11, 120).
32. "Gracias sean dadas al saludable consejo que Sancho Panza dio a su amo" (II, 11, 120).
33. "Así es verdad—replicó don Quijote" (II, 12, 121).
34. "Cada día, Sancho,... te vas haciendo menos simple y más discreto" (II, 12, 121).
35. "Dígote, Sancho, que si como tienes buen natural y discreción, pudieras tomar un púlpito en la mano y irte por ese mundo predicando lindezas" (II, 20, 195).
36. "Confieso,... que todo lo que dices, Sancho, sea verdad" (II, 28, 259).
37. "De que Sancho el bueno sea gracioso lo estimo yo en mucho, porque es señal que es discreto; que las gracias y los donaires... no asientan sobre ingenios torpes; y pues el buen Sancho es gracioso y donairoso, desde aquí le confirmo por discreto" (II, 30, 272).
38. "Por vida del duque—dijo la duquesa—, que no se ha de apartar de mí Sancho un punto: quiérole yo mucho, porque sé que es muy discreto" (II, 31, 279).
39. "[Sancho] es uno de los más graciosos escuderos que jamás sirvió a caballero andante; tiene a veces unas simplicidades tan agudas, que el pensar si es simple o agudo causa no pequeño contento; tiene malicias que le condenan por bellaco, y descuidos que le confirman por bobo; duda de todo, y créelo todo; cuando pienso que se va a despeñar de tonto, sale con unas discreciones, que le levantan al cielo. Finalmente, yo no le trocaría con otro escudero, aunque me diesen de añadidura una ciudad.... Veo en él una cierta aptitud para esto de gobernar, que atusándole tantico el entendimiento, se saldría con cualquier gobierno" (II, 32, 293).
40. "Sancho Panza tiene razón en todo cuanto ha dicho, y la tendrá en todo cuanto dijere" (II, 32, 295).
41. "Bien haya tal señor y tal criado, el uno, por norte de la andante caballería, y el otro, por estrella de la escuderil fidelidad" (II, 32, 296).
42. "[No] dejó de admirarse [la duquesa] en oír las razones y refranes de Sancho" (II, 33, 300).
43. "Así es, como Sancho dice—dijo el duque" (II, 37, 328).
44. "Razón tienes, Sancho—dijo don Quijote" (II, 39, 336).
45. "¡Oh Sancho Panza gracioso" (II, 40, 339).
46. "Con vos me entierren, Sancho, que sabéis de todo—respondió el duque—, y yo espero que seréis tal gobernador como vuestro juicio promete" (II, 42, 356).
47. "Por solas estas últimas razones que has dicho juzgo que mereces ser gobernador de mil ínsulas: buen natural tienes" (II, 43, 365).
48. "Apenas se hubo partido Sancho, cuando don Quijote sintió su soledad" (II, 44, 368).

49. "Quedaron todos admirados, y tuvieron a su gobernador por un nuevo Salomón" (II, 45, 379).
50. "Los presentes quedaron admirados, y el que escribía las palabras, hechos y movimientos de Sancho no acababa de determinarse si le tendría y pondría por tonto, o por discreto" (II, 45, 379-80).
51. "Los circunstantes quedaron admirados de nuevo de los juicios y sentencias de su nuevo gobernador" (II, 45, 382).
52. "Todos los que conocían a Sancho Panza se admiraban oyéndole hablar tan elegantemente, y no sabían a qué atribuirlo, sino a que los oficios y cargos graves, o adoban, o entorpecen los entendimientos" (II, 49, 404).
53. "El suave modo de governar que en estos principios vuesa merced ha dado no les da lugar [a los insulanos] de hacer ni de pensar cosa que en deservicio de vuesa merced redunde" (II, 49, 405).
54. "Estoy admirado de ver que un hombre tan sin letras como vuesa merced...diga tales y tantas cosas llenas de sentencias y de avisos, tan fuera de todo aquello que del ingenio de vuesa merced esperaban los que nos enviaron y los que aquí venimos" (II, 49, 406).
55. *"Con dificultad se halla un buen gobernador en el mundo, y tal me haga a mí Dios como Sancho gobierna"* (II, 50, 418).
56. "He oído decir que en [el tal gobierno] se porta valentísimamente el tal Sancho" (II, 50, 423).
57. "El mayordomo ocupó lo que [de la noche] faltaba en escribir a sus señores lo que Sancho Panza hacía y decía, tan admirado de sus hechos como de sus dichos" (II, 51, 425).
58. "Tengo para mí que el mismo Licurgo...no pudiera dar mejor sentencia que la que el gran Panza ha dado" (II, 51, 427).
59. "Cumplió su palabra el mayordomo, pareciéndole ser cargo de conciencia matar de hambre a tan discreto gobernador" (II, 51, 427).
60. *"Cuando esperaba oír nuevas de tus descuidos e impertinencias,...las oí de tus discreciones"* (II, 51, 428).
61. "[Sancho] ordenó cosas tan buenas, que hasta hoy se guardan en aquel lugar, y se nombran: Las constituciones del gran gobernador Sancho Panza" (II, 51, 433).
62. "[La carta de Sancho] puso en duda la sandez del gobernador" (II, 52, 439).
63. "[El] gran Sancho Panza, flor y espejo de todos los insulanos gobernadores" (II, 52, 440).
64. "Par Dios que tiene razón el gran Sancho" (II, 53, 446).
65. "Abrazáronle todos, y él...abrazó a todos, y los dejó admirados, así de sus razones como de su determinación tan resoluta y tan discreta" (II, 53, 446).
66. "Tú dices bien, Sancho—dijo don Quijote" (II, 58, 474).
67. "Yo apostaré que este buen hombre...es un tal Sancho Panza,...a cuyas gracias no hay ningunas que se le igualen" (II, 58, 478).
68. "Hízolo así don Quijote, pareciéndole que las razones de Sancho más eran de filósofo que de mentecato" (II, 59, 483).
69. "Apartóse Roque a una parte y escribió una carta a un su amigo

[diciéndole que]...los donaires de...Sancho Panza no podían dejar de dar gusto general a todo el mundo" (II, 60, 504-05).

70. "Los donaires de Sancho fueron tantos, que de su boca andaban como colgados todos los criados de casa y todos cuantos le oían" (II, 62, 509).

71. "Muy filósofo estás, Sancho,...muy a lo discreto hablas" (II, 66, 541).

72. "¡Voto a tal—dijo un labrador que escuchó la sentencia de Sancho—que este señor ha hablado como un bendito y sentenciado como un canónigo! (II, 66, 544).

73. "[Los labradores se quedaron] admirados de haber visto y notado...la discreción [del criado de don Quijote]" (II, 66, 544).

74. "Tú has dicho muy bien—dijo don Quijote" (II, 67, 548).

75. "Nunca te he oído hablar, Sancho—dijo don Quijote—, tan elegantemente como ahora" (II, 68, 553).

76. "A ti, [Sancho—dijo Altisidora—] ¡oh el más compasivo escudero que contiene el orbe!, te agradezco la vida que poseo" (II, 69, 562).

77. "Tú tienes razón, Sancho amigo" (II, 71, 570).

78. "¡Oh Sancho bendito! ¡Oh Sancho amable—respondió don Quijote—, y cuán obligados hemos de quedar Dulcinea y yo!" (II, 71, 571).

79. "Tienes razón, Sancho—dijo don Quijote" (II, 71, 574).

80. "Le diera [a Sancho el gobierno de un reino], porque la sencillez de su condición y fidelidad de su trato lo merece" (II, 74, 589).

81. "Así es—dijo Sansón—, y el buen Sancho Panza está muy en la verdad destos casos" (II, 74, 590).

Appendix 18

Catholicism

1. "Qué dé al diablo vuestra merced tales juramentos, señor mío—replicó Sancho—; que son muy en daño de la salud y muy en perjuicio de la conciencia" (I, 10, 151).

2. "A dos cosechas [de la caballería] quedaremos inútiles para la tercera, si Dios, por su infinita misericordia, no nos socorre" (I, 15, 194).

3. "He oído predicar al cura de nuestro lugar" (I, 20, 239).

4. "Mal cristiano eres, Sancho,...porque nunca olvidas la injuria que una vez te han hecho" (I, 21, 256).

5. "Yo cristiano viejo soy" (I, 21, 263).

6. "Quien ha infierno—respondió Sancho—, nula es retencio, según he oído decir" (I, 25, 310).

7. "Yo...querría amar y servir [a Nuestro Señor] por lo que pudiese" (I, 31, 388).

8. "Soy cristiano viejo" (I, 47, 563).

9. "Si hubiera dicho de mí cosas que no fueran muy de cristiano viejo, como soy, que nos habían de oír los sordos" (II, 3, 63).

10. "Todo lo que pienso decir son sentencias del padre predicador que la cuaresma pasada predicó en este pueblo" (II, 5, 77-78).

11. "Por estas mesmas razones lo dijo el padre" (II, 5, 78).

12. "Según nos lo dicen por esos púlpitos" (II, 7, 87).

13. "Creo, firme y verdaderamente en Dios y en todo aquello que tiene y cree la santa Iglesia Católica Romana" (II, 8, 94).
14. "A nuestro cura he oído decir..." (II, 20, 194).
15. "No acabo de entender ni alcanzar cómo siendo el principio de la sabiduría el temor de Dios, tú, que temes más a un lagarto que a Él, sabes tanto" (II, 20, 195).
16. "Juzque vuesa merced, señor, de sus caballerías,...y no se meta en juzgar de los temores o valentías ajenas; que tan gentil temeroso soy yo de Dios como cada hijo de vecino" (II, 20, 195).
17. "[Sancho] se acogió a las tinajas, donde había sacado su agradable espuma, pareciéndole aquel lugar como sagrado, que había de ser tenido en respeto" (II, 21, 201).
18. "Púsose Sancho de rodillas, pidiendo devotamente al cielo lo librase de tan manifiesto peligro.... Puesto de rodillas, las manos juntas y los ojos clavados al cielo, pidió a Dios con una larga y devota plegaria le librase de allí adelante de los atrevidos deseos y acometimientos de su señor" (II, 29, 266-67).
19. "Podré encomendarme a nuestro Señor o invocar los ángeles que me favorezcan.... ¡Ea, pues—dijo Sancho—, Dios me ayude y la Santísima Trinidad de Gaeta!" (II, 41, 346).
20. "[Sancho pidió] que le ayudasen en aquel trance con sendos paternostres y sendas avemarías" (II, 41, 348-49).
21. "[Sancho] había oído contar otro caso como aquél al cura de su lugar" (II, 45, 379).
22. "[Como gobernador pienso], sobre todo, tener respeto a la religión y a la honra de los religiosos" (II, 49, 406).
23. "[Sancho] ordenó que ningún ciego cantase milagro en coplas si no trujese testimonio auténtico de ser verdadero, por parecerle que los más que los ciegos cantan son fingidos, en perjuicio de los verdaderos" (II, 51, 433).
24. "[Sancho] de todo corazón se encomendaba a Dios que de aquel peligro le sacase" (II, 53, 442).
25. "Al tiempo de caer, [Sancho] se encomendó a Dios de todo corazón.... [Después], viéndose bueno, entero y católico de salud, no se hartaba de dar gracias a Dios Nuestro Señor de la merced que le había hecho" (II, 55, 455).
26. "He oído decir al cura de nuestro pueblo que no es de personas cristianas ni discretas mirar en [agüeros]" (II, 73, 582).

Appendix 19

Complaints

1. "Fue de pesadumbre para Sancho no llegar a poblado" (I, 10, 153).
2. "[Sancho se levantó] despidiendo treinta ayes, y sesenta sospiros, y ciento y veinte pésetes y reniegos de quien allí le había traído" (I, 15, 197).
3. "¡Desdichado de mí,...de todas las malandanzas me cabe la mayor parte!" (I, 17, 208).

4. "[Sancho] maldecía el bálsamo y al ladrón que se lo había dado" (I, 17, 211).

5. "A los escuderos, que se los papen duelos" (I, 18, 217).

6. "[Sancho] arrancábase las barbas, maldiciendo la hora y el punto en que la fortuna se le había dado a conocer" (I, 18, 224).

7. "El que ayer mantearon, ¿era otro que el hijo de mi padre? Y las alforjas que hoy me faltan, con todas mis alhajas, ¿son de otro que del mismo?" (I, 18, 225).

8. "Noramala alcanzaré yo el condado [si no se casa con la princesa Micomicona],...y en siendo rey [vuestra merced], hágame marqués o adelantado.... [Pero] no siéndolo, ¿qué mercedes me puede hacer? Esto es de lo que yo me quejo" (I, 30, 377-78).

9. "Los escuderos de los caballeros andantes estamos sujetos a mucha hambre y a mala ventura, y aun a otras cosas que se sienten mejor que se dicen" (I, 31, 391).

10. "Si al cabo de haber andado caminos y carreras, y pasado malas noches y peores días, ha de venir a coger el fruto de nuestros trabajos el que se está holgando en esta venta, no hay para qué darme priesa" (I, 46, 552).

11. "El sonsacado, y el destraído, y el llevado por esos andurriales soy yo, que no tu amo;...él me sacó de mi casa con engañifas, prometiéndome una ínsula, que hasta agora la espero" (II, 2, 53).

12. "[Nosotros] comemos [el pan] en el hielo de nuestros cuerpos; porque ¿quién más calor y más frío que los miserables escuderos de la andante caballería? Y aun menos mal si comiéramos,...pero tal vez hay que se nos pasa un día y dos sin desayunarnos, si no es del viento que sopla" (II, 13, 128).

13. "[Sancho] rehusaba de volver a la hambre que se usa en las florestas" (II, 18, 176).

14. "[Don Quijote] se desvió un poco del camino, bien contra la voluntad de Sancho, viniéndosele a la memoria el buen alojamiento que había tenido en...casa de don Diego" (II, 19, 185).

15. "¡Ah bodas de Camacho y abundancia de la casa de don Diego, y cuántas veces os tengo de echar [de] menos!" (II, 24, 226).

16. "[No pondré silencio] en dejar de decir que los caballeros andantes huyen, y dejan a sus buenos escuderos molidos como alheña, o como cibera, en poder de sus enemigos" (II, 28, 256).

17. "A la fe, señor nuestro amo,...cada día voy descubriendo tierra de lo poco que puedo esperar de la compañía que con vuestra merced tengo; porque si esta vez me ha dejado apalear, otra y otras ciento volveremos a los manteamientos de marras,...[a andar] por caminos sin camino y por sendas y carreras que no las tienen, bebiendo mal y comiendo peor" (II, 28, 257 and 258).

18. "Los que servimos a labradores,...a la noche cenamos olla y dormimos en cama; en la cual no he dormido después que ha que sirvo a vuestra merced. Si no ha sido el tiempo breve que estuvimos en casa de don Diego de Miranda, y la jira que tuve con la espuma que saqué de las ollas de Camacho, y lo que comí y bebí y dormí en casa de Basilio, todo el otro tiempo he dormido en la dura tierra, al cielo abierto, sujeto a lo que dicen

inclemencias del cielo, sustentándome con rajas de queso y mendrugos de pan, y bebiendo aguas, ya de arroyos, ya de fuentes" (II, 28, 258-59).

19. "También debe de ser castigo del cielo...que a los escuderos de los caballeros vencidos los puncen moscas, los coman piojos y les embista la hambre. Si los escuderos fuéramos hijos de los caballeros a quien servimos, o parientes suyos muy cercanos, no fuera mucho que nos alcanzara la pena de sus culpas hasta la cuarta generación; pero ¿qué tienen que ver los Panzas con los Quijotes?" (II, 68, 554).

20. "A mí, que la salud ajena me cuesta gotas de sangre, mamonas, pellizcos, alfilerazos y azotes, no me dan un ardite, Pues yo les voto a tal que si me traen a las manos otro algún enfermo, que antes que le cure, me han de untar las mías" (II, 71, 570).

APPENDIX 20

LOVE OF FOOD

1. "[Después de una] pobre y seca comida,... [Sancho] se fue tras el olor que despedían de sí ciertos tasajos de cabra que hirviendo al fuego en un caldero estaban; y...él quisiera en aquel mesmo punto ver si estaban en sazón de trasladarlos del caldero al estómago" (I, 10 and 11, 153).
2. "[Don Quijote y Sancho] con mucho donaire y gana, embaulaban tasajo como el puño.... No estaba...ocioso el cuerno" (I, 11, 155).
3. "Ni Sancho llevaba otro cuidado...sino de satisfacer su estómago con los relieves,...y así, iba...sacando de un costal y embaulando en su panza" (I, 23, 280-81).
4. "[Sancho] no quiso entrar [a la venta], aunque llegó a hora que lo pudiera y debiera hacer, por ser la del comer y llevar en deseo de gustar algo caliente; que había grandes días que todo era fiambre" (I, 26, 321).
5. "Yo a aquel arroyo me voy con esta empanada, donde pienso hartarme por tres días" (I, 50, 589-90).
6. "¿Qué son ínsulas, [Sancho]? ¿Es alguna cosa de comer, golosazo, comilón que tú eres?" (II, 2, 53).
7. "Sancho [iba] sobre su antiguo rucio, proveídas las alforjas de cosas tocantes a la bucólica" (II, 7, 91).
8. "Comió Sancho sin hacerse de rogar, y tragaba a escuras bocados de nudos de suelta" (II, 13, 132).
9. "Estaba [Sancho] comprando unos requesones que los pastores le vendían; y acosado de la [mucha] priesa de su amo, no supo qué hacer dellos, ni en qué traerlos, y, por no perderlos, que ya los tenía pagados, acordó de echarlos en la celada de su señor" (II, 17, 157-58).
10. "Quedó el agua de color de suero, merced a la golosina de Sancho y a la compra de sus negros requesones" (II, 18, 170).
11. "[Sancho] se hallaba muy bien con la abundancia de la casa de don Diego, y rehusaba de volver a la hambre que se usa en las florestas, despoblados y a la estrecheza de sus mal proveídas alforjas. Con todo esto, las llenó y colmó de lo más necesario que le pareció" (II, 18, 176).
12. "De la parte desta enramada...sale un tufo y olor harto más de torrez-

nos asados que de juncos y tomillos: bodas que por tales olores comienzan, para mi santiguada que deben de ser abundantes y generosas. —Acaba, glotón—dijo don Quijote" (II, 20, 186).

13. "Todo lo miraba Sancho Panza, y todo lo contemplaba, y de todo se aficionaba. Primero le cautivaron y rindieron el deseo las ollas, de quien él tomara de bonísima gana un mediano puchero; luego le aficionaron la voluntad los zaques; y últimamente, las frutas de sartén,...y así, sin poderlo sufrir ni ser en su mano hacer otra cosa, se llegó a uno de los solícitos cocineros, y con corteses y hambrientas razones le rogó le dejase mojar un mendrugo de pan en una de aquellas ollas.... [el cual] asió de un caldero, y encajándole en una de las medias tinajas, sacó en él tres gallinas y dos gansos, y dijo a Sancho: —Comed, amigo, y desayunaos con esta espuma, en tanto que se llega la hora del yantar" (II, 20, 188-89).

14. "Nunca de ollas de Basilio sacaré yo tan elegante espuma como es esta que he sacado de las de Camacho, [respondió Sancho], y enseñóle el caldero lleno de gansos y de gallinas, y asiendo de una, comenzó a comer con mucho donaire y gana, y dijo: —...a Camacho me atengo, de cuyas ollas son abundantes espumas gansos y gallinas, liebres y conejos... Y diciendo esto, comenzó de nuevo a dar asalto a su caldero, con tan buenos alientos, que despertó los de don Quijote" (II, 20, 193-95).

15. "[Sancho] se acogió a las tinajas, donde había sacado su agradable espuma, pareciéndole aque lugar como sagrado" (II, 21, 201).

16. "A sólo Sancho se le escureció el alma, por verse imposibilitado de aguardar la espléndida comida...de Camacho,...y así, asenderado y triste siguió a su señor,...y así se dejó atrás las ollas de Egipto, aunque las llevaba en el alma; cuya ya casi consumida y acabada espuma, que en el caldero llevaba, le representaba la gloria y la abundancia del bien que perdía; y así, congojado y pensativo, aunque sin hambre, sin apearse del rucio, siguió las huellas de Rocinante" (II, 21, 202).

17. "Sancho se refociló tres días a costa de los novios" (II, 22, 203).

18. "Suma era la alegría que llevaba consigo Sancho,...siempre aficionado a la buena vida; y así, tomaba la ocasión por la melena en esto del regalarse cada y cuando que se le ofrecía" (II, 31, 273).

19. "Así me sustentaré Sancho a secas con pan y cebolla, como gobernador con perdices y capones" (II, 43, 365).

20. "Denme de comer, o si no, tómense su gobierno, que oficio que no da de comer a su dueño no vale dos habas" (II, 47, 389).

21. "Lo que agora se ha de hacer,...es meter en un calabozo al doctor Recio; porque si alguno me ha de matar ha de ser él, y de muerte adminícula y pésima, como es la de la hambre" (II, 47, 390).

22. "Por ahora denme un pedazo de pan y obra de cuatro libras de uvas,... porque, en efecto, no puedo pasar sin comer" (II, 47, 391).

23. "¿Sería posible,...maestresala, que agora que no está aquí el doctor Pedro Recio, que comiese yo alguna cosa de peso y de sustancia, aunque fuese un pedazo de pan y una cebolla?" (II, 47, 392).

24. "Si hubiera comido, no hubiera mejor postre para mí que vuestro retrato" (II, 47, 393).

25. "[Sancho] esperaba con grande ansia llegase la noche y la hora de cenar; y aunque el tiempo, al parecer suyo, se estaba quedo, sin moverse de un lugar, todavía se llegó por él el tanto deseado, donde le dieron de cenar un salpicón de vaca, con cebolla, y unas manos cocidas de ternera algo entrada en días. Entregóse en todo, con más gusto que si le hubieran dado francolines de Milán,...y entre la cena, volviéndose al doctor, le dijo:

    —De aquí adelante no os curéis de darme a comer cosas regaladas ni manjares esquisitos, porque será sacar a mi estómago de sus quicios, el cual está acostumbrado a cabra, a vaca, a tocino, a cecina, a nabos y a cebollas, y si acaso le dan otros manjares de palacio, los recibe con melindre, y algunas veces con asco. Lo que el maestresala puede hacer es traerme estas que llaman ollas podridas, que mientras más podridas son, mejor huelen, y en ellas puede embaular y encerrar todo lo que él quisiere, como sea de comer" (II, 49, 404-05).

26. "Le hicieron desayunar con un poco de conserva y cuatro tragos de agua fría, cosa que la trocara Sancho con un pedazo de pan y un racimo de uvas; pero viendo que aquello era más fuerza que voluntad, pasó por ello, con harto dolor de su alma y fatiga de su estómago" (II, 51, 425).

27. "Padecía hambre Sancho, y tal, que en su secreto maldecía el gobierno y aun a quien se le había dado; pero con su hambre y con su conserva se puso a juzgar aquel día" (II, 51, 425).

28. "Denme de comer, y lluevan casos y dudas sobre mí, que yo las despabilaré en el aire" (II, 51, 427).

29. "*No te muestres, aunque por ventura lo seas—lo cual yo no creo—,...glotón*" (II, 51, 429).

30. "*En este gobierno...tengo más hambre que cuando andábamos los dos por las selvas y por los despoblados...* [Hay] *un cierto doctor...* [que] *no cura las enfermedades cuando las hay, sino que las previene,...y las medicinas que usa son dieta y más dieta, hasta poner la persona en los huesos mondos.... Pensé venir a este gobierno a comer caliente y a beber frío, y...he venido a hacer penitencia, como si fuera ermitaño*" (II, 51, 430-31).

31. "[Ofreciéronle] todo aquello que quisiese para el regalo de su persona y para la comodidad de su viaje. Sancho dijo que no quería más de un poco de cebada para el rucio y medio queso y medio pan para él; que pues el camino era tan corto, no había menester mayor ni mejor repostería" (II, 53, 446).

32. "Me paso al servicio de mi señor don Quijote; que, en fin, en él, aunque como el pan con sobresalto, hártome, a lo menos; y para mí, como yo esté harto, eso me hace que sea de zanahorias que de perdices" (II, 55, 461).

33. "Sancho no osaba tocar a los manjares que delante tenía, de puro comedido, y esperaba a que su señor hiciese la salva" (II, 59, 482).

34. "Pero viendo que, llevado de sus imaginaciones, [su amo] no se acordaba de llevar el pan a la boca, no abrió la suya, y atropellando por todo género de crianza, comenzó a embaular en el estómago el pan y queso que se le ofrecía" (II, 59, 482).

35. "Desa manera—dijo Sancho, sin dejar de mascar apriesa,...yo, a lo menos, no pienso matarme a mí mismo;...yo tiraré mi vida comiendo hasta que llegue al fin que le tiene determinado el cielo" (II, 59, 483).
36. "Don Quijote, comió algo, y Sancho mucho" (II, 59, 483).
37. "Mi señor es delicado y come poco, y yo no soy tragantón en demasía" (II, 59, 484).
38. "Quedóse Sancho con la olla con mero mixto imperio; sentóse en cabecera de mesa, y con él el ventero, que no menos que Sancho estaba de sus manos y de sus uñas [de vaca] aficionado" (II, 59, 488).
39. "Que me maten, señores, si el autor deste libro que vuesas mercedes tienen quiere que no comamos buenas migas juntos; yo querría que ya que me llama comilón,...no me llamase también borracho,...[que el Sancho y el don Quijote de Cide Hamete], que somos nosotros: mi amo, valiente, discreto y enamorado; y yo, simple gracioso, y no comedor ni borracho" (II, 59, 488-89).
40. "Tenemos noticia, buen Sancho, que sois tan amigo de manjar blanco y de albondiguillas, que si os sobran las guardáis en el seno para el otro día.
    —No, señor, no es así,...porque tengo más de limpio que de goloso,...y quienquiera que hubiere dicho que yo soy comedor aventajado y no limpio, téngase por dicho que no acierta.
    —Por cierto—dijo don Quijote—, que la parsimonia y limpieza con Sancho come se puede escribir y grabar en láminas de bronce...Verdad es que cuando él tiene hambre, parece algo tragón, porque come apriesa y masca a dos carrillos; pero la limpieza siempre la tiene en su punto, y en el tiempo que fue gobernador aprendió a comer a lo melindroso: tanto, que comía con tenedor las uvas y aun los granos de la granada" (II, 62, 509-10).
41. "Quiero el envite [del vino]—dijo Sancho—,...y escancie el buen Tosilos.
    —En fin—dijo don Quijote—, tú eres, Sancho, el mayor glotón del mundo.
    Rióse el lacayo,...desalforjó sus rajas, y sacando un panecillo, él y Sancho...despabilaron y dieron fondo con todo el repuesto de las alforjas, con tan buenos alientos, que lamieron el pliego de las cartas, sólo porque olía a queso" (II, 66, 545-46).
42. "Cenaron tarde y mal, bien contra la voluntad de Sancho, a quien se le representaban las estrechezas de la andante caballería usadas en las selvas y en los montes, si bien tal vez la abundancia se mostraba en los castillos y casas, así de don Diego de Miranda como en las bodas del rico Camacho y de don Antonio Moreno; pero consideraba no ser posible ser siempre de día ni siempre de noche" (II, 67, 551).

APPENDIX 21

GULLIBILITY

1. "Sólo Sancho Panza pensaba que cuanto su amo decía era verdad,...lo que dudaba algo era en creer aquello de la linda Dulcinea del Toboso, porque nunca tal nombre ni tal princesa había llegado jamás a su noticia" (I, 13, 177).

2. "Tengo para mí que aquellos que se hólgaron conmigo no eran fantasmas ni hombres encantados,...sino hombres de carne y de hueso" (I, 18, 216).
3. "Y con tanto ahínco afirmaba don Quijote que eran ejércitos, que Sancho lo vino a creer" (I, 18, 218).
4. "No puedo sufrir ni llevar en paciencia algunas cosas que vuestra merced dice, y que por ellas vengo a imaginar que todo cuanto me dice de caballerías, y de alcanzar reinos e imperios, de dar ínsulas y de hacer otras mercedes y grandezas, como es uso de caballeros andantes, que todo debe de ser cosa de viento y mentira, y todo pastraña, o patraña, o como lo llamáremos" (I, 25, 306).
5. "Sería yo de parecer que, ya que a vuestra merced le parece que son aquí necesarias calabazadas y que no se puede hacer esta obra sin ellas, se contentase, pues todo esto es fingido y cosa contrahecha y de burla,... con dárselas en el agua, o en alguna cosa blanda" (I, 25, 309).
6. [Sancho believes the priest ("Esta hermosa señora—respondió el cura—...es, como quien no dice nada, la heredera...del gran reino de Micomicón," I, 29, 362), and accepts the story of princess Micomicona, but see below no. 12].
7. "Socorred a mi señor, que anda envuelto en la más reñida y trabada batalla que mis ojos han visto.... Ha dado una cuchillada al gigante enemigo de la señora princesa Micomicona.... Yo vi correr la sangre por el suelo, y la cabeza cortada y caída a un lado , que es tamaña como un gran cuero de vino" (I, 35, 437 and 438).
8. "El gigante muerto es un cuero horadado; y la sangre, seis arrobas de vino tinto" (I, 37, 457).
9. "Todo lo creyera yo...si también mi manteamiento fuera cosa dese jaez; mas no lo fue, sino real y verdaderamente" (I, 37, 457-58).
10. "¡Vive el Señor, que es verdad cuanto mi amo dice de los encantos deste castillo, pues no es posible vivir una hora con quietud en él!" (I, 45, 547).
11. "Sancho, que a todo estaba presente, dijo, menando [la] cabeza a una parte y a otra:
    —¡Ay señor, señor, y cómo hay más mal en el aldegüela que se suena" (I, 46, 551).
12. "Yo tengo por cierto y por averiguado que esta señora que se dice ser reina del gran reino Micomicón no lo es más que mi madre" (I, 46, 551).
13. "Así lo creo yo—dijo Sancho—, excepto aquello de la manta, que realmente sucedió por vía ordinaria" (I, 46, 553).
14. "[Sancho] no dejó de conocer quién eran todas aquellas contrahechas figuras; más no osó descoser su boca" (I, 46, 555).
15. "Osaría afirmar y jurar que estas visiones...no son del todo católicas" (I, 47, 557).
16. "Así va encantado mi señor...como mi madre.... Siendo esto ansí, ¿cómo quieren hacerme a mí entender que va encantado?...¡Ah señor cura, señor cura! ¿Pensaba vuestra merced que no le conozco?" (I, 47, 562).
17. "Viendo Sancho que podía hablar a su amo sin la continua asistencia del cura y el barbero, que tenía por sospechosos,...le dijo:
    —Aquestos dos que vienen aquí cubiertos los rostros son el cura de nuestro lugar y el barbero" (I, 48, 573).

18. "[Sancho] dio voces [al moledor de su amo] que no le diese otro palo, porque era un pobre caballero encantado, que no había hecho mal a nadie en todos los días de su vida" (I, 52, 600).

19. "Hay quien diga que anduvistes demasiadamente de crédulo en creer que podía ser verdad el gobierno de aquella ínsula ofrecida por el señor don Quijote" (II, 3, 62).

20. "Si sucediese, lo cual ni lo creo ni lo espero, que vuesa merced me diese la ínsula que me tiene prometida" (II, 7, 88).

21. "Este mi amo...he visto que es un loco de atar.... Siendo, pues, loco, como lo es, y de locura que las más veces toma unas cosas por otras, y juzga lo blanco por negro y lo negro por blanco, como se pareció cuando dijo que los molinos de viento eran gigantes, y las mulas de los religiosos dromedarios, y las manadas de carneros ejércitos de enemigos, y otras muchas cosas a este tono..." (II, 10, 106-07).

22. "Querían aconsejar [a mi amo] personas discretas, aunque, a mi parecer mal intencionadas" (II, 13, 128).

23. "La aprehensión que en Sancho había hecho lo que su amo dijo de que los encantadores habían mudado la figura del Caballero de los Espejos en la del bachiller Carrasco no le dejaba dar crédito a la verdad que con los ojos estaba mirando. Finalmente, se quedaron con este engaño amo y mozo (II, 15, 145).

24. "[A Sancho] no le satisfacían las quimeras de su amo" (II, 16, 149).

25. "Perdóneme vuestra merced, señor mío, si le digo que de todo cuanto aquí ha dicho...le creo cosa alguna.... Bien se estaba...con su entero juicio,...y no agora, contando los mayores disparates que pueden imaginarse.... Vuelva por su honra, y no dé crédito a esas vaciedades que le tienen menguado y descabalado el sentido" (II, 23, 219, 220, and 223).

26. "¿Es posible que...[mi amo] diga que ha visto los disparates imposibles que cuenta de la cueva de Montesinos?" (II, 24, 229).

27. "[Sancho tenía lo que su amo dijo que había visto en la cueva de Montesinos] por la mesma mentira" (II, 29, 261).

28. "Vuestra merced quiere dar a cada paso en estos que no sé si los llame disparates" (II, 29, 262).

29. "Renovóse la admiración...en Sancho, en ver que, a despecho de la verdad, querían que estuviese encantada Dulcinea" (II, 34, 310).

30. "Señor, ¿cómo dicen éstos que vamos tan altos, si alcanzan acá sus voces, y no parecen sino que están aquí hablando, junto a nosotros?" (II, 41, 349).

31. "Señor, o a mí me ha de llevar el diablo de aquí de donde estoy,...o vuestra merced me ha de confesar que el rostro deste mayordomo del duque, que aquí esta, es el mesmo de la Dolorida...Denantes le oí hablar, y no pareció sino que la voz de la Trifaldi me sonaba en los oídos. Ahora bien: yo callaré; pero no dejaré de andar advertido de aquí adelante, a ver si descubre otra señal que confirme o desfaga mi sospecha" (II, 44, 367-68).

32. "El enemigo que yo hubiere vencido quiero que me le claven en la frente.... [Quiero] pedir y suplicar a algún amigo, si es que le tengo [en esta ínsula], que me dé un trago de vino" (II, 53, 443).

33. "En la opinión de don Quijote y de Sancho Panza, la cabeza quedó por encantada y por respondona, más a satisfación de don Quijote que de Sancho" (II, 62, 517).

34. "No podía imaginar Sancho cómo pudiesen tener tantos pies aquellos bultos [galeras] que por el mar se movían" (II, 61, 507). "Cuando Sancho vio a una moverse tantos pies colorados, que tales pensó él que eran los remos, dijo entre sí:
—Éstas sí son verdaderamente cosas encantadas, y no las que mi amo dice" (II, 63, 523).

35. "Si va a decir la verdad, yo no me puedo persuadir que los azotes de mis posaderas tengan que ver con los desencantos de los encantados" (II, 67, 547).

APPENDIX 22

QUIXOTIFICATION

1. "Y lo mesmo hizo Sancho Panza, incitado y movido del ejemplo de su amo" (I, 15, 191).

2. "Será de provecho para los quebrantamientos de huesos como lo es para las feridas [—respondió Sancho]" (I, 15, 192).

3. "Sabed...que caballero aventurero es una cosa que en dos palabras se ve apaleado y emperador. Hoy está la más desdichada criatura del mundo y la más menesterosa, y mañana tendría dos o tres coronas de reinos que dar a su escudero" (I, 16, 199-200).

4. "Para curar uno de los mejores caballeros andantes que hay en la tierra, el cual yace en aquella cama, malferido por las manos del encantado moro que está en esta venta" (I, 17, 209).

5. "Por un solo Dios, señor mío, que non se me faga tal desaguisado; y ya que del todo no quiera vuestra merced desistir de acometer este fecho, dilátelo, a lo menos, hasta la mañana" (I, 20, 239).

6. "Ayudó Sancho...a la soltura de Ginés" (I, 22, 274).

7. "Se admiraron de nuevo, considerando cuán vehemente había sido la locura de don Quijote, pues había llevado tras de sí el juicio de [Sancho]" (I, 26, 324-25).

8. "*Resuelto* has de decir, mujer—dijo Sancho—, y no *revuelto*" (II, 5, 78).

9. "Señor, las tristezas no se hicieron para las bestias, sino para los hombres; pero si los hombres las sienten demasiado, se vuelven bestias: vuestra merced se reporte, y vuelva en sí, y coja las riendas a Rocinante, y avive y despierte, y muestre aquella gallardía que conviene que tengan los caballeros andantes. ¿Qué diablos es esto? ¿Qué descaecimiento es éste? ¿Estamos aquí, o en Francia? Mas que se lleve Satanás a cuantas Dulcineas hay en el mundo, pues vale más la salud de un solo caballero andante que todos los encantos y transformaciones de la tierra" (II, 11, 114).

10. "Cada día, Sancho,...te vas haciendo menos simple y más discreto.
—Sí, que algo se me ha de pegar de la discreción de vuestra merced,...y con esto espero de dar frutos de mí que sean de bendición, tales que no desdigan ni deslicen de los senderos de la buena crianza que vuesa

merced ha hecho en el agostado entendimiento mío" (II, 12, 121-22).
11. "Habéis aprendido a ser cortés en la escuela de la misma cortesía, [Sancho]; bien parece...que os habéis criado a los pechos del señor don Quijote" (II, 32, 296).
12. "Puedo meterme como escudero que ha aprendido los términos de la cortesía en la escuela de vuesa merced,...y en estas cosas, según he oído decir a vuesa merced, tanto se pierde por carta de más como por carta de menos" (II, 37, 328).
13. "Sancho, todo triste, todo apesarado, no sabía qué decirse ni qué hacerse: parecíale que todo aquel suceso pasaba en sueños y que toda aquella máquina era cosa de encantamento. Veía a su señor rendido y obligado a no tomar armas en un año; imaginaba la luz de la gloria de sus hazañas escurecida, las esperanzas de sus nuevas promesas deshechas" (II, 64, 535).
14. "Muy filósofo estás, Sancho—respondió don Quijote—; muy a lo discreto hablas; no sé quién te lo enseña" (II, 66, 541).
15. "Nunca te he oído hablar, Sancho,...tan elegantemente como ahora; por donde vengo a conocer ser verdad el refrán que tú algunas veces sueles decir: 'No con quien naces, sino con quien paces'" (II, 68, 553).
16. "Mire, [señor], no sea perezoso, sino levántese desa cama, y vámonos al campo vestidos de pastores, como tenemos concertado: quizá tras de alguna mata hallaremos a la señora doña Dulcinea desencantada, que no haya más que ver" (II, 74, 589-90).

Appendix 23

Wordplay

1. "feo Blas" for "Fierabrás" (I, 15, 192).
2. "Malandrino" for "Mambrino" (I, 19, 228).
3. "Martino" for "Mambrino" (I, 21, 256).
4. "hilo" for "Fili" (I, 23, 282).
5. "Magimasa" for "Madásima" (I, 25, 300).
6. "abad" for "Elisabat" (I, 25, 300).
7. "Moro" for "Medoro" (I, 25, 305).
8. "sobajada" for "soberana" (I, 26, 324).
9. "Pandahilado" for "Pandafilando" (I, 30, 376).
10. "baciyelmo" for "bacía" and "yelmo" (I, 44, 540).
11. "tocadas honradas" for "tocas honradas" (I, 46, 551).
12. "Berenjena" for "Benengeli" (II, 2, 57).
13. "grama" and "tica" for "gramática" (II, 3, 63).
14. "Almohadas" for "Almohades" (II, 5, 77).
15. "Julios o Agostos" for Julio César (II, 8, 97).
16. "altivez" for "alteza" (II, 10, 109).
17. "patio...espeso" for "pacto...espreso" (II, 25, 237).
18. "leña" for "línea" (II, 29, 264).
19. "puto y gafo,...meón, o meo" for "cómputo del cosmógrafo Ptolomeo" (II, 29, 264).

20. "condesa Tres Faldas, o Tres Colas" for "condesa Trifaldi" (II, 37, 326).
21. "verde" for "verídico" (II, 41, 347).
22. "Magallanes o Magalona" for "Magalona" (II, 41, 351).
23. "tortolitas...barberos...estropajos...perritas" for "trogloditas...bárbaros...antropófagos...scitas" (II, 68, 556).

APPENDIX 24

SEXUAL TEMPERANCE

1. "Tenía [a Rocinante] por persona casta...como yo" (I, 15, 194).
2. "Pues ¡monta que es mala la reyna [Micomicona]! ¡Así se me vuelvan las pulgas de la cama!" (I, 30, 376).
3. *"No te muestres, aunque por ventura lo seas—lo cual yo no creo—,...mujeriego"* (II, 51, 429).
4. "Yo de mí sé decir que me rindiera y avasallara la más mínima razón amorosa [de Altisidora]" (II, 58, 475).
5. "[Celebrando] yo en mis versos [a mi mujer] vengo a descubrir mis castos deseos, pues no ando a buscar pan de trastrigo por las casa ajenas" (II, 67, 549).
6. "¡A fee que si las hubieras conmigo, [Altisidora], que otro gallo te cantara!" (II, 70, 569).

APPENDIX 25

MEMORY

1. "Los golpes...me han de quedar tan impresos en la memoria como en las espaldas" (I, 15, 195).
2. "Todas estas desventuras que...nos han sucedido...han sido pena del pecado cometido por vuestra merced contra la orden de su caballería, no habiendo cumplido el juramento que hizo de no comer pan a manteles ni con la reina folgar...hasta quitar aquel almete de Malandrino, o como se llama el moro, que no me acuerdo bien" (I, 19, 228).
3. "Has de saber, ¡oh Sancho amigo!, que yo nací, por querer del cielo, en esta nuestra edad de hierro, para resucitar en ella la dorada, o de oro. Yo soy aquel para quien están guardados los peligros, las hazañas grandes, los valerosos fechos...'
   Y por aquí fue repitiendo todas o las más razones que don Quijote dijo la vez primera que oyeron los temerosos golpes (I, 20, 248).
   [Sancho amigo, has de saber que yo nací, por querer del cielo, en esta nuestra edad de hierro, para resucitar en ella la de oro, o la dorada, como suele llamarse. Yo soy aquel para quien están guardados los peligros, las grandes hazañas, los valerosos hechos..." (I, 20, 238-39.]
4. "También...tengo yo [en la memoria la receta del benditísimo brebaje]" (I, 21, 256).
5. "Pensar que yo [he de tomar la carta] en la memoria es disparate; que la tengo tan mala, que muchas veces se me olvida cómo me llamo" (I, 25, 314).

6. "Todo lo escuchó Sancho, y lo tomó muy bien en la memoria" (I, 27, 329).
7. "Así fuera—respondió Sancho—, si no...hubiera yo tomado [la carta] en la memoria cuando vuestra merced me la leyó,...[pero] después que la di, como vi que no había de ser de más provecho, di en olvidalla" (I, 30, 381-82).
8. "A fee que no os falta memoria cuando vos queréis tenerla" (II, 3, 62).
9. "Todo lo que pienso decir son sentencias del padre predicador que la cuaresma pasada predicó en este pueblo, el cual, si mal no me acuerdo, dijo..." (II, 5, 77-78).
10. "A mí bardas me parecieron, si no es que soy falto de memoria" (II, 8, 93).
11. "Bástame tener el *Christus* en la memoria para ser buen gobernador.
    —Con tan buena memoria—dijo el duque—, no podrá Sancho errar en nada" (II, 42, 356).
12. "Atentísimamente...escuchaba Sancho [a su amo], y procuraba conservar en la memoria sus consejos, como quien pensaba guardarlos" (II, 43, 360).
13. "*Erutar* diré de aquí adelante—respondió Sancho—, y a fee que no se me olvide" (II, 43, 361).
14. "Bien veo que todo cuanto vuestra merced me ha dicho son cosas buenas, santas y provechosas; pero ¿de qué han de servir, si de ninguna me acuerdo?" (II, 43, 363).
15. "[Sancho dijo] que él tenía tan gran memoria, que a no olvidársele todo aquello de que quería acordarse, no hubiera tal memoria en toda la ínsula" (II, 45, 379).
16. "En este caso no he hablado de mío, sino que se me vino a la memoria un precepto...que me dio mi amo don Quijote" (II, 51, 427).

Appendix 26

Lies

1. "[Sancho respondió al ventero] que no era nada, sino que [su amo] había dado una caída de una peña abajo" (I, 16, 198).
2. "No fueron golpes,...sino que la peña tenía muchos picos y tropezones" (I, 16, 199).
3. "No caí,...sino que del sobresalto que tomé de ver caer a mi amo, de tal manera me duele a mí el cuerpo, que me parece que me han dado mil palos" (I, 16, 199).
4. "El cielo, conmovido de mis lágrimas y plegarias, ha ordenado que no se pueda mover Rocinante" (I, 20, 240).
5. "¿Qué rumor es ése, Sancho?
    —No sé, señor.... Alguna cosa nueva debe de ser" (I, 20, 245).
6. "¿De qué te ríes, Sancho?
    —Ríome...de considerar la gran cabeza que tenía el pagano dueño deste almete, que no semeja sino una bacía de barbero pintiparada" (I, 21, 255).
7. "También [hallé yo la maletilla], y no quise llegar a ella con un tiro de piedra: allí la dejé, y allí se queda como se estaba; que no quiero perro con cencerro" (I, 23, 286-87).

8. "¿Cómo que no...has visto [a Dulcinea], traidor blasfemo?...Pues, ¿no acabas de traerme ahora un recado de su parte?

   —Digo que no la he visto tan despacio...que pueda haber notado particularmente su hermosura y sus buenas partes punto por punto; pero así, a bulto, me parece bien" (I, 30, 378-79). [See also I, 30 and 31, 381-86, and all other related passages.]

9. "[Sancho] ya estaba cansado de mentir tanto" (I, 31, 388).

10. "No será muy difícil [hacer creer a mi amo] que una labradora, la primera que me topare por aquí, es la señora Dulcinea" (II, 10, 107) [See also II, 10, 107-113, and all other related passages.]

11. "Querían aconsejar [a mi señor] personas discretas...que procurase ser arzobispo...y yo estaba entonces temblando si le venía en voluntad de ser de la Iglesia" (II, 13, 128).

12. "Si son requesones, démelos vuesa merced; que yo me los comeré.... Pero cómalos el diablo, que debió de ser el que ahí los puso.... A lo que Dios me da a entender, también debo yo de tener encantadores que me persiguen" (II, 17, 159).

13. "Debiérase acordar de los capítulos de nuestro concierto antes que esta última vez saliésemos de casa: uno de ellos fue que me había de dejar hablar todo aquello que quisiese, con que no fuese contra el prójimo ni contra la autoridad de vuesa merced" (II, 20, 187).

14. "Yo, señora, sentí que íbamos, según mi señor me dijo, volando por la región del fuego,...[y yo], bonitamente y sin que nadie lo viese, por junto a las narices aparté tanto cuanto el pañizuelo que me tapaba los ojos, y por allí miré hacia la tierra, y parecióme que toda ella no era mayor que un grano de mostaza, y los hombres que andaban sobre ella, poco mayores que avellanas; porque se vea cuán altos debíamos de ir entonces" (II, 41, 353). [See also II, 41, 353-55, and all other related passages.]

15. "Pero el socarrón dejó de [darse los azotes] en las espaldas, y daba en los árboles, con unos suspiros de cuando en cuando, que parecía que con cada uno dellos se le arrancaba el alma" (II, 71, 572). [See also II, 71, 573-75, below no. 16, and all other related passages.]

16. "Abre los ojos, deseada patria, y mira que vuelve a ti Sancho Panza tu hijo, si no muy rico, muy bien azotado" (II, 72, 580).

Appendix 27

Opinion of, and Attitude towards, Don Quixote

1. "[El nombre de mi amo es] don Quijote de la Mancha,...y es caballero aventurero, y de los mejores y más fuertes que de luengos tiempos acá se han visto en el mundo" (I, 16, 199).

2. "Si acaso quisieren saber esos señores quién ha sido el valeroso que tales los puso, diráles...que es el famoso don Quijote de la Mancha" (I, 19, 234).

3. "[Sancho] determinó de no [dejar a su amo] hasta el último tránsito y fin de aquel negocio" (I, 20, 247).

4. "Puede estar seguro que de aquí adelante no despliegue mis labios para hacer donaire de las cosas de vuestra merced, si no fuere para honrarle, como a mi amo y señor natural" (I, 20, 251).

5. "Si no nos sucediese bien, tiempo nos queda para volvernos a la jaula, en la cual prometo, a ley de buen y leal escudero, de encerrarme juntamente con vuestra merced" (I, 49, 576).

6. "Sólo Sancho Panza se desesperaba, porque no se podía desasir de un criado del canóngio, que le estorbaba que a su amo no ayudase" (I, 52, 597).

7. "Sancho no hizo otra cosa que arrojarse sobre el cuerpo de su señor, haciendo sobre él el más doloroso y risueño llanto del mundo" (I, 52, 600-01).

8. "Unos pergaminos escritos... daban noticia... de la fidelidad de Sancho" (I, 52, 604).

9. "No pienso granjear fama de valiente, sino del mejor y más leal escudero que jamás sirvió a caballero andante" (II, 4, 70-71).

10. "Este mi amo... he visto que es un loco de atar.... Siendo, pues, loco, como lo es..." (II, 10, 106).

11. "Sancho, que consideró el peligro en que iba su amo de ser derribado, saltó del rucio, y a toda priesa fue a valerle" (II, 11, 117).

12. "Este mentecato de mi amo, de quien sé que tiene más de loco que de caballero" (II, 13, 130).

13. "[El escudero del Caballero del Bosque] sirve a otro amo tan tonto como el mío" (II, 13, 131).

14. "[Mi amo] no tiene nada de bellaco; antes tiene un alma como un cántaro; no sabe hacer mal a nadie, sino bien a todos, ni tiene malicia alguna,... y por esta sencillez le quiero como a las telas de mi corazón, y no me amaño a dejarle, por más disparates que haga" (II, 13, 131).

15. "[Mi amo] no es loco—respondió Sancho—, sino atrevido" (II, 17, 160).

16. "Este mi amo... cuando comienza a enhilar sentencias y a dar consejos, no sólo puede tomar púlpito en las manos, sino dos en cada dedo, y andarse por esas plazas a ¿qué quieres, boca? ¡Válate el diablo por caballero andante, que tantas cosas sabe!" (II, 22, 204).

17. "[Creyendo Sancho que su señor se quedaba dentro] lloraba amargamente y tiraba con mucha priesa por desengañarse" (II, 22, 210).

18. "Cuando Sancho Panza oyó decir esto a su amo... acabó de conocer indubitablemente que su señor estaba fuera de juicio y loco de todo punto" (II, 23, 220).

19. "¿Es posible que hombre que sabe decir tales, tantas y tan buenas cosas como aquí ha dicho, diga que ha visto los disparates imposibles que cuenta de la cueva de Montesinos?" (II, 24, 229).

20. "Yo tengo a mi señor don Quijote por loco rematado,... [y], verdaderamente y sin escrúpulo, a mí se me ha asentado que es un mentecato,... [pero] somos de un mismo lugar, he comido su pan, quiérole bien, es agradecido, diome sus pollinos y, sobre todo, yo soy fiel" (II, 33, 297 and 298).

21. "[Sancho] propuso en su corazón de acompañar a su señor hasta las últimas partes del mundo" (II, 40, 344).

22. "Bien puede buscar mi señor otro escudero que le acompañe,...que yo no soy brujo para gustar de andar por los aires" (II, 41, 345).
23. "[Sancho] venía caminando sobre el rucio a buscar a su amo, cuya compañía le agradaba más que ser gobernador de todas las ínsulas del mundo" (II, 54, 447).
24. "Quedó Sancho...admirado de lo que sabía [su señor], pareciéndole que no debía de haber historia en el mundo ni suceso que no lo tuviese cifrado en la uña y clavado en la memoria" (II, 58, 473).
25. "¿Es posible que haya en el mundo personas que se atrevan a decir y a jurar que este mi señor es loco? Digan vuestras mercedes, señores pastores: ¿hay cura de aldea, por discreto y por estudiante que sea, que pueda decir lo que mi amo ha dicho, ni hay caballero andante, por más fama que tenga de valiente, que pueda ofrecer lo que mi amo aquí ha ofrecido?" (II, 58, 479).
26. "Bien [veo que mi amo es un loco], y bien se lo digo a él" (II, 66, 546).
27. "Se le arraigó una calentura [a don Quijote], que le tuvo seis días en la cama,...sin quitársele de la cabecera Sancho Panza, su buen escudero" (II, 74, 586).

APPENDIX 28

FROM *loco* TO *gracioso*

1. "El cuadrillero...[tuvo a Sancho] por hombre falto de seso" (I, 17, 209).
2. "[Don Quijote] había llevado tras sí el juicio de [Sancho]" (I, 26, 324-25).
3. "Estaba peor Sancho despierto que su amo durmiendo" (I, 35, 439).
4. "¿Qué es lo que dices, loco?...¿Estás en tu seso?" (I, 37, 457).
5. "[A Sancho] le faltaba bien poco para tener la mesma enfermedad de su amo" (I, 46, 554-55).
6. "¿También vos, Sancho, sois de la cofradía de vuestro amo?...Le habéis de tener compañía en la jaula" (I, 47, 563).
7. "[Sansón] nunca creyó que [Sancho] era tan gracioso como [en la primera parte] le pintan" (II, 7, 91).
8. "[Sansón] dijo entre sí que tales dos locos como amo y mozo no se habrían visto en el mundo" (II, 7, 91).
9. "[Cide Hamete] dice...que desde este punto comienzan...[los]donaires de [Sancho]" (II, 8, 92).
10. "Los pescadores y molineros...teniéndolos por locos, les dejaron y se recogieron en sus aceñas" (II, 29, 267).
11. "No tuvo caballero andante en el mundo escudero...más gracioso del que yo tengo" (II, 30, 272).
12. "De que Sancho...sea gracioso lo estimo yo en mucho" (II, 30, 272).
13. "Hermano, si sois juglar—replicó la dueña—, guardad vuestras gracias para donde lo parezcan y se os paguen" (II, 31, 275).
14. "Perecía de risa la duquesa en oyendo hablar a Sancho, y en su opinión le tenía por más gracioso y por más loco que a su amo; y muchos hubo en aquel tiempo que fueron deste mismo parecer" (II, 32, 286).
15. "¡Oh Sancho Panza gracioso!" (II, 40, 339).

16. "Yo apostaré que este...[es] Sancho Panza,...a cuyas gracias no hay ningunas que se le igualen" (II, 58, 478).
17. "Los donaires de [Sancho]...no podían dejar de dar gusto general a todo el mundo" (II, 60, 505).
18. "Los donaires de Sancho fueron tantos, que de su boca andaban como colgados todos los criados de casa y todos cuantos le oían" (II, 62, 509).
19. "Con [la salud de don Quijote perdemos las gracias] de Sancho Panza,... que cualquiera dellas puede volver a alegrar a la misma melancolía" (II, 65, 537).
20. "El verdadero Sancho Panza soy yo, que tengo más gracias que llovidas,...que se me caen a cada paso, y tales y tantas, que sin saber yo las más veces lo que me digo, hago reír a cuantos me escuchan" (II, 72, 577).
21. "Más gracias habéis dicho vos, amigo, en cuatro razones que habéis hablado que el otro Sancho Panza en cuantas yo le oí hablar" (II, 72, 577).

APPENDIX 29

HOMESICKNESS AND EAGERNESS TO CONTINUE THEIR ADVENTURES

1. "Lo que sería mejor y más acertado,...fuera el volvernos a nuestro lugar, ahora que es tiempo de la siega y de entender en la hacienda" (I, 18, 216).
2. "[Sancho] propuso en su corazón de dejar a su amo y volverse a su tierra" (I, 18, 225).
3. "Me quiero volver a mi casa, y a mi mujer, y a mis hijos" (I, 25, 300).
4. "Sería bien que vuestra merced probase a salir desta cárcel...[y] probásemos otra vez la suerte de buscar más aventuras" (I, 49, 576).
5. "Volvamos a mi aldea,...y allí daremos orden de hacer otra salida" (I, 52, 601).
6. "Siendo Dios servido de que otra vez salgamos en viaje a buscar aventuras,...[que] no hay cosa más gustosa en el mundo que ser un hombre honrado escudero de un caballero andante buscador de aventuras,...[y] es linda cosa esperar los sucesos atravesando montes, escudriñando selvas, pisando peñas, visitando castillos, alojando en ventas a toda discreción, sin pagar ofrecido sea al diablo el maravedí" (I, 52, 603).
7. "Si mi señor tomase mi consejo, ya habíamos de estar en esas campañas deshaciendo agravios y enderezando tuertos" (II, 4, 69).
8. "Estoy alegre porque tengo determinado de volver a servir a mi amo don Quijote,...y yo vuelvo a salir con él, porque lo quiere así mi necesidad" (II, 5, 73).
9. "Harto mejor haría yo...en volverme a mi casa, y a mi mujer, y a mis hijos, y sustentarla y criarlos con lo que Dios fue servido de darme, y no andarme tras vuesa merced" (II, 28, 258).
10. "[Sancho] buscaba ocasión de que, sin entrar en cuentas ni en despedimientos con su señor, un día se desgarrase y se fuese a su casa" (II, 30, 268).
11. *"Tengo grandísimo deseo de saber del estado de mi casa, de mi mujer y de mis hijos"* (II, 51, 432).
12. "Volvámonos a nuestra casa y dejémonos de andar buscando aventuras por tierras y lugares que no sabemos" (II, 65, 537).

13. "Abre los ojos, deseada patria, y mira que vuelve a ti Sancho Panza tu hijo" (II, 72, 580).
14. "Mire, [señor], no sea perezoso, sino levántese desa cama, y vámonos al campo vestidos de pastores, como tenemos concertado" (II, 74, 589-90).

APPENDIX 30

SAYINGS AND PROVERBS

1. "A los escuderos, que se los papen duelos" (I, 18, 217).
2. "Váyase el muerto a la sepultura y el vivo a la hogaza" (I, 19, 236).
3. "Quien busca el peligro perece en él" (I, 20, 239).
4. "La cudicia rompe el saco" (I, 20, 239).
5. "Será enojar a la Fortuna, y dar coces, como dicen, contra el aguijón" (I, 20, 240).
6. "El bien que viniere para todos sea, y el mal, para quien lo fuere a buscar" (I, 20, 241). [See also below no. 7.]
7. "El mal, para quien le fuere a buscar,... viene aquí como anillo al dedo" (I, 20, 242).
8. "Las aventuras y desventuras nunca comienzan por poco" (I, 20, 245).
9. "Todo saldrá en la colada" (I, 20, 249-50).
10. "Ese te quiere bien, que te hace llorar" (I, 20, 250).
11. "Orégano sea, y no batanes" (I, 21, 253).
12. "No pidas de grado lo que puedes tomar por fuerza;...más vale salto de mata que ruego de hombres buenos [II, 67, 550]" (I, 21, 262-63).
13. "No quiero perro con cencerro" (I, 23, 287).
14. "Allá se lo hayan; con su pan se lo coman;...de mis viñas vengo, no sé nada; el que compra y miente, en su bolsa lo siente;...desnudo nací, desnudo ma hallo: ni pierdo ni gano [II, 8, 94-95; II, 53, 444; II, 57, 467; see also below no. 109];...muchos piensan que hay tocinos y no hay estacas [see also below nos. 44, 119, and 139];...¿quién puede poner puertas al campo?;...de Dios dijeron" (I, 25, 302).

    "¡Válame Dios,...y qué de necedades vas, Sancho, ensartando! ¿Qué va de lo que tratamos a los refranes que enhilas?" (I, 25, 302).
15. "No se ha de mentar la soga en casa del ahorcado;...y a Dios, que me mudo" (I, 25, 314).
16. "Lo eche todo a doce, aunque nunca se venda" (I, 25, 316). [See also below no. 132.]
17. "Más vale pájaro en mano que buitre volando [II, 12, 120; see also below no. 138];...quien bien tiene y mal escoge, por bien que se enoja no se venga" (I, 31, 387).
18. "Ciertos son los toros" (I, 35, 440).
19. "Al freír de los huevos lo verá" (I, 37, 460).
20. "Hay más mal en el aldegüela que se suena" (I, 46, 551).
21. "Cada puta hile, y comamos" (I, 46, 552).
22. "Donde reina la envidia no puede vivir la virtud, ni adonde hay escaseza la liberalidad" (I, 47, 562).
23. "La rueda de la Fortuna anda más lista que una rueda de molino;...los que ayer estaban en pinganitos hoy están por el suelo" (I, 47, 562).

24. "Cada uno es hijo de sus obras;...algo va de Pedro a Pedro;...a mí no se me ha de echar dado falso [see also below no. 80];...es peor meneallo [II, 12, 127]" (I, 47, 563).
25. "A Dios y veámonos, como dijo un ciego a otro" (I, 50, 587).
26. "No es la miel para la boca del asno" (I, 52, 603).
27. "Aún la cola falta por desollar" (II, 2, 57).
28. "Hasta aquí son tortas y pan pintado" (II, 2, 57; II, 17, 162).
29. "Ni me tiro ni me pago" (II, 3, 63).
30. "Nos habían de oír los sordos" (II, 3 63; II, 60, 492).
31. "Nos dormimos aquí en las pajas;...ténganos el pie al herrar, y verá del que cosqueamos" (II, 4, 69).
32. "Santiago, y cierra España!" (II, 4, 70; II, 58, 474).
33. "No ha de vivir el hombre en hoto de otro sino de Dios" (II, 4, 71).
34. "Cuando te dieren la vaquilla, corre con la soguilla [see also below nos. 89 and 117];...cuando viene el bien, mételo en tu casa" (II, 4, 71).
35. "Todo esto fuera flores de cantueso" (II, 5, 74).
36. "El que no sabe gozar de la ventura cuando le viene,...no se debe quejar si se le pasa" (II, 5, 75).
37. "Estaos siempre en un ser, sin crecer ni menguar, como figura de paramento" (II, 5, 76).
38. "Hablen cartas y callen barbas;...quien destaja no baraja [II, 43, 362];...más vale un toma que dos te daré[II, 72, 575];...el consejo de la mujer es poco, y el que no le toma es loco" (II, 7, 87).
39. "Hoy somos y mañana no;...tan presto se va el cordero como el carnero [see also below no.65];...la muerte es sorda" (II, 7, 87).
40. "Sobre un huevo pone la gallina;...muchos pocos hacen un mucho;...mientras se gana algo no se pierde nada" (II, 7, 88).
41. "El pan comido y la compañía deshecha" (II, 7 90).
42. "A coche acá, cinchado, y...al estricote" (II, 8, 94).
43. "En cada tierra su uso" (II, 9, 101).
44. "Buen corazón quebranta mala ventura;...donde no hay tocinos, no hay estacas;...donde no [se] piensa, salta la liebre" (II, 10, 105).
45. "Déjenme a mí con ella" (II, 10, 105).

   "Por cierto, Sancho,...que siempre traes tus refranes tan a pelo de lo que tratamos" (II, 10, 105).

46. "¡Allá darás, rayo!;...[buscarle] tres pies al gato;...[buscar] a Marica por Ravena, o al bachiller en Salamanca" (II, 10, 106).
47. "Todas las cosas tienen remedio, si no es la muerte" (II, 10, 106). [See also below no. 92]
48. "Dime con quién andas, decirte he quién eres [II, 23, 219];...no con quien naces, sino con quien paces [II, 32, 284]" (II, 10, 106).
49. "Tener la [de uno] siempre sobre el hito" (II, 10, 107).
50. "[Tener] los ojos en el colodrillo" (II, 10, 109).
51. "Quien la vido y la vee ahora, ¿cuál es el corazón que no llora?" (II, 11, 114).
52. "[El] tiempo...es el mejor médico destas y de otras mayores enfermedades" (II, 11, 115).

"En lo que [Sancho] se mostraba más elegante y memorioso era en traer refranes, viniesen o no [viniesen] a pelo de lo que trataba" (II, 12, 122).

53. "Los duelos con pan son menos" (II, 13, 128).

54. "No hay camino tan llano... que no tenga algún tropezón o barranco; en tras casas cuecen habas, y en la mía, a calderadas;... más acompañados y paniaguados debe de tener la locura que la discreción;... el tener compañeros en los trabajos suele servir de alivio en ellos" (II, 13, 131).

55. "Tiene un alma como un cántaro;... le quiero como a las telas de mi corazón" (II, 13, 131).

56. "Cada uno mire por el virote;... tal suele venir por lana que vuelve tresquilado[see below nos. 92 and 125];... Dios bendijo la paz y maldijo las riñas;... un gato acosado, encerrado y apretado se vuelve en león" (II, 14, 139).

57. "Aunque se la den entre dos platos" (II, 16, 150; II, 53, 445).

58. "Han dado salto en vago" (II, 17, 159).

59. "Cada oveja con su pareja [II, 53, 445];... buen siglo hayan y buen poso" (II, 19, 180).

60. "Dios, que da la llaga, da la medicina;... de aquí a mañana muchas horas hay;... en una [hora] y aun en un momento, se cae la casa; yo he visto llover y hacer sol, todo a un mesmo punto; tal se acuesta sano la noche, que no se puede mover otro día;... ¿habrá quien se alabe que tiene echado un clavo a la rodaja de la fortuna?;... entre el *sí* y el *no* de la mujer no me atrevería yo a poner una punta de alfiler, porque no cabría;... el amor... mira con unos anteojos, que hacen parecer oro al cobre, a la pobreza riqueza, y a las lagañas perlas" (II, 19, 181).

"¿Adónde vas a parar, Sancho, que seas maldito?... Que cuando comienzas a ensartar refranes... no te puede esperar sino el mesmo Judas, que te lleve. Dime, animal, ¿qué sabes tú de clavos, ni de rodajas, ni de otra cosa ninguna?

—¡Oh! Pues si no me entienden... no es maravilla que mis sentencias sean tenidas por disparates. Pero no importa: yo me entiendo, y sé que no he dicho muchas necedades en lo que he dicho" (II, 19, 181).

61. "No pedir cotufas en el golfo:... más que las tenga el conde Dirlos;... sobre un buen cimiento se puede levantar un buen edificio, y el mejor cimiento y zanja del mundo es el dinero" (II, 20, 186-87).

62. "El rey es mi gallo" (II, 20, 193).

63. "Tanto vales cuanto tienes, y tanto tienes cuanto vales [II, 43, 364];... dos linajes solos hay en el mundo,... el tener y el no tener;... antes se toma el pulso al haber que al saber; un asno cubierto de oro parece mejor que un caballo enalbardado" (II, 20, 193-94).

64. "Estaré yo mascando barro" (II, 20, 194).

65. "No hay que fiar en la descarnada,... la cual también come cordero como carnero,... que con igual pie [pisa] las altas torres de los reyes como las humildes chozas de los pobres. Tiene esta señora más de poder que de melindre; no es nada asquerosa, de todo come y a todo hace, y de toda suerte de gentes, edades y preeminencias hinche sus alforjas. No es

segador que duerme las siestas; que a todas horas siega, y corta así la seca como la verde yerba; y no parece que masca, sino que engulle y traga cuanto se le pone delante, porque tiene hambre canina, que nunca se harta; y aunque no tiene barriga, da a entender que está hidrópica y sedienta de beber solas las vidas de cuantos viven, como quien se bebe un jarro de agua fría.

—No más, Sancho...Tente en buenas, y no te dejes caer; que... lo que has dicho de la muerte por tus rústicos términos es lo que pudiera decir un buen predicador" (II, 20, 194-95).

66. "Bien predica quien bien vive" (II, 20, 195).
67. "Pasar por los bancos de Flandes" (II, 21, 196).
68. "Andarse por esas plazas a ¿qué quieres, boca?" (II, 22, 204).
69. "El buey suelto bien se lame" (II, 22, 204).
70. "En manos está el pandero que le sabrá bien tañer" (II, 22, 208).
71. "El mal ajeno de pelo cuelga" (II, 28, 257).
72. "Quien yerra y se enmienda, a Dios se encomienda" (II, 28, 261).
    "Maravillárame yo, Sancho, si no mezclaras algún refrancico en tu coloquio" (II, 28, 261).
73. "Haz lo que tu amo te manda, y siéntate con él a la mesa" (II, 29, 262).
    "Mira, Sancho, cómo hablas, y ten cuenta de no encajar algún refrán de los tuyos en tu embajada" (II, 30, 268).
74. "Al buen pagador no le duelen prendas [II, 34, 307; II, 59, 486; II, 71, 572];...en casa llena presto se guisa la cena [II, 43, 362]" (II, 30, 269).
75. "Donde menos se piensa se levanta la liebre;...esto que llaman naturaleza es como un alcaller que hace vasos de barro, y el que hace un vaso hermoso también puede hacer dos, y tres, y ciento" (II, 30, 272).
76. "A buen salvo está el que repica" (II, 31, 279; II, 43, 362).
77. "Júntate a los buenos, y serás uno dellos;...quien a buen árbol se arrima, buena sombre le cobija;...viva él y viva yo" (II, 32, 284).
78. "Es bueno vivir mucho, por ver mucho;...el que larga vida vive, mucho mal ha de pasar" (II, 32, 288).
79. "Por su mal le nacieron alas a la hormiga [there is an allusion to this saying in II, 53, 445];...tan buen pan hacen aquí como en Francia;...de noche todos los gatos son pardos;...asaz de desdichada es la persona que a las dos de la tarde no se ha desayunado;...no hay estómago que sea un palmo mayor que otro...[y] se puede llenar...de paja y de heno;...las avecitas del campo tienen a Dios por su proveedor y despensero;...más calientan cuatro varas de paño de Cuenca que otras cuatro de límiste de Segovia;...al dejar este mundo y meternos la tierra adentro, por tan estrecha senda va el príncipe como el jornalero;...no ocupa más pies de tierra el cuerpo del Papa que el del sacristán, aunque sea más alto el uno que el otro, que al entrar en el hoyo todos nos ajustamos y encogemos, o nos hacen ajustar y encoger, mal que nos pese y a buenas noches;...detrás de la cruz está el diablo;...no es oro todo lo que reluce;...de entre los bueyes, arados y coyundas sacaron al labrador Wamba para ser rey de España, y de entre los broacados, pasatiempos y riquezas sacaron a Rodrigo para ser comido de culebras" (II, 33, 298-99).

80. "A quien cuece y amasa, no le hurtes hogaza;...no me han de echar dado falso;...soy perro viejo, y entiendo todo tus, tus [see also below no. 130],...y no consiento que me anden musarañas ante los ojos, porque sé dónde me aprieta el zapato" (II, 33, 300).
81. "Sobre ello, morena;...ándense a cada triquete conmigo a dime y direte;...más vale el buen nombre que las muchas riquezas" (II, 33, 302).
82. "Aunque las calzo, no las ensucio;...dan por ella un ojo" (II, 33, 303).
83. "El buen gobernador, la pierna quebrada, y en casa" (II, 34, 307). [See also below no. 99.]
84. "Más vale al que Dios ayuda que al que mucho madruga;...tripas llevan pies, que no pies a tripas [see also below no. 96];...pónganme el dedo en la boca, y verán si aprieto o no" (II, 34, 307-08).

"¡Maldito seas,...Sancho maldito,...y cuándo será el día...donde yo te vea hablar sin refranes una razón corriente y concertada" (II, 34, 308).

"—Los refranes de Sancho Panza-dijo la duquesa-,...[son] de estimar, por la brevedad de las sentencias. De mí sé decir que me dan más gusto que otros, aunque sean mejor traídos y con más sazón acomodados" (II, 34, 308).

85. "Asno cargado de oro sube ligero por una montaña;...dádivas quebran-tan peñas;...a Dios rogando y con el mazo dando [II, 72, 575];...más vale un «toma» que dos «te daré»;...como quien dice «bebe con guindas» " (II, 35, 317).
86. *"Pon lo tuyo en concejo, y unos dirán que es blanco, y otros que es negro"* (II, 36, 322).
87. "Será mejor no menear el arroz, aunque se pegue" (II, 37 , 327).
88. "Tanto se pierde por carta de más como por carta de menos;...al buen entendedor, pocas palabras" (II, 37, 328).
89. "En la tardanza va el peligro;...cuando te dieren la vaquilla acudas con la soguilla;...bien se está San Pedro en Roma [II, 53, 444; II, 59, 487]" (II, 41, 345).
90. "¡En priesa me vees y doncellez me demandas!" (II, 41, 347).

"No has de mezclar en tus pláticas la muchedumbre de refranes que sueles; que puesto que los refranes son sentencias breves, muchas veces los traes tan por los cabellos, que más parecen disparates que sentencias.

—Eso Dios lo puede remediar,...porque sé más refranes que un libro, y viénenseme tantos juntos a la boca cuando hablo, que riñen, por salir, unos con otros; pero la lengua va arrojando los primeros que encuentra, aunque no vengan a pelo" (II, 43, 361-62).

91. "El dar y el tener, seso ha menester" (II, 43, 362). [See also below no. 111.]

"¡Eso sí, Sancho!...¡Encaja, ensarta, enhila refranes; que nadie te va a la mano! ¡Castígame mi madre, y yo trómpogelas! Estoyte diciendo que escuses [refranes], y en un instante has echado aquí una letanía dellos, que así cuadran con lo que vamos tratando como por los cerros de Úbeda. Mira, Sancho, no te digo yo que parece mal un refrán traído a propósito; pero cargar y ensartar refranes a troche moche hace la plática desmayada y baja" (II, 43, 362).

92. "Para todo hay remedio, si no es para la muerte;...que el que tiene el padre alcalde...;...¡llegaos, que la dejan ver!;...no, sino popen y calóñenme;...vendrán por lana, y volverán trasquilados;...a quien Dios quiere bien, la casa le sabe;...las necedades del rico por sentencias pasan en el mundo;...haceos miel, y paparos han moscas [see also below no. 97];...del hombre arraigado no te verás vengado" (II, 43, 363-64).

"¡Oh, maldito seas de Dios, Sancho!...¡Sesenta mil satanases te lleven a ti y a tus refranes! Una hora ha que los estás ensartando y dándome con cada uno tragos de tormento. Yo te aseguro que estos refranes te han de llevar un día a la horca!...Dime, ¿dónde los hallas, ignorate, o cómo los aplicas, mentecato, que para decir yo uno y aplicarle bien, sudo y trabajo como si cavase?

—¿A qué diablos se pudre de que yo me sirva de mi hacienda, que ninguna otra tengo, ni otro caudal alguno, sino refranes y más refranes?" (II, 43, 364).

93. "Venían...como peras en tabaque;...al buen callar llaman Sancho" (II, 43, 364).

94. "Entre dos muelas cordales nunca pongas tus pulgares;...a idos de mi casa y qué queréis con mi mujer, no hay responder;...si da el cántaro en la piedra o la piedra en el cántaro, mal para el cántaro;...vienen a pelo;...el que vee la mota en el ojo ajeno, vea la viga en el suyo;... [espantose] la muerte de la degollada;...más sabe el necio en su casa que el cuerdo en la ajena" (II, 43, 364-65).

95. "Mientras se duerme, todos son iguales" (II, 43, 365).

96. "Tripas llevan corazón, que no corazón tripas" (II, 47, 391).

97. "O somos, o no somos;...vivamos todos, y comamos en buena paz compaña;...cuando Dios amanece, para todos amanece;...sin perdonar derecho ni llevar cohecho;...el diablo está en Cantillana;...haceos miel, y comeros han moscas" (II, 49, 405).

98. "¿Digo algo, o quiébrome la cabeza?" (II, 49, 406).

99. "La doncella honrada, la pierna quebrada, y en casa;...la mujer y la gallina, por anda se pierden aína;...la que es deseosa de ver, también tiene deseo de ser vista" (II, 49, 414).

"El señor gobernador Sancho a cada paso...dice [refranes],...aunque muchos no vienen a propósito" (II, 50, 423).

100. "Siempre es alabado más el hacer bien que mal" (II, 51, 427).

101. "Eso pido, y barras derechas" (II, 51, 427).

102. "¡Tarde piache!" (II, 53, 445).

103. "Nadie tienda más la pierna de cuanto fuere larga la sábana;...déjenme pasar, que se me hace tarde" (II, 53, 445).

104. "Lo bien ganado se pierde, y lo malo, ello y su dueño" (II, 54, 453).

105. "Se fue a mesa puesta y a cama hecha" (II, 55 455).,

106. "Todos los duelos con pan son buenos" (II, 55, 456).

107. "Bien vengas mal, si vienes solo" (II, 55, 457).

108. "El hombre pone y Dios dispone;...Dios sabe lo mejor y lo que le está bien a cada uno;...cual el tiempo, tal el tiento;...nadie diga «desta agua no beberé»;...adonde se piensa que hay tocinos, no hay estacas" (II, 55, 459-60).

109. "Entré desnudo, y desnudo me hallo; ni pierdo, ni gano" (II, 55, 460).

110. "Lo que has de dar al mur, dalo al gato, y sacarte ha de cuidado" (II, 56, 465).

111. "Para dar y tener, seso es menester" (II, 58, 472).

112. "Dios lo oiga y el pecado sea sordo" (II, 58, 473). [See also below no. 120.]

113. "Muera Marta, y muera harta" (II, 59, 483).

114. "Hasta la muerte, todo es vida" (II, 59, 483).

115. "Quien las sabe las tañe" (II, 59, 487).

116. "Ni quito rey, ni pongo rey" (II, 60, 492).

117. "[Cuando] me sucede que me den la vaquilla, corro con la soguilla" (II, 62, 509).

118. "Del dicho al hecho hay gran trecho" (II, 64, 532).

119. "Donde las dan las toman;...no siempre hay tocinos donde hay estacas" (II, 65, 537).

120. "El pecado sea sordo;...más vale buena esperanza que ruin posesión" (II, 65, 538).

121. "Viva la gallina, aunque con su pepita;...hoy por ti y mañana por mí;...el que hoy cae puede levantarse mañana" (II, 65, 538).

122. "Tan de valientes corazones es...tener sufrimiento en las desgracias como alegría en las prosperidades;...esta que llaman por ahí Fortuna es una mujer borracha y antojadiza, y, sobre todo, ciega" (II, 66, 541).

123. "La culpa del asno no se ha de echar a la albarda" (II, 66, 543).

124. "Como si dijésemos: «Si os duele la cabeza, untaos las rodillas»" (II, 67, 548).

125. "No querría que [Sanchica] fuese por lana y volviese trasquilada;... suelen andar los amores y los no buenos deseos por los campos como por las ciudades, y por las pastorales chozas como por los reales palacios;...quitada la causa se quita el pecado;...ojos que no veen, corazón que no quiebra" (II, 67, 550).

"No más refranes...pues cualquiera de los que has dicho basta para dar a entender tu pensamiento; y muchas veces te he aconsejado que no seas tan pródigo de refranes y que te vayas a la mano en decirlos; pero paréceme que es predicar en desierto, y «castígame mi madre, y yo trómpogelas»" (II, 67, 551).

126. "Dijo la sartén a la caldera; Quítate allá, ojinegra" (II, 67, 551).

"[Tú traes los refranes] tan por los cabellos, que los arrastras, y no los guías,...y el refrán que no viene a propósito, antes es disparate que sentencia" (II, 67, 551).

127. "Bien haya el que inventó el sueño, capa que cubre todos los humanos pensamientos, manjar que quita la hambre, agua que ahuyenta la sed, fuego que calienta el frío, frío que templa el ardor, y, finalmente,

moneda general con que todas las cosas se compran, balanza y peso que iguala al pastor con el rey y al simple con el discreto. Sola una cosa tiene mala el sueño, según he oído decir, y es que se parece a la muerte, pues de un dormido a un muerto hay muy poca diferencia.

—Nunca te he oído hablar, Sancho, ... tan elegantemente como ahora.

—Debe de haber entre [mis refranes] y los suyos esta diferencia: que los de vuestra merced vendrán a tiempo y los míos a deshora" (II, 68, 553).

128. "Amanecerá Dios, y medraremos" (II, 68, 554).
129. "A mal viento va esta parva; ... todo el mal nos viene junto, como al perro los palos" (II, 68, 556).
130. "¡Esas burlas, a un cuñado; que yo soy perro viejo, y no hay conmigo tus, tus!" (II, 69, 560).
131. "Esto me parece argado sobre argado, y no miel sobre hojuelas" (II, 69, 561).
132. Tengo yo de ser la vaca de la boda; ... lo eche todo a trece, aunque no se venda" (II, 69, 561-62).
133. "Los diablos, jueguen o no jueguen, nunca pueden estar contentos, ganen o no ganen" (II, 70, 566).
134. "Si las hubieras conmigo, ... otro gallo te cantará" (II, 70, 569).
135. "El abad de donde canta yanta; ... no quiero [comunicar mis virtudes] con otros de bóbilis, bóbilis" (II, 71, 570).
136. "A dineros pagados, brazos quebrados" (II, 71, 573).
137. "¡Aquí morirás, Sansón, y cuantos con él son!" (II, 71, 573).
138. "A sangre caliente y cuando estaba picado el molino; ... más [vale] un «toma» que dos «te daré», y el pájaro en la mano que el buitre volando" (II, 71, 575).

"No más refranes, Sancho, por un solo Dios—dijo don Quijote—; que parece que te vuelves al *sicut erat;* habla a lo llano, a lo liso, a lo no intricado, ... y verás como te vale un pan por ciento.

—No sé qué mala ventura es esta mía ... que no sé decir razón sin refrán, ni refrán que no me parezca razón" (II, 71, 575).

139. "Muchas veces donde hay estacas no hay tocinos" (II, 73, 583).

APPENDIX 31

SANCHO WEEPS

1. "[Sancho] comenzó a llorar con la mayor ternura del mundo" (I, 20, 239).
2. "De nuevo tornó a llorar Sancho" (I, 20, 247).
3. "No sin muchas lágrimas de entrambos, se despidió [Sancho de su señor]" (I, 25, 317).
4. "Hasta Sancho Panza lloraba" (I, 36, 455).
5. "Miré por el jumento, y no le vi; acudiéronme lágrimas a los ojos" (II, 4, 67).

6. "Si digno—respondió Sancho, enternecido y llenos de lágrimas los ojos" (II, 7, 90).

7. "Sancho, con lágrimas en los ojos le suplicó desistiese de tal empresa" (II, 17, 162).

8. "Lloraba Sancho la muerte de su señor, que aquella vez sin duda creía que llegaba en las garras de los leones" (II, 17, 162).

9. "[Sancho] lloraba amargamente" (II, 22, 210).

10. "Miraba Sancho a don Quijote...en tanto que los tales vituperios le decía, y compungióse de manera que le vinieron las lágrimas a los ojos" (II, 28, 260).

11. "Y en esto, comenzó [Sancho] a llorar tan amargamente, que don Quijote, mohíno y colérico, le dijo:

—¿De qué temes, cobarde criatura? ¿De qué lloras, corazón de mantequillas?" (II, 29, 263).

12. "Dijo esto con tanto sentimiento la Trifaldi, que...arrasó los [ojos] de Sancho" (II, 40, 344).

13. "Mirando a todos los del jardín tiernamente y con lágrimas, dijo [Sancho] que le ayudasen en aquel trance" (II, 41, 348).

14. "[Sancho] tomó la bendición de su señor, que se la dio con lágrimas y [él] la recibió con pucheritos" (II, 44, 368).

15. "Llegándose al rucio, [Sancho] le abrazó,...no sin lágrimas en los ojos" (II, 53, 444).

16. "Abrazáronle todos, y él, llorando, abrazó a todos" (II, 53, 446).

17. "A mí me hizo llorar, que no suelo ser muy llorón [—dijo Sancho]" (II, 54, 454).

18. "Dio la duquesa las cartas de su mujer a Sancho Panza, el cual lloró con ellas" (II, 57, 467).

19. "[Sancho comenzó] a llorar tiernamente, como si ya [tuviera a su amo] muerto delante" (II, 74, 587).

20. "Hallando [Sancho] a la ama y a la sobrina llorosas, comenzó a hacer pucheros y a derramar lágrimas" (II, 74, 589).

21. "Estas nuevas dieron un terrible empujón a los ojos preñados...de Sancho Panza,...de tal manera, que [le] hizo reventar las lágrimas de los ojos y mil profundos suspiros del pecho" (II, 74, 589).

22. "¡Ay!—respondió Sancho, llorando—. No se muera vuestra merced" (II, 74, 589).

23. "[Déjase] de poner aquí [el llanto de Sancho por la muerte de don Quijote]" (II, 74, 591).

APPENDIX 32

REFERENCES TO SALARY

"[Don Quijote le dijo a Sancho que] en lo que tocaba a la paga de sus servicios, no tuviese pena, porque él había dejado hecho su testamento antes que saliera de su lugar, donde se hallaría gratificado de todo lo tocante a su salario, rata por cantidad, del tiempo que hubiese servido" (I, 20, 247).

"Las mercedes y beneficios que yo os he prometido llegarán a su tiempo; y si no llegaren, el salario, a la mesmo, no se ha de perder, como ya os he dicho" (I, 20, 251).

1. "Querría yo saber, por si acaso no llegase el tiempo de las mercedes y fuese necesario acudir al de los salarios, cuánto ganaba un escudero,... y si se concertaban por meses, o por días, como peones de albañir" (I, 20, 251).

"[Que te] he señalado [salario] a ti en el testamento cerrado que dejé en mi casa...por lo que podía suceder" (I, 20, 251).

"[El salario de Sancho] no podrá perderse; que en mi testamento, que ya está hecho, dejo declarado lo que se le ha de dar" (I, 46, 556).

2. "Vuesa merced me señale salario conocido,...que no quiero estar a mercedes" (II, 7, 87).

3. "Si me he puesto en cuentas de tanto más cuanto acerca de mi salario, ha sido por complacer a mi mujer" (II, 7, 90).

"Dineros tenéis míos [—dijo don Quijote—], mirad cuánto ha que esta tercera vez salimos de nuestro pueblo, y mirad lo que podéis y debéis ganar cada mes, y pagaos de vuestra mano" (II, 28, 258).

4. "A mi parecer,...con dos reales más que vuestra merced añadiese cada mes [a los dos ducados que ganaba sirviendo a Tomá Carrasco] me tendría por bien pagado" (II, 28, 259).

"En mi buena suerte, [Sancho], te tenía librada la paga de tus servicios (II, 42, 357).

APPENDIX 33
COMPASSION

1. "Túvole Sancho tanta compasión, que sacó un real de a cuatro del seno y se le dio de limosna" (I, 22, 270).
2. "Sacó de su repuesto Sancho un pedazo de pan y otro de queso,... dándoselo [a Andrés]" (I, 31, 391).
3. "Fueron los [cuatro reales] que tú, Sancho, me diste el otro día para dar limosna a los pobres que topase por los caminos" (II, 23, 222).
4. "Enternecióse Sancho Panza con las razones de maese Pedro, y díjole: —No llores,...ni te lamentes, que me quiebras el corazón" (II, 26, 246).
5. "Yo soy caritativo de mío y tengo compasión de los pobres" (II, 33, 300).

6. "[La caza] consiste en matar a un animal que no ha cometido delito alguno,... [y no hace] con mi conciencia" (II, 34, 307).
7. "Las barbas y lágrimas destas señoras las tengo clavadas en el corazón" (II, 41, 347).
8. "Como [Sancho], según dice Cide Hamete, era caritativo además, sacó de sus alforjas medio pan y medio queso,... y dióselo" (II, 54, 447).
9. "[Don Quijote] desesperábase de ver la flojedad y caridad poca de Sancho... pues, a lo que creía, solos cinco azotes se había dado" (II, 60, 491).
10. "Roque... contó el trágico suceso de Claudia Jerónima, de que le pesó en estremo a Sancho" (II, 60, 502).
11. "Yo imagino, [Sancho], que eres hecho de mármol, o de duro bronce, en quien no cabe movimiento ni sentimiento alguno... ¡Oh alma endurecida! ¡Oh escudero sin piedad!" (II, 68, 552).
12. "Sacó Sancho cuatro cuartos de la faltriquera y dióselos al mochacho por la jaula" (II, 73, 581).

APPENDIX 34
LOQUACITY

1. "Querer... que vaya... por estas soledades de día y de noche, y que no... hable cuando me diere gusto, es enterrarme en vida" (I, 25, 300).
2. "Ya te tengo dicho... que eres muy grande hablador" (I, 25, 313).
3. "En mí la gana de hablar siempre es primero movimiento, y no puedo dejar de decir, por una vez siquiera, lo que me viene a la lengua" (I, 30, 379).
4. "No me faltarán escuderos... no tan... habladores como vos" (II, 7, 89).
5. "Nunca he visto yo escudero... que se atreva a hablar donde habla su señor" (II, 12, 127).
6. "Yo le diré... quién soy, para que vea si puedo entrar en docena con los más hablantes escuderos" (II, 12, 127).
7. "Por quien Dios es, Sancho,... que concluyas con tu arenga; que tengo para mí que si te dejasen seguir en las que a cada paso comienzas, no te quedaría tiempo para comer ni para dormir; que todo le gastarías en hablar" (II, 20, 187).
8. "¿Has acabado tu arenga, Sancho?
   —Habréla acabado,... porque veo que vuestra merced recibe pesadumbre con ella; que si esto no se pusiera de por medio, obra había cortada para tres días.
   —Plega a Dios, Sancho,... que yo te vea mudo antes que me muera" (II, 20, 194).
9. "Nunca llegará tu silencio a do ha llegado lo que has hablado, hablas y tienes de hablar en tu vida;... y así, jamás pienso verte mudo, ni aun cuando estés bebiendo o durmiendo" (II, 20, 194).
10. "Si hablo mucho, más procede de enfermedad que de malicia" (II, 28, 261).
11. "No tuvo caballero andante en el mundo escudero más hablador... del que yo tengo" (II, 30, 272).
12. "Hasta ahora—dijo el eclesiástico—,más os tengo por hablador que por mentiroso" (II, 31, 279-80).

Lengths of Sancho's longer speeches:

11 lines:	Part I	48, 573
	Part II	5, 73-74; 12, 121-22; 13, 128; 20, 193-94; 30, 269; 68, 553; 70, 563
12 lines:	Part I	49, 575; 52, 601
	Part II	13, 132; 32, 295; 47, 391-92; 59, 483
13 lines:	Part I	10, 151; 37, 460; 47, 563; 49, 576; 52, 603
	Part II	7, 87-88; 31, 279; 33, 300; 43, 365; 47, 394-95; 71, 570
14 lines:	Part I	21, 262-63; 25, 310; 30, 377
	Part II	2, 57; 4, 66-67; 5, 73; 8, 98; 17, 159; 19, 181; 32, 294; 49, 405-06; 53, 445; 58, 475; 65, 537-38; 67, 550; 71, 571
15 lines:	Part I	15, 194; 25, 300; 25, 306
	Part II	4, 67-68; 5, 77; 11, 112; 11, 114-15; 14, 138; 14, 139; 20, 194-95; 57, 467; 74, 589-90
16 lines:	Part I	11, 154; 31, 386-87
	Part II	13, 130: 35, 318-19; 39, 336; 43, 364-65; 47, 389; 54, 453-54; 72, 577
17 lines:	Part II	20, 186-87; 21, 196; 33, 297-98; 33, 301; 41, 345-46; 43, 363-64
18 lines:	Part I	18, 216
	Part II	28, 258-59; 41, 353-54; 49, 405
19 lines:	Part I	25, 316-17; 31, 384
	Part II	8, 94-95; 33, 302; 49, 404
20 lines:	Part I	21, 258
	Part II	47, 391
24 lines:	Part II	5, 77-78; 13, 133; 53, 444-45
25 lines:	Part I	47, 562-63
30 lines:	Part II	28, 257-58; 35, 316-17
31 lines:	Part I	20, 239-40
33 lines:	Part II	55, 455-56
35 lines:	Part II	4, 70-71
37 lines:	Part I	25, 312-13
	Part II	33, 298-99
39 lines:	Part II	55, 460-61

INDEX

See also Bibliography I